What Does Athens Have to Do with Jerusalem?

Eight Interdisciplinary Conversations Integrating Faith and Reason

By

Matthew R.S. Todd

Mill Lake Books

Copyright © 2018 Matthew R.S. Todd
No part of this book may be reproduced in any form without written permission, except for brief quotations in critical reviews.

Published by Mill Lake Books
Abbotsford, BC
Canada

Printed by Lightning Source, distributed by Ingram

Cover design by Dean Tjepkema

Unless otherwise noted, Scripture verses are taken from THE HOLY BIBLE, NEW INTERNATIONAL VERSION®, NIV® Copyright © 1973, 1978, 1984, 2011 by Biblica, Inc.® Used by permission. All rights reserved worldwide.

Scripture verses marked NASB are taken from the NEW AMERICAN STANDARD BIBLE®, Copyright © 1960, 1962, 1963, 1968, 1971, 1972, 1973, 1975, 1977, 1995 by The Lockman Foundation. Used by permission.

Scripture verses marked The Message are taken from *The Message*. Copyright © 1993, 1994, 1995, 1996, 2000, 2001, 2002. Used by permission of NavPress Publishing Group.

Scripture verses marked KJV are taken from the King James Version.

Scripture verses marked NMB are taken from the New Matthew Bible, Copyright © 2016 by Ruth Magnusson (Davis). All rights reserved.

ISBN 978-0-9951983-7-1

"Many leaders are recognizing that the time for new wineskins is now if we are going to have relevant structures to assimilate what God is doing around the world by His Spirit. In Todd's characteristically thoughtful and insightful approach, the quality of the gospel is not in dispute. But he challenges the reader to wrestle with the appropriateness of our wineskins. As a coach in various cultural contexts over the last three decades, I can attest that this is not an easy (or even a welcome) conversation, but nevertheless a crucial one.

"Of any period, the early Church had the greatest impact on its society, yet it was at this time that the Church was the most marginalized and persecuted. From Constantine in the fourth century until today, the Church has been at the center of Western civilization. Ironically, during this time, it has never had the influence and spiritual power of its early predecessor. The period dominated by the modern worldview is in decline, and, particularly in the West, we are seeing the rise of a postmodern worldview.

"The point Todd makes across several disciplines is that reason and faith are not mutually exclusive. Modernity and postmodernity as worldviews may have similarities—they may be the same light reflecting at different angles through the same prism. As the domination of Athenian modernism (rationalism) fades, postmodernism (experientialism) may very well be the context in which the Church can regain its Jerusalem roots. The sky is not falling. A new day may very well be dawning."

Phillip T. Jeske, PhD,
President, ICM Canada

"I recently heard someone comment that just as he had figured out the answers, all the questions had changed. This sentiment may well describe the current position of the Church in the context of Western culture. In *What Does Athens Have to Do with Jerusalem?* Dr. Todd identifies and addresses significant issues at the intersection of Church and culture. Particularly in Chapter 8, Todd challenges traditional and accepted church practices, including how we organize, communicate, educate, and train leaders. He presents meaningful ideas to reveal a way forward while at the same time maintaining and honoring the message and truth of the Kingdom of God. Todd is uniquely equipped and experienced, and he comes from a place of authenticity and authority on these subjects. Church leaders in our changing culture would do well to take heed of his analysis and ideas regarding the path forward."

Douglas Friesen,
President, CLIMB Intercultural Society

About the Author

Matthew Todd, BTh, BGS, MTS, MA, DTL, DMin (cand.), is the author of *Hope Alive: Going and Growing through Pain* (Mill Lake Books, 2016), *Developing Transformational English Ministries in Chinese Churches* (Friesen Press, 2016), *English Ministries Crisis in Chinese Canadian Churches* (Wipf & Stock Publishers, 2015), *Historical Attitudes That Have Shaped the Church's Use of the Arts* (Word Alive Press, 2010), and *The Interface of Percussive Arts, Religious Experience, and Sacred Association* (Word Alive Press, 2008). Todd has served for over thirteen years as an adjunct theology, philosophy, and ethics teacher with L.I.F.E. College and P.L.B.C. Canada, has pastored in two congregations, has served as a speaker in multiple cross-cultural contexts, has written for numerous theological and popular journals, and has served on the executive of the Mennonite Brethren Chinese Churches Association (as English pastors liaison) and on the former Greater Vancouver English Ministries Fellowship (VCEMF, now called Shepherds Circle). Currently, he serves as an officer and overseer with the CLIMB Intercultural Society with the goal of developing and mobilizing effective leaders for intercultural challenges. His hobbies include drumming with a big band in the Greater Vancouver area, reading books on cultural studies and theology, and maintaining an itinerant speaking schedule.

Dedication
To Lin and Paul

I trust you are enjoying your retirement from departments at the University of Toronto.
Here is an extension of some of our more casual table conversations.

Table of Contents

Introduction:
What Does Athens Have to Do with Jerusalem?....... 9

1. Perceiving the Beauty of God 23

2. Making a Case for the Resurrection from
Ground Zero 65

3. The Potential for Christian Fantasy
Literature to Promote Enchantment and
Religious Experience 121

4. Why Is God Good to All People? 153

5. Conversations with Cultured Pagans:
The God Question 159

6. Saint Augustine's Philosophy of Time:
The Enduring Contemporary Debate 179

7. Lessons from the Fall of Constantinople 231

8. Signs of Hope as Christendom Declines
(A Chapter for Those Weary of the Church's
Cultural Captivity) 249

Epilog: Athens to Jerusalem 287

Bibliography 295

INTRODUCTION
What Does Athens Have to Do with Jerusalem?

What does *Athens* have to do with *Jerusalem*? What does *reason* have to do with *faith?* When the Russian astronaut Gherman Titoy returned from a trip in space, he commented:

> Some people say there is a God out there...but in my travels around the earth all day long, I looked around and didn't see Him...I saw no God or angels. The rocket was made by our own people. I don't believe in God, I believe in man, his strength, his possibilities, his reason.[1]

In more subtle and more articulate terms, British philosopher Bertrand Russel said something similar in a BBC interview:

> When you are studying any subject or considering any philosophy, ask yourself only: What are the facts and what is the truth that the facts bear out? Never let yourself be diverted either by what you wish to believe or what you think would have beneficent social effects if it were believed. But look only and solely at what are the facts."[2]

---

[1] Alan Stein, "Soviet cosmonaut Gherman Titov begins a two-day visit to Century 21 Exposition on May 5, 1962," History Link.org, http://www.historylink.org/File/10104, accessed November 15, 2017.

[2] BBC interview with Bertrand Russell (1959) on *Face to Face*, https://www.youtube.com/watch?v=yw8n2asHj7Q

Both of these statements assume that observation plus reason leads to truth and that this approach is diametrically opposed to faith and belief (that Athens has nothing to do with Jerusalem). But this means that both of these statements are based on some a priori presuppositions about what is true and these presuppositions flow out of people's worldviews, which themselves are compendiums of faith and reason. Worldviews carry presuppositions about what is real; what it means to be human; what comes after death; the nature of knowledge and rationality; ethics; whether we should attach any meaning to human history; and much else.[3] The big presupposition, of course, is what we think the *basis* of reality is. Two branches of philosophy that address this issue are metaphysics and epistemology (being and knowing). But philosophy has also provided arguments for why reason might lead the thinker to bridge over into faith. These include teleological arguments (from design in nature), cosmological arguments (dealing with universal causation), ontological arguments (based in being and existence), arguments from consciousness, arguments from the existence of beauty, arguments from miracles, arguments from love, morality, and natural law, and so forth.[4] Worldviews inevitably address interactions between faith and reason.

---

[3] James W. Sire, *The Universe Next Door* (Downers Grove, IL: InterVarsity Press, 1988), 18. See also David K. Naugle, *Worldview: The History of a Concept* (Grand Rapids, MI: Wm. B. Eerdmans, 2002).

[4] To see a much larger list of 34 philosophical categories used in the argument for the existence of God, see "Category: Arguments for the existence of God," Wikipedia, https://en.wikipedia.org/wiki/Category:Arguments_for_the_existence_of_God), accessed December 9, 2017. See also: J.P. Moreland and William Lane Craig, *Philosophical Foundations for a Christian Worldview* (Downers Grove, IL: InterVarsity Press, 2003).

The predominant Western worldview is rationalism, essentially the idea that reason (and not faith) is the only path to truth. This worldview has several different formulations. For instance, logical positivism says that only statements verifiable by empirical observation can be considered meaningful or truthful. Material monism tries to explain the physical world without dependence on the supernatural. Empiricism is the theory that knowledge comes only or primarily from sensory experience, from what can be seen, heard, smelled, tasted, or touched, that is, from what can be directly observed.

However, research has shown that even theories in the sciences can and do become independent of sense perceptions[5]—in order for observed data to become systematized and formulated into theories that can be useful, scientists must at some point posit unobservable entities; that is to say, they must launch from the dock of reason into faith. Logical positivists have sought to avoid introducing metaphysical terms into science and have always tried to ensure that the terms they use refer to observables. Because of this, logical positivism is reductionist. The scientific community has carefully worked out a structure delimiting which unobservable or theoretical entities, which types of theories, are admissible. This structure, this conceptual perspective, determines which questions are deemed worth investigating and what sorts of answers are acceptable. But this structure, of course, is essentially a conceptual worldview, a set of philosophical a priori assumptions. When we consider the vocabulary of scientific theories, there are three classes: observation terms, terms expressing logical connections, and theoretical terms. For example,

---

[5] Phillip H. Wiebe, *Theism in an Age of Science* (Lanham, MD: University Press of America, 1988), 29-39.

atomism makes use of both observation terms and theoretical terms. The theoretical terms include electron, electron orbit, electron jump, proton, and nucleus—entities whose existence is logically inferred but which cannot be directly observed. These theoretical terms bridge gaps between observations or empirical terms; that is, they apply reason to what is observed to posit the existence of entities which cannot be observed. As well, theories are dynamic and not static—they keep developing, which is something that Thomas Kuhn brought attention to in his discussion of the structure of scientific revolutions (paradigm shifts).[6] Theories are also affected by the received view (the currently accepted paradigm) rather than being solely based on observed data. Thus, theoretical terms are equivalent to metaphysical concepts as we cannot see the bridging links between the physical events and the theories that are developed to explain them. Even mental states are included as theoretical entities in such scientific theories. An example is the Diagnostic and Statistical Manual of Mental Disorders (DSM) used by psychologists (which at one time defined homosexuality as a mental illness). Theories can be false or true.

Theism, the worldview that argues for the existence of God, also posits unobservables to account for observable events. However in response to such arguments, rationalism, the predominant Western worldview, demonstrates its bias. Those in the theistic camp are told by rationalists, "We can have our unobservables but you cannot have yours," or "We can have our faith beliefs, but you cannot have yours." This book challenges the legitimacy of those kinds of statements. Kuhn recognized that paradigm shifts

---

[6] Thomas S. Kuhn, "Revolutions as changes of worldview," *The Structure of Scientific Revolutions* (Chicago: University of Chicago Press, 1962), 111-135.

happen because humans simply can't and won't know everything—we are finite creatures always in process. [7] I share the view of philosopher Alvin Plantinga that belief in God can be justified independent of evidence and is a properly basic starting point, similar to the belief that there are other minds and planets without ever having seen or experienced them.[8] Blaise Pascal argued that reason can begin again by recognizing what it can never know.[9] It was Pascal who said, "The heart is aware of God, not reason. This is what faith is. The heart has its reasons which are unknown to reason." Pascal felt that it was actually reason that had its limits and faith that had no limits.

That brings us to the next question: are there some people who are able to emerge from reason and extend into the realm of faith more easily? Some researchers, such as Dean Hamer, who wrote the book *The God Gene: How Faith Is Hardwired into Our Genes,* seem to think so. [10] Charles Templeton, the author of *Farewell to God,*[11] was a classic figure of the late twentieth century who flip-flopped from a faith-based worldview to a rationalist worldview and then expressed, at the end of his life, that he missed Jesus.

So the relationship between faith and reason has a messy history in the Western world and in most religious traditions—and for a good reason. Faith

---

[7] Ibid.
[8] Alvin Plantinga, "Religious Belief without Evidence" in Louis P. Pojman, ed., *Philosophy of Religion,* 4th ed. (Cengage Learning, 2002.), 468.
[9] Blaise Pascal, "Reason can begin again by recognizing what it can never know," *The Mind on Fire* (Portland, OR: Multnomah Press, 2006), 129-134.
[10] Dean Hamer, *The God Gene: How Faith Is Hardwired into Our Genes* (Toronto: Random House of Canada, 2004).
[11] Charles Templeton, *Farewell to God: My reasons for rejecting the Christian faith* (Toronto: McClelland & Stewart, 1996).

takes us into metaphysics—the why questions, not the what questions. Everyone makes metaphysical assumptions, that is, assumptions about what is real. Most people are metaphysical dualists, believing that spirit and matter represent the two fundamental categories into which all real things can be sorted. When I ask the question, "What does reason have to do with faith?" I am inquiring into something that goes beyond Kant's question regarding *Religion within the Limits of Reason*.[12] Faith in God is more than just a basis for establishing ethics or promoting social cohesion. As Rudolf Otto pointed out, central to an understanding of faith is the idea of the holy, the nonrational numinous, the *mysterium tremendum* (the terrible mystery), that which is "wholly other."[13]

A sample of Canonical texts [14] might help illuminate what is involved in integrating faith and reason. Isaiah 1:18 (NASB) gives an invitation: "Come now, and let us reason together." Yet Paul, in Colossians 2:8, warned, "See to it that no one takes you captive through hollow and deceptive philosophy, which depends on human tradition," and, in 1 Corinthians 1:21, he stated, "In the wisdom of God the world through its wisdom did not know him." Theists tend to vacillate between reason and faith when arguing for the historical reliability of the biblical Canon on the basis of archeological finds and biblical criticism. They draw from apologetics, which is a branch of theology related to the philosophy of religion. A variety of apologetic methods are used to

---

[12] Immanuel Kant, *Religion within the Limits of Reason Alone*, trans. Theodore Greene and Hoyt Hudson (New York: Harper and Row, 1960).
[13] Rudolf Otto, *The Idea of the Holy*, 2nd ed. (London: Oxford University Press, 1958).
[14] That is, "the authoritative list of books accepted as Holy Scripture" (*Merriam-Webster's Collegiate Dictionary*, 11th ed.), the Bible.

communicate the reasonableness of faith, including literature, expertise, power events, justice and charity, and the quality of community.[15] Deeply related to this book's thesis are the arguments of philosophers such as Soren Kierkegaard, Alvin Plantinga, Michael Polanyi, and William Alston, who use rational arguments to persuade their readers that there is more to learning about life than solitary learning can deliver—we must also draw on experience and our life journey as we process the mystery of existence and intuitively apprehend spiritual realities.[16]

What does *Athens* have to do with *Jerusalem*? What does *reason* have to do with *faith*? I can remember my first visit to Jerusalem in 1980 as a drummer with a band that had traveled to that part of the world to give musical performances throughout the country of Israel. It was a thrill to play concerts at military bases, in concert halls (in places such as Tel Aviv, Arad, Haifa, and Jerusalem), and in communities. Our playlist was about fifty percent Jewish faith/culture songs (such as "Hatikvah," "Am Yisrael Chai," "Jerusalem," and "Hava Nagilah"), and the rest were Old Testament Afro-American faith songs (such as, "Go Down, Moses," "Swing Low, Sweet Chariot," and "Ain't Gonna Study War No More"). We packed concert halls and other venues. Our audiences included decorated military leaders and important visitors such as Colonel Yehuda Levi, the US ambassador to Israel, and his wife, and the Minister of Agriculture. By the age of twenty, I had read through the Old and New Testaments at least once and was aware that Jerusalem was an ancient city of faith pilgrimage, prophecy, and promise. Its

---

[15] See John Stackhouse, *Humble Apologetics* (New York: Oxford University Press, 2002), 206-232.
[16] Ibid, 150-151.

significance to Jews, Christians, and Muslims cannot be understated. Jerusalem has been a focal point for drawing people into the mystery of faith and hope. It is almost hard for me to describe the feeling of awe I experienced while spending my first night in Jerusalem at the King David Hotel watching the sunset from the Golden City. The places I visited—Solomon's Steps, the Eastern Gate, the Wailing Wall, Lazarus's tomb, King David's tomb, the Church of the Nativity, the Garden of Gethsemane, the Garden Tomb (presumed to be the burial place of Christ), the Mount of Olives, the Sea of Galilee, the Dead Sea, Masada, Jericho, Megiddo, Mount Carmel, and the Mediterranean Sea—all had ancient faith stories attached to them. These stories of faith were reinforced by further visits to the Chief Rabbi of Jerusalem, the Orthodox section of Israel, the Holocaust Memorial, and the Knesset.

It was to Israel that the words of Proverbs 3:5 were spoken: "Trust in the LORD with all your heart and lean not on your own understanding." The point is that no matter how much knowledge and education we obtain, God has fixed it so that we do not understand all truth through reason. We never will "know it all." Israel's sages pointed out that we stand in a place of wisdom if we accept that we will never mine the depths of the mystery of existence and why anything exists at all. It is implied that we were never intended to figure everything out; rather, we were intended to depend on a Sovereign who characteristically is good and orchestrates the big picture of life. A pilgrimage to Jerusalem metaphorically represents a faith journey of practicing an awareness of the presence of God, bringing our trust and veneration to a God who spoke the cosmos into existence.

Decades after I had traveled to Israel, I journeyed to Athens, Greece, a place that had an entirely different feel to it. I traveled there after I had completed a Master of Arts in a university philosophy department, which had given me some appreciation for Greece's philosophic traditions. In Athens, I visited the Acropolis, a UNESCO world heritage site that contains the remains of several ancient buildings of great architectural and historic significance, the most famous being the Parthenon. Next to that area was the Areopagus (Mars Hill). It was here that the apostle Paul, recognizing the potential significance of the Athenian altar to the Unknown God, delivered his famous speech:

> You are ignorant of the very thing you worship, and this is what I am going to proclaim to you. The God who made the world and everything in it is the Lord of heaven and earth and does not live in temples built by human hands (Acts 17:24).

Close to that location were other temples still standing from the time of Plato and Aristotle. A visit to this area brings the tourist into conversations about the famous philosophers and rationalists associated with its history. Athens has a rich history in metaphysics (epic tales of the gods) and philosophy (Socrates, Plato, and Aristotle).

Athens and Jerusalem—I cannot think of two cities that evoke more polarized associations in my mind, Athens and its association with philosophy and reason, and Jerusalem and its association with faith, hopes, dreams, tears, longing, passion, and piety. The title of this book is drawn from a statement by one of the ancient Church Fathers, Tertullian (c. 160-240 AD). Tertullian expressed his concern over the strange yoking of faith and reason: "What is there in common between Athens and Jerusalem? What between the

Academy and the Church?"[17] This question is a motif woven throughout the chapters of this book—the backdrop of every chapter is the assumption that there are linkages between faith and reason. As Tertullian did, I will use Jerusalem as a metaphor for faith, and I will use Athens as a metaphor for reason. Linking the two is the all-inclusive integration of heart, mind, and soul. I embrace the conviction that both faith and reason are gifts intended to open up a holistic life experience and that we must be willing to live with the tension of different ways of knowing.[18] As Blaise Pascal argued in "The Wager," we should see the reasonableness of hedging our bets.

The following eight chapters address a variety of topics that I have wrestled with during my journey over the course of the last twenty years. Several of these chapters offer an apologetic for the existence of something more than just a material world. A couple of the chapters specifically address the need for a deeper understanding of the Christian mission.

Chapter One, Perceiving the Beauty of God, asserts that beauty points to the probability of God's existence. The phrase "beauty of God" is frequently used, but the meaning often seems obscure. This chapter looks at some of the reasons philosophers and philosopher-theologians ascribe beauty to God, as well as some of the objections to that proposition. Two key areas of focus are religious language and religious experience. Every building block in the case for perceiving the beauty of God can be contested, yet the

---

[17] Henry Bettenson, ed., "Christianity and Ancient Learning," *Documents of the Christian Church*, 2nd ed. (London: Oxford University Press, 1963), 7.
[18] There are other ways of knowing besides reason and faith. These include EQ (emotional intelligence), ESP (extra sensory perception), intuition, and the way we know we are loved by someone else.

premises put forward are relative to their own domains of knowing (ways of knowing) truth.

Chapter Two, Making a Case for the Resurrection from Ground Zero, makes a plausible case for the resurrection of Christ. It addresses some foundational philosophical objections to miracles presented by David Hume and Immanuel Kant. The chapter defines the term "resurrection" and discusses allegations that the resurrection was a transformation to a spiritual body, a resuscitation, or a vision. It thus counters arguments against the resurrected Christ having a physical, immortal body. The chapter then makes a case for the historicity of the resurrection based on the biblical Canon but also taking into consideration some primary, secondary, and peripheral historical facts. The chapter concludes with the question: if the resurrection of Christ is plausible, what might be the implication of that for one's life?

Chapter Three, The Potential for Christian Fantasy Literature to Promote Enchantment and Religious Experience, investigates some of the objections to Christian fantasy literature. Drawing on insights from historical and contemporary Christian authors who have used this genre, the article probes the ability of fantasy literature to facilitate enchantment or a sense of the numinous. The chapter concludes that Christian fantasy literature is an expression of the Christian imagination, which is rooted in humans being made in the image of God (*imago Dei*).

Chapter Four asks, **Why Is God Good to All People?** That all people know some good things in life is a reasonable conclusion based on observation and experience; that those good things come to us from a Transcendent Source is a matter of faith. It is easily observed that peoples of diverse worldviews are blessed in talents, skills, vocational and artistic predispositions, and financial prosperity. Why is it that there seems to be no favoritism in the bestowing of such gifts, talents, and capacities on people who have little regard for piety or a transcendent ethos? The question assumes that God exists and has willed all peoples into existence. Some people ask, "If we are part of the faith family, then why doesn't God bless us in greater measure in talent, gifting, mastery, expertise, and prosperity?" This chapter is thus a discussion and celebration of common grace.

Chapter Five, Conversations with Cultured Pagans: The God Question, takes a critical look at how the apostle Paul intentionally and strategically engaged alternative worldviews while visiting Athens, the world center of pagan philosophy and religion in the first century AD. In a conversation on the question of who God is, a good starting place would be to define the participants' worldviews. In a society that is increasingly multicultural, pluralist, and religiously diverse, it is important that we understand both our own worldview and the worldviews of the people we are talking to.

Chapter Six, Saint Augustine's Philosophy of Time: The Enduring Contemporary Debate, takes as its starting point the discussion in Book 11 of Augustine's *The Confessions*. Many of us struggle with understanding time and the mystery of past, present, and future. Is time subjective reality, objective reality, or both? What was the Divine doing before Creation, and what is His current relationship to time? The chapter explains the traditional view of timeless eternity along with the contemporary view of divine temporalism, offering a way forward in the discussion.

Chapter Seven, Lessons from the Fall of Constantinople, examines some of the factors that led to the collapse of this once great city, a remnant of the Byzantine Empire. How do we come to terms with the demise of faith that the fall of Constantinople represented, as well as the interrelationship of faith and reason that Constantinople attempted to embrace? From a socio-evolutionary point of view, Christianity is seen as unnecessary scaffolding that can be kicked away once a culture has evolved philosophically, reached the peak of social development, and embraced rationalism. But what replaces Christianity is empire building of another kind and faith in another belief system that ignores human limitations and the profound mystery that is inherent in the human condition.

Chapter Eight, Signs of Hope as Christendom Declines, explores the purer forms of orthodox practice and community that might emerge after the institution of the Church becomes fully marginalized in an evolving secular society. The chapter describes the current cultural captivity of the gospel as a result of churches compromising with their surrounding contexts. This has led to public caricatures of the Church, which prevent people from being able to hear the Good News. However, as Christendom declines in Western society, there is hope that new and better forms and practices will emerge—a Church that is a more inclusive institution for the marginalized; a focus on relationships rather than programs; reinvigorated patterns of discipleship; more appropriate linkages between Church and State; a less distorted understanding of pastoral identity; serious engagement with social justice issues; and ways of making theological training available to all.

CHAPTER 1
Perceiving the Beauty of God

The concept of beauty raises a number of questions. Does the existence of beauty point to the probability of God's existence? Where do our ideas of beauty come from? What do people, especially Christians, mean when they say, "We perceive the *beauty* of God"? The phrase is frequently used to describe some aspects of Christian experience, and Christians commonly use the phrase in sermons and songs,[19] but what does the phrase actually mean?

This chapter begins by looking at biblical references and some of the reasons philosopher-theologians ascribe beauty to God. It then explores some of the main objections to the proposition that one may perceive the beauty of God. An attempt will be made to get past the objections and point a way forward. Two key areas of focus are religious language and religious experience. Every building block in the case for perceiving the beauty of God can be contested, yet the premises put forward are relative to their own domains of knowing (ways of knowing) truth. Smart's words hover over this chapter in that "all premises and methodology can be questioned as there are no knock down arguments in philosophy."[20]

---

[19] Some examples of such songs are "Beautiful, beautiful, Jesus is beautiful," "O Lord, you're beautiful," and "Fairest Lord Jesus."
[20] J.J.C. Smart and J.J. Haldane, *Atheism and Theism* (Oxford: Blackwell Publishers, 1996), 76.

1. The Case for Perceiving the Beauty of God
The case for perceiving the beauty of God is supported by both faith and reason. Following are some of the key arguments.

A. Beauty in the Bible
The Christian Church has inherited ideas on beauty from both the biblical and the Greek contexts. Christians drink deeply from the well of Scripture when ascribing beauty to God. The idea of divine beauty is connected to the biblical concept of "glory." Early in biblical history it is associated with visible, physical, sensory phenomena such as the pillar of cloud and fire (Exodus 16:10, 24:16-17), a bright light in the tabernacle and temple (Exodus 40:34-35, 1 Kings 8:11, 2 Chronicles 5:14, 7:1-3), and other manifestations (Numbers 14:2). In these experiences, the Israelites recalled that they saw no form or image. The glory of God was something independent of their perception, for it was something that had to be revealed. One could not just casually look into God's glory; God had to choose to visibly manifest His reality. Scripture is full of claimed revelations of God's beauty, many of which could be referred to as epiphanies of divine glory.

Scripture indicates that God made creation a good, dynamic, finite, dependent, and orderly system upheld by the power of His word. goodness being a broad concept which includes beauty (Genesis 1, Isaiah 40:26, 45:18-19, Psalm 104:24,27-29, Romans 11:36, Hebrews 1:3, Psalm 33:6,8-9). The Bible speaks of the beauty of God's creation (Psalm 19) and of God making everything "beautiful in its time" (Ecclesiastes 3:11). Job 38:4-7 indicates that creation owes its beauty to God and that His wisdom and goodness can be judged from what is made; that is, God is a supremely beautiful Being who reflects His beauty onto creation.

Jonathan Edwards picked up on this idea by saying,
> All the beauty to be found throughout the whole of creation is but the reflection of the diffused beams of that Being who hath an infinite fullness of brightness and glory [and] is the foundation and fountain of all being and beauty.[21]

The implication is that God's beauty must exceed the most beautiful things in His creation. Contemplation of creation's beauty is presented as a stimulus to prayer and praise (Psalm 148:1-6).

The majority of verses in the Bible that speak of the beauty of God are found in the Old Testament but not in its didactic (teaching) literature. Biblical references to God as "beautifying," "beautiful," or a "Beauty" are not necessarily trying to describe a physical, sensory experience in the way one would describe shapes and colors. Descriptions of the beauty of God often use metaphor to describe experiential and existential personal and intersubjective community experiences.

There are a number of supporting concepts to the idea of "perceiving the beauty of God." In the Bible, beauty is treated as something that is integrated into the larger purposes of God for His people. It has been argued that "beauty can serve as a pointer or natural sign of God, thereby enabling indirect perception of God's existence and attributes."[22] Beauty is often associated with the ethical, moral, and spiritual character of God.[23] Scripture advocates that one

---

[21] Jonathan Edwards, "The Nature of True Virtue," quoted in Leland Ryken, *Triumphs of the Imagination: Literature in Christian Perspective* (Downers Grove, IL.: InterVarsity Press, 1979), 36.
[22] Ryan West and Adam C. Pelser, "Perceiving God through Natural Beauty," *Faith and Philosophy* 32 (July 2015): 294.
[23] Ibid., 298, 305-306.

should seek "to behold the beauty of the LORD" (Psalm 27:4 KJV), for "the beauty of the LORD [can come upon] us" if we pursue Him (Psalm 90:17 KJV). Beauty also refers to attributes of God such as His glory and His strength in acts of deliverance (Isaiah 63:12, Psalm 149:4).

The ability to perceive the beauty of God is also attributed to places associated with God's presence. Scripture states that "strength and beauty are in His sanctuary" (Psalm 96:6 NASB) and that "From Zion, perfect in beauty, God shines forth" (Psalm 50:2). The beauty of the Lord can also be perceived in the experience of corporate worship and life with God. 1 Chronicles 16:29 and Psalm 29:2 and 96:9 all indicate that the believer should "Worship the Lord in the beauty of holiness" (KJV). Community life that is obedient to God's Word is intended to qualitatively reflect the fact that God gives "beauty for ashes" (Isaiah 61:3 KJV). Those who proclaim the Good News of God (Romans 10:15) are described as "beautiful" because what they are doing is an extension of The Beautiful One's activities (Isaiah 52:7). The Old Testament particularly associates beauty with Jesus Christ, and yet that beauty is not linked with his phenotype (his literal appearance). Christians draw on Isaiah 53:2 that states, "He had no beauty...to attract us to him." Scripture indicates that God's eternal beauty became a man in the *kenosis*, a veiled beauty, to transform what is ugly and deformed into something beautiful.[24] God intends to give people "the

---

[24] Physical beauty is not a necessary condition for something to be excellent. Although people love beauty, it is obvious that not all creation is filled with beauty. So what does God love? Romans 8:28 indicates that God draws beauty out of ugliness, and resulting out of the horrific ugliness of the cross we can see supreme beauty. Nicholas Wolterstorff, *Art in Action* (Grand Rapids, MI: Wm. B. Eerdmans, 1980), 161-163. Annie Dillard, *Holy the Firm* (New York: Harper and Row, 1977), 73-74.

light [experience] of the knowledge of God's glory in the face of Christ" (2 Corinthians 4:6). Perceiving the beauty of God becomes associated with spiritual and intellectual illumination, which in turn is connected with transformation and the acquisition of wisdom, insight, and truth.

B. Philosophers and Theologians

In the West, there is a difference of opinion before and after Kant on whether beauty points to God. Beauty was perceived and conceptualized in very different terms during the Ancient, Medieval, and Modern epochs.

Plato's understanding of beauty, in part, seems to have been assimilated into Christian thought, particularly the notion that "If something is beautiful, it is so because it 'participates' in the absolute Form of Beauty."[25] Plato attributed the order and beauty found in the world to a divine Craftsman or Demiurge.[26] Hence "Beauty has a separate existence from those changing things which move in and out of Beauty" and is a "reflection of a reality existing independently of our knowledge whether or not the order is precisely comprehensible." [27] Perhaps one of Plato's most important ideas assimilated by Christianity is the way he connected love with both the aesthetic and the intellectual urge. In passages of the *Dialogues*, Plato seemed to understand the urge to self-transcendence. For example, in his analysis of love in the "Symposium," he defined love as the desire for the

---

[25] Richard Tarnas, *The Passion of the Western Mind*, (New York: Ballantine Books, 1991), 6-7.
[26] Samuel E. Stumpf, *Socrates to Sartre* (New York: McGraw-Hill, 1994), 77.
[27] Ibid., 59. See also Robert Banks and Paul Stevens, *The Complete Book of Everyday Christianity* (Downers Grove, IL: InterVarsity Press, 1997), 63.

perpetual possession of beauty.[28] Aristotle, perhaps foreshadowing Kant, did not agree with Plato that beauty pointed to a transcendent idea of beauty.[29]

Mediaeval and Renaissance thought seemed to build on Plotinus's central place for beauty. Plotinus was a philosopher very much in the Platonic tradition. He wrote an essay "On Beauty" in the *Enneads* advocating that all people seek union with divinity. He suggested that God is inaccessible to the senses but aesthetic experience can advance one from ignorance to mystical transcendence. This is possible because beauty emanates from God and is bestowed onto material things. Material things become beautiful by "communicating in the thought that flows from the Divine."[30] Hence beauty points to God, who transcends everything in the world and can only be substantially revealed through a contemplative, inner, mystical experience that is independent of any rational or sense experience.[31] (Similarly, the ancient Church Father Irenaeus felt that beauty reflected the Creator's artwork and could never be contemplated in isolation from its true artistic intention. Although humans have fallen short of the glory of God, human life is found in perceiving God.[32]) Plotinus regarded non-sensible beauty as being of a higher order and claimed that, by ascending through a hierarchy of beauty-inducing

---

[28] Linda Zagzebski, "Vocatio Philosophiae," in Kelly James Clark, ed., *Philosophers Who Believe,* (Downers Grove, IL: InterVarsity Press, 1993), 256-257. "Symposium," *Great Dialogues of Plato,* ed. Philip Rouse (New York: Penguin Books, 1984), 69-117, 107.
[29] Tarnas, 56.
[30] Plotinus, "First Ennead, Sixth Tractate on 'Beauty,'" *Enneads,* trans. Stephen Mackenna and B.S. Page, available from: http://www.vt98/academic/books/plotinus/enneads; accessed November 15, 2017.
[31] Ibid.
[32] Hans Urs Von Balthasar, "Irenaeus," *The Glory of the Lord,* vol. 2 (San Francisco: Ignatius Press, 1984), 70-90.

forms, one could find the pathway to a mystical union with the One who has no form and cannot be confined by language or ideas. A person must become godlike to capture a vision of God, who dwells in unspeakable light and beauty.[33]

Pseudo-Dionysius also connected Christian thought on beauty with Neoplatonic philosophy, advocating that God relates to the world through emanations. He taught that the knowledge of God can be approached in two ways—a "positive way" that ascribes to God the perfect attributes of creatures and creation such as beauty, unity, light, and so on, and a "negative way" in which one considers God's nature by dismissing things least compatible with Him.[34] As a person contemplatively ascends closer to God, the ordinary forms of human knowledge are annihilated by the blindness caused by the excess of His beauty and light. Pseudo-Dionysius felt that, ultimately, God was beyond the knowable.

Despite the fact that Augustine had a Platonic tendency to suppress the senses and imagination, he felt that the chief characteristics of "sensation" and material bodies were that they pointed beyond themselves because creation is the art of the Supreme Artist. Divine beauty confers truth, virtue, harmony, goodness, and wisdom on everything, resulting in a love for the beautiful in humanity.[35] God is absolute beauty, and when humans enter into relationship with God, they can experience indescribable beauty above

---

[33] Stumpf, 125-126. Jerrold Levinson, "Plotinus," in David E. Cooper and Robert Hopkins, eds., *A Companion to Aesthetics* (Malden, MA: Blackwell Publishers, reprint 1997), 335-336.

[34] Stumpf, 155.

[35] Von Balthasar, "Beauty," *The Glory of the Lord,* 114-123. Authors who believe beauty points to truth and is a function of truth include: Arthur Koestler, *The Act of Creation* (London: Penguin Books, reprint 1989), 331, and Thomas Dubay, *The Evidential Power of Beauty* (San Francisco: Ignatius Press, 1999).

beauty. Augustine felt that perception of the beauty of God could also come by illumination, which would help one make judgments about eternal things. [36] Augustine's doctrine of beauty was deeply connected with the experiential. We encounter beauty in the experience of light-giving truth, in the experience of holy character, and in the experience of vision. Perhaps Augustine's cautiousness over the sensual enjoyment of worldly beauty may not have been a form of asceticism but a preparation for something more exhilarating.

Anselm leaned on rational metaphysics and natural theology in his ontological argument for proving the existence of God. He felt that we could perceive God's beauty through both the senses of the body and the senses of the soul. However, one may not perceive the beauty of God if the soul is hardened or blocked by sin.[37]

> Saint Edmund Rich encouraged the Church to:
> Recognize [God's] beauty. To do this consider the great beauty there is in earthly creatures. There are many things, which delight our earthly [senses] by their beauty. Seeing this beauty, there must be in a spiritual creature beauty, which is everlasting, for there is so much beauty in things that exist today and tomorrow will pass away. On the other hand, if there is so much beauty in every created thing, how much beauty must there be in its Creator who made all things out of nothing. How great and beyond measure the difference must be.[38]

---

[36] Stumpf, 138-140.
[37] Von Balthasar, "Anselm," *The Glory of the Lord,* 218, 213-237. Stumpf, 165-168.
[38] Elmer O'Brien, "St. Edmund Rich," *Varieties of Mystic Experience* (Canada: Mentor-Omega Books, 1965), 114-116.

Rich also built a case for perceiving God's beauty on natural theology, but he bridged into mysticism by arguing that the beauty of God could be perceived beyond images and reason.

Bonaventure discussed the structure of beauty and argued that beauty was a transcendent property found in the true and good. The beautiful could be sensed through the bodily and spiritual senses. He spoke of a hierarchy of beauty that begins with the physical world and leads to the inner and invisible world of souls, angels, and the Trinity. Bonaventure suggested that there are higher and lower forms of beauty and that the lower forms of beauty must be abandoned for the sake of the higher forms. Because the most spiritual forms of beauty are more hidden, one needs to renounce, at times, all familiar beauty and undertake a contemplative ascent to perceive the beauty of God. The soul can only experience "inner beauty" when it is purified and mirrors God. He viewed physical and sensual beauty as pointers to absolute beauty, for nature has its roots in God, and he suggested several ways a believer could approach the theologically beautiful. Beauty is an expression of God, who is "beauty past all hope."[39] Bonaventure strongly advocated that the Christian keep his senses under control on the path to God and keep the heart free, not imprinting any images of visible things on it. He stated that:

> Man must lift himself above all that is of the senses, all that can be imagined and conceived. He must reflect, and say that He whom he loves is not physical, for He cannot be seen, heard, smelled, tasted or touched but

---

[39] Von Balthasar, "Bonaventure," *The Glory of the Lord,* 352. Beauty is also an imaginative idea. Bonaventure made the serious charge that "if God does not think the Ideas of the world, he could not have created it" (Stumpf, 179).

can only be longed for. Next, he must say that he is not imaginable, for He cannot be held in boundaries, forms, numbers, outlines, or figures of speech. He is not conceivable, for He cannot be proved, defined, or investigated. As a whole, He can only be longed for.[40]

Bonaventure felt that to the extent that one longs for God beyond vain temporal forms of beauty, that will be the extent to which God reveals His beauty to that person.

Aquinas offered proofs for the existence of God that all had their foundation in sense experience, proofs from order, design, and degrees of perfection, which all have connections to the concept of beauty. Beauty is the result of harmony, unity, goodness, and truth and implies teleology, with a final cause in a transcendent reality.[41] Aquinas described God as beauty itself and the source of beauty in all things. Each thing is beautiful to the extent that it manifests its proper form.[42]

For Descartes, knowledge of self and God come before sense impressions of beauty. Beauty points to perfection, which implies the existence of a perfect Being.[43]

Spinoza, a pantheist, felt that beauty was a part of God, for "God contains everything" and is expressed in various modes through which we grasp His beauty through intuition.[44] Although Spinoza did not separate the Creator from creation, he did try to incorporate a metaphysical explanation for beauty.

---

[40] Von Balthasar, "Bonaventure," *The Glory of the Lord*, 349-350.
[41] John Haldane, "Thomas Aquinas," in Cooper and Hopkins, 9-10. See also Dabney Townsend, "Harmony and Symmetry," in Cooper and Hopkins, 179-182.
[42] A representative contemporary argument for this is found in West and Pelser, 298, 305-306.
[43] Stumpf, 244-245.
[44] Ibid., 251.

The empiricist Berkeley felt that there were some things, encountered occasionally in experience, which are external to our minds and exist even when we do not perceive them. He concluded that:

> There is therefore some other mind wherein they exist...Because all human minds are intermittently diverted from things, there [must be] an Omnipresent eternal Mind which knows and comprehends all things and exhibits them to our view...according to...the laws of nature.[45]

For Berkeley, the existence of beauty depended on the existence of God, who is the cause of orderliness and goodness in the things of nature.

Ruskin stated that the ability to perceive "typical beauty" and "vital beauty" was a gift from God.[46] Contemporaries such as Weil believed that beauty was eternity here below and almost the only way in which we can allow God to penetrate us. She felt that "the soul's natural inclination to love beauty is the trap God most frequently uses in order to win" the soul and open it to transcendence.[47] A "longing for the beauty of the world is essentially a longing for the Incarnation."[48]

Dubay referred to the "evidential power of beauty" in which there is a convergence of science and theology, based upon a growing agreement that beauty is a powerful objective pointer to truth. Beauty is seen as triggering a search for explanations and causes. Dubay suggested that God has left divine traces in both spheres (science and theology) to point to their

---

[45] Ibid., 279.
[46] Michael Wheeler, "John Ruskin," in Cooper and Hopkins, 372-374.
[47] Simone Weil, "Forms of the Implicit Love of God," *Waiting on God* (London: Routledge and Kegan Paul, 1950), 103.
[48] Ibid., 109.

single origin. Both disciplines assume that beauty is not merely "in the eye of the beholder" but is primarily something "out there." Dubay mainly argued for perceiving beauty based on contemporary design arguments, focusing on both the micro and the macro levels of nature. He considered beauty and design to be the language of God.[49]

Early Dutch Neo-Calvinists such as Kuyper, Bavinck, Dooyeweerd, Rookmaaker, and Seerveld, also embraced this idea that the concept of beauty was objective, embedded in the fabric of the created world and rooted in God Himself.[50]

A shared idea among many Christian philosopher-theologians is that divine beauty is perceived in powerful experiences of natural or artistic beauty, which reflect the nature of their Creator. West and Pelser argued that "emotions enable us to...recognize, and thus to understand and appreciate various kinds of value in the world, including moral, religious, and aesthetic value."[51] In other words, we seem to be "wired" to perceive beauty. They contended that

> If God exists, and created the beauty of the natural world, and did so, at least in part, in order to make himself known, it would make sense for God to constitute humans in such a way that we would naturally move from the sign of beauty to the God signified by the beauty.[52]

C. Further Appeals to Experience

Many defend the idea of "perceiving the beauty of God" by appealing to personal experiences that they

---

[49] Dubay, *The Evidential Power of Beauty*.
[50] Jeremy S. Begbie, *Voicing Creation's Praise: Towards a Theology of the Arts* (Edinburgh: T. & T. Clark, 1991), 97-156.
[51] West and Pelser, 300.
[52] Ibid., 308.

consider to be manifestations of divine glory. Testimony to this can be found in the mystical literature of the Church. Saint Bernard and Saint John of the Cross spoke of visions of beauty as anticipations of the beatific vision.[53] Saint Catherine described perceiving the beauty of God in mystic experience as being immersed in a kind of "Sea Pacific."[54] Many mystics in the history of the Church have indicated that they have perceived the beauty of God in immediate and direct terms not mediated through creation or nature. These individuals often indicated that they were wholly passive in the process of receiving such knowledge and insight.

The experience of encountering the beauty of God while in a mystical state seems to be very different from encountering the beauty of God through sense perception or reasoning. Mystics mentioned states of ecstasy in which they experienced boundless and incomprehensible kinds of beauty.[55] Pseudo-Dionysius described an experience of a cosmic vision of beauty this way:

> A vision in ecstasy of a sacral universe, pouring forth wave upon wave from out of the unfathomable abyss of inaccessible divinity, spreading abroad in ever-lengthening undulations until it touches the shores themselves of Nothingness. A cosmos gyrating in a dance of ceremonial liturgic adoration about the luminous darkness of that innermost mystery, aware of the

---

[53] *The Collected Works of St. John of the Cross,* trans. Kieran Kavnaugh and Otilio Rodriguez (Washington, D.C.: ICS Publications, 1979), 78, 557, 590, 607. O'Brien, "St. John of the Cross," *Varieties of Mystic Experience,* 217-226.

[54] Roger Schmidt, "Patterns and Varieties of Faith," *Exploring Religion* (Belmont, CA: Wadsworth Publishing Co., 1988), 362.

[55] Evelyn Underhill, *The Essentials of Mysticism* (New York: E.P. Dutton, 1961), 1-24.

awesome nearness of this center...and of the ever-widening distance from that One which is beyond essence and inconceivability. This beautiful vision inebriates even while it clears the mind. It is as though in the sudden glare of a lightning bolt there was revealed the existential compenetration of all the kingdoms of the cosmos, their hierarchies, their mutual relationship, the ceaseless movement of ascension and descent from the invisible summit to the base plunged in matter...A vision of such amplitude situated within the stable majesty of peace.[56]

In seeking union with God and knowledge of His transcendent beauty, these mystics seemed to be saying that it is necessary to abandon all sensation, all objects, and all intellectual and ordinary thought. That is, one should pray to see and know, but not by using sight, sense, reason, or any other common way of knowing, since God is beyond all normal seeing and knowing. Pseudo-Dionysius spoke of God as the transcendent "divine dark" who dwells invisibly in inaccessible light beyond all sensing and understanding; therefore, only those who go beyond ordinary sensing and knowing will get the opportunity to know and look upon the beauty of God.[57]

Saint Gregory of Nyssa suggested that "a closer awareness of hidden things, beyond what can be grasped by sense and reason, guides us through sense phenomena to the world of the invisible."[58] Gregory encouraged believers to climb a ladder from earthly beauty to the vision of Beauty itself with the aid of the

---

[56] O'Brien, "The Pseudo-Dionysius," *Varieties of Mystic Experience*, 66-67.
[57] Ibid., 65-78.
[58] O'Brien, "St. Gregory of Nyssa," *Varieties of Mystic Experience*, 44-51.

Holy Spirit. He saw the Holy Spirit as helping seekers to "suspend bodily perception and leave surface appearances," which would result in awakening the soul to the beauty of God.[59]

Many other thinkers—including Evagrius, Augustine, the desert monks, Eckhart, Rich, and Ruysbroek—suggested that, in order for one to be receptive to experiencing the beauty of God in a mystical experience, one must get beyond visible bodily things, forms, and images and go to the immaterial. Ruysbroek felt that earthly images were a distraction, and that because God is the Father of light, dwelling in incomprehensible and unspeakable light, He wants to illuminate the eyes of one's spirit.[60]

Saint Edmund Rich encouraged contemplation and introspection in striving to see the beauty of God. Those who want to perceive the beauty of God must "learn to subdue every image, corporeal, earthly and celestial, (and) reject (tread down) whatever may come to (them) through sight, hearing, touch, taste, or any other bodily sensation."[61]

Richard of Saint Victor also felt that capturing a glimpse of the beatific vision required a "complete forgetfulness of oneself."[62]

Eckhart felt that the seat of mystical experience was "reason" but that the soul only "attains to perfect beatitude by throwing itself into the desert of the Godhead where there are no forms," for only then can it be dead to itself and alive to God.[63]

Augustine, influenced by Plotinus and his followers, promoted seven steps in the ascent to truth. The sixth step he called the "Entrance into Light"

---

[59] Ibid., 44-51.
[60] O'Brien, 57, 60-61, 83-84, 151-157.
[61] Ibid., 114-116.
[62] Ibid., 108.
[63] Ibid., 123-128.

because of the experience of illumination. More interestingly, Augustine admitted that although one could see "the things which God has made, God Himself he does not see." He perceived God to be higher than his own soul and not to be found in physical things.[64]

Augustine was a small voice in the Ancient Church in recognizing the limitations of natural theology. Other mystics, such as William of Saint Thierry, Saint Teresa of Avila, and Marie of the Incarnation, spoke of the beauty of God being "imprinted" on the soul. William of Saint Thierry said that because "man is [made] in the image and likeness of God, [man] is capable of receiving the imprint of the Trinity."[65] Marie of the Incarnation spoke of thirteen states of prayer which she passed through to a point where she experienced a beautiful intimacy with God that was impossible to describe. However, she also indicated that the experience flowed over into the senses.[66] Saint Teresa of Avila elaborated on how joy suspends the faculties in the beautiful union and rapture of a mystic experience. The human spirit is elevated and given flight. In the beauty of a "nonimaginative vision," a kind of knowledge is impressed or engraved on the mind that is considered authentic. A person "understands that God is present by the effects [and experience] He grants to the soul."[67] Teresa felt that this was a foretaste of the secret delights and grandeurs that go on in heaven. Teresa often described her mystical experiences of the Lord in terms of being full of beauty, splendor, dazzle, whiteness, and

---

[64] Ibid., 59-61.
[65] Ibid., 95.
[66] Ibid., 227-231.
[67] *Saint Teresa of Avila: Collected Works,* trans. Kieran Kavanaugh and Otilio Rodriguez (Washington, D.C.: ICS Publications, 1976), 172-242.

brilliance that were beyond imagination.[68]

Saint Ignatius Loyola, who had personally experienced God flood his intellect with knowledge, made a distinction between mystic experience and visions.[69]

In the view of Saint Bernard of Clairvaux, one can perceive the beauty of God if God causes the soul to experience His love. The beauty of God's presence can enter and leave a person's being without the person being initially aware of it. Bernard said:

> Although He has entered into me several times He has never made His coming apparent to sight, hearing, or touch...I could not tell by any of my senses...Only by the movement of my heart was I able to recognize His Presence (the departure of vices, restraint on carnal affections, conviction of secret faults). In the renewal of the spirit of my mind and inward man I have perceived in some degree the loveliness of His beauty.[70]

Swinburne concluded that there are five kinds of religious experience that occur publicly or privately and affect people's perceptions of God. People can claim to perceive God through perceiving ordinary nonreligious objects such as things in nature or through perceiving unusual public events such as the resurrection. People may claim to perceive God in a way that engages the five senses or in a way that is not mediated via any sensations (the person experiencing only a strong awareness). Finally, people may experience sensations that are indescribable with normal vocabulary. One may recognize that he perceives God, as through a sixth sense, but be

---

[68] Ibid., 227-242.
[69] O'Brien, "St. Ignatius Loyola," *Varieties of Mystic Experience*, 194-199.
[70] O'Brien, 101, 105.

incapable of describing that perception other than through an analogy.[71]

2. Objections and Concerns with Advocating that One May "Perceive the Beauty of God"

The notion of beauty changed with the rise of modernity, so that the perception of beauty was no longer connected to a celebration of God's creation. With the change came problems with appealing to experience, revelation, and the perception of beauty as pointing toward God. In speaking of a "self-subsistent Being," it was asked if causes always had to have the qualities of their effects. In other words, beauty in nature did not necessarily imply that the Creator was beautiful. In fact, people questioned whether the definition of beauty was a cultural or subjective one.

A. Philosophers

Many philosophers have felt that arguments from natural theology leave the nature of divine beauty unclear; at best, they tell us that God is beautiful or beauty. Few contemporary philosophers would view any perception of beauty as proof of God's reality. This is partly because of a recognition that even good philosophical arguments rarely amount to proof and partly because of a recognition of the complexity of belief in God.

There is a difference of opinion before and after Kant on the question of perceiving the beauty of God. Beauty is conceptualized differently and is based on different premises and terms. Forebears of Kant were already constructing some contrary ideas to the mediaeval idea of beauty. Descartes felt that appreciation of beauty and aesthetic enjoyment were

---

[71] Richard Swinburne, *The Existence of God* (Oxford: Clarendon Press, 1991), 248-252.

merely sensual pleasures and not reliable pointers to truth. Truth is subjective, and one should not try to use a religious conscience to pursue God in an objective way or to bring God to light objectively. Descartes felt that the senses had the ability to stimulate an active imagination and thus mislead judgment.[72]

Empiricists of the seventeenth and eighteenth centuries accounted for the perception of beauty as being purely based on sensual stimulation. Beauty came to be viewed as a pleasurable feeling brought on by people's identification with and appreciation of certain kinds of order and harmony. Hume rejected any lingering connection with metaphysics and associated beauty solely with sensations. He felt that impressions of beauty are internal subjective states and therefore should not be offered as proof of an external reality. Any argument for the perception of God, including one starting from beauty—which he described as a "phantasm of the senses"[73]—should be categorized as an uncertain inference "beyond the reach of human experience."[74] According to Begbie, rationalist and empiricist philosophy had a tendency to weaken the ties between beauty and any reality external to the self and to drive a wedge between aesthetic experience and knowledge.[75] There are a number of philosophical assumptions that have encouraged the contemporary tendency to perceive beauty as intrinsically independent of other dimensions of human experience.

Kant developed some of the ideas on perception circulating in his time. Those ideas encapsulate many of the key assumptions on beauty that are currently

---

[72] Stumpf, "Existentialism," 485-487. Also see: Begbie, 187, 189.
[73] Joseph Margolis, "David Hume," in Cooper and Hopkins, 198.
[74] Stumpf, 286.
[75] Begbie, 188.

taken for granted. Kant believed that objects conform to the operations of the mind in that the mind brings something to the objects it experiences. He believed that we can only know things as they appear to us and not as they are in themselves because the mind is an active agent, imposing its way of knowing upon experiences and objects. He believed that thinking involves making judgments about what we experience, that the mind imposes its ideas on our experiences, and that human knowledge is limited to the world of experience. His hope was that reason based on universal laws would help us determine what is real.[76] Kant felt that God was beyond our experience. Therefore, he argued that we should not use transcendental ideas and theoretical principles (reason) that have no application beyond the field of sense experience to demonstrate the existence of God.[77] When people claim that they have perceived beauty, Kant believed that they are confusing subjective judgments of taste with claims to knowledge. He separated the enjoyment of beauty from the sphere of knowledge and moral experience, classifying such perceptions as "fictitious knowledge."

One of the obvious outcomes of Kant's views was the isolation of beauty from everyday life. The best that we can hope to achieve is perhaps an intersubjective validity. His synthesis of rationalism and empiricism provided an impetus to modern agnosticism, and his ideas have greatly influenced the history of philosophy, especially in metaphysics. Naturalists clearly welcomed Kant's ideas, and they have built their theories, in part, on his anti-supernaturalism. Rousseau and the Romantic Movement picked up on Kant's idea that beauty is an

---

[76] Stumpf, 306-324. Also see Begbie, 186-197.
[77] Stumpf, 306-324.

expression of feeling.[78] Darwinians and Naturalists extended Kant's thought into materialistic pantheistic monism. It is in the shadow of this historical backdrop that philosophers such as Kai Nielsen and J.J.C. Smart presented their case against the possibility of perceiving God. Rorty and postmodern philosophy confounded the topic even more by rejecting the idea that the mind is a mirror reflecting an abstract eternal pattern that is "out there," external to the mind. The traditional idea was that there is an essence to reality and to grasp that essence is to know the truth; postmodernists regarded that idea as pure fiction.[79]

B. Biblical Language

Locke stated, "All nonliteral figurative language should be banned when talking about objects of knowledge"—he considered beauty to be a subjective experience and not something inherent in an object.[80] He dismissed biblical language that refers to God's beauty as being full of ambiguity.

Hume was a forerunner of the Logical Positivists in contending that a statement is only meaningful if it is rational or subject to verification by the physical senses. Logical Positivists set up a standard of meaning whereby all language, including theological statements, was subject to measurement. According to their standard, the only meaningful use of language is language that meets the rational verifiability principle. Biblical texts that allude to perceiving the beauty of God were dismissed as empty rhetoric void of both rational validity and intelligibility.[81]

---

[78] E.F. Carritt, "Beauty as Expression," in John Hospers, ed., *Introductory Readings in Aesthetics* (New York: The Free Press, 1969), 129-141. Stumpf, 298.
[79] Stumpf, 473-480.
[80] Banks and Stevens, 62-65. Also see Begbie, 188.
[81] John P. Newport, *Life's Ultimate Questions* (Dallas: Word

Wittgenstein subjected religious language to linguistic analysis, classifying it as irrelevant and meaningless, expressing only the feelings of the speaker. Language's meaningfulness was determined by the accuracy with which the words represented facts. Wittgenstein emulated Kant in assuming that there should be a convergence between language and reality, in which language mirrors the world. The logical extension of this position was that abstract metaphysical propositions about God could not be expressed as objective fact. The presuppositions of analytic philosophy emasculated religious language, making it meaningless by attempting to force it to be expressed in the same way that propositions in natural science are. Wittgenstein claimed that books of divinity and metaphysics were full of abstract sophistry and illusion and should be committed to the flames.[82]

Carnap, Russell, and the Neo-Wittgensteinian group also attacked biblical metaphysical propositions, contending that they asserted nothing. Neo-Wittgensteinian philosophers viewed religious language as an autonomous language game. Russell stated that there is not enough evidence to substantiate the claims of abstract biblical language.[83] Nielsen added that since we cannot speak of God in a literal sense and since symbolic and analogical talk of God is illegitimate, then the claim that God can be experienced and similar "God talk" are nonsense.[84]

Phillips felt that it was philosophy's legitimate

Publishing, 1989), 96-112.
[82] Stumpf, 448.
[83] John Blanchard, "Glory and Rubbish," *Does God Believe in Atheists?* (Darlington, England: Evangelical Press, 2000), 310-313. Stumpf, "Analytic Philosophy," 449-453.
[84] Kai Nielsen, *Philosophy and Atheism: In Defense of Atheism* (Buffalo, NY: Prometheus Books, 1985), 77-106.

task to use the kind of language involved in religious belief and the notions of reality embedded in it, but he recognized that religious beliefs and practices are expressed in language that cannot be questioned in any straightforward empirical way.[85] Rorty recognized that we normally think of language as a means of representing reality to the mind. He refused to believe that the mind is a mirror that receives accurate representations of reality and that to know is to know truth, for this assumes that out there are fixed and stable realities capable of being described.[86]

C. Problems with Appealing to Experience

Schleiermacher attempted to analyze religious experience and extract from it the essence of religion, which he interpreted as a sense of absolute dependence and a taste for the Infinite. In his attempt to be empirical in his approach, he rejected the abstract in favor of analyzing religious experience in terms of feelings.[87] Theorists such as William James, Smart, and Nielsen resonated with Schleiermacher and analyzed religious experiences based on naturalistic preconceptions and explanations. They concluded that religious experience is subjective and can be explained by neurophysiology and the psychology of sensation and perception. These theorists claimed that there is no valid inference from religious thoughts to the proposition that God exists.[88]

---

[85] See D.Z. Phillips, *Religion without Explanation* (Oxford: Basil Blackwell, 1976).

[86] Stumpf, 477.

[87] Colin Brown, *Philosophy and the Christian Faith* (London: InterVarsity Press, 1973), 108-116.

[88] William James, *The Varieties of Religious Experience: A Study in Human Nature* (London: Collins, 1960), 104-257. Smart and Haldane, 48-51. Also see Kai Nielsen, "Perceiving God", in J.J. MacIntosh and H.A. Meynell, eds., *Faith, Scepticism, and Personal Identity* (Calgary: University of Calgary Press, 1994).

Nielsen refused to believe "that in some cases in which people take themselves to be directly aware of God, they are in fact perceiving God." Thus, he attempted to differentiate between perceiving an object and subjective thinking about an object. He attributed "perceiving God" to a conscious cognitive state, perhaps even a subconscious altered state, rooted in neurophysiology. Nielsen questioned the phenomenology of anyone who claimed to "perceive the beauty of God," suggesting that the agent having the experience got the ontology incorrect. [89] Nielsen argued that what a theist claims to have experienced is just a subjective feeling in reaction to what the subject took to be the presence of God. He stated that feelings cannot form a legitimate basis for a direct knowledge of God. The bottom line for him was that if the whole phenomenal content of the experience of God is affective, based on an emotional response rather than what is actually out there, then there is good reason for doubting that one could have a perception of God. Nielsen accused people of confusing their emotions with what they attributed them to.[90]

Wiebe observed that Nielsen's focus was on mundane perceptual experiences that have an affective tone, which are often thought to be explicable in naturalistic terms. Wiebe noted that perceptions from ordinary experience are going to be less convincing to those who hear secondhand about such experiences.[91]

3. Getting Past Objections to the Idea that People Might "Perceive the Beauty of God"

Christianity is not so much based on a single

---

[89] Kai Nielsen, "Perceiving God," 1-16.
[90] Ibid.
[91] Phillip H. Wiebe, "Kai Nielsen on Perceiving God" (unpublished paper presented at Trinity Western University, fall 2001).

proposition as on a complex web of assertions about God's reality and His relationship with creation. Perhaps it is unreasonable to think that a single argument could be sufficient for building the case for God's existence. Rather, particular arguments could be seen as providing lesser and greater degrees of support for the case for "perceiving the beauty of God." I will now present some arguments that could be useful in a *cumulative case* for "perceiving the beauty of God"; it is my conviction that these will increase the plausibility of belief in God by providing support for some elements of theism.

A. Addressing the Philosophers

I will begin by briefly addressing the guiding principles of Kant, for he has promoted the now widely accepted assumption that beauty has nothing to do with knowledge and truth. The dominant conceptions of human rationality inherited from the Enlightenment need to be challenged. That is, we need to move beyond the traditional extremes of objectivism and relativism.

Other philosophers have suggested approaches that lead to very different conclusions from those of Kant. Gadamer, for example, suggested that people respond to beauty because it mediates meaning as a unity; therefore, perceptions of beauty should not be classified as mere subjective consciousness but as ontological disclosures in which the meaning is realized in the encounter.[92]

Polyani believed that perceptions of beauty are cognitive apprehensions of the objectively real, and that it is necessary to have a wider conception of knowledge than Kant allowed. He proposed a very different attitude to the senses in that he viewed all

---

[92] Begbie, 199-200.

human knowing as a fully self-involving activity, engaging all of our faculties, senses, mind, and reason.[93]

Davis also affirmed that the cognitive and affective aspects of religious life should be considered together. He argued that, through our senses, we have a range of awareness that engages with what is beyond. Although our senses do not give us complete certainty, they do give us access to what is objectively real.[94]

West and Pelser maintained that "our belief in the objectivity of beauty is a first principle of common sense, a foundationally justified belief."[95]

Although Santayana found it problematic to call beauty a "manifestation of God to the senses," he did feel that an analysis of what is meant by God might reveal how the attributes of God could be an appropriate way to reach an understanding of beauty.[96] An example of this would be Balthasar, who started with the beauty of God in Revelation and not with the beauty of creation to come to an understanding of beauty.

Swinburne made use of probability calculus in order to make his claims about theism more plausible. While one argument might not provide convincing evidence, when arguments are combined, the probability increases; there is a cumulative effect as the arguments offer confirmation for each other. The probability becomes greater when many arguments are combined. Swinburne included in his list of examples the argument that if God exists, we would

---

[93] Ibid., 201-202.
[94] Stephen T. Davis, *God, Reason and Theistic Proofs* (Grand Rapids, MI: Wm. B. Eerdmans, 1997), 46-59.
[95] West and Pelser, 310. The authors argue that "this view is embedded in common sense and ordinary language and is not undercut by the fact that people's tastes differ widely" (311).
[96] Morris Grossman, "George Santayana," in Cooper and Hopkins, 375-376.

expect Him to make a beautiful world, and that is just what we find. Therefore, the existence of a beautiful world is one of the reasons to think God exists. He also felt that religious experience could be evidence of the reality of what religion claims exists.[97]

B. Addressing Language

Wittgenstein, who had earlier in his career thought that some theological statements were meaningless, later opened up a new understanding of the purpose and function of religious language. Wittgenstein recognized that, while some transcendent ideas are not expressible, that does not mean that a person cannot know anything about God. He believed that we are locked in a "language bubble" that tells us little about God or ultimate reality. He viewed religious and scientific language as being very different and subject to different rules. He said that one problem with the verifiability principle laid down by the linguistic analysts is that they failed to recognize other forms of language as legitimate and meaningful. A functional analysis of religious language allows it be assessed fairly, based on its own purpose, without the rules from another category of language being superimposed on it. Words carry meanings in different ways, and the meaning of a word is relative to the context. Religious language serves the practical purpose of giving meaningful expression to religious experience.[98] Religious language is not intended to serve the purpose of providing technical and scientific insights. However, the truth of the argument that the idea of beauty is objective "is suggested by...ordinary language."[99]

---

[97] Swinburne, *The Existence of God*, 116-244.
[98] Jerry Gill, "Wittgenstein and Religious Language," *Theology Today* 21 (April, 1964), 64.
[99] West and Pelser, 309.

Hick did not feel that Wittgenstein would have endorsed certain Neo-Wittgensteinian developments that contradict the normal intentions of most language users. Wittgenstein noted that there are no limits on thought; hence placing limits on language seems to differentiate which ideas are meaningful and which ideas are nonsense based on a subjective conceptual preference. Thus Hick argued that the Neo-Wittgensteinian philosophy of religion embodies a misinterpretation of religion. Religious people use language and religious pictures in metaphorical and mythical ways and as pointers to transcendent realities, and denying the legitimacy of this practice does violence to religious speech.[100] Hick discussed how Wittgenstein talked about the "religious way of experiencing" and the ways this was expressed. He pointed to two senses of the word "see." One has to do with the physical sense and the other with interpretive activity. Finding meaning does not only occur through physical sight. "Experiencing-as" refers to our ordinary multi-dimensional awareness of the world, which includes thought and interpretation. Hick noted that physical objects or situations can exhibit meaning to which language refers. One dimension of significance that transcends the physical meaning of the environment is the religious. Hick focused on the religious dimension, a kind of "experiencing-as" in which people perceive that they are living in the unseen presence of God. This can be sensed occasionally in a particular place or situational context or felt pervasively. Hick tended to define this as an existential experience.[101] It is important to note that although common language is full of metaphors that transfer meaning, that meaning can only be

---

[100] John Hick, "Seeing-as and Religious Experience," in Terence Penelhum, ed., *Faith* (New York: Macmillan, 1989), 183-192.
[101] Ibid., 183-192.

partially explained. Because interpretative activity enters into all conscious experience, it is reasonable to suggest that religious language should be seen as being a meaningful expression of religious experience. Therefore, allowance should be made for making choices in epistemological analysis, in which there can be a hierarchy of interpretations. Hick concluded that faith is an uncompelled interpretation and a mode of "experiencing-as" based on our inherited language and system of concepts. Hick was alluding to the fact that there is a realm of value beyond language.[102]

Schoen felt that one way forward in dealing with controversial religious phraseology would be to specify the range of phenomena in nonreligious terminology and then functionally define God in that way. If an analogous mechanism from outside the religious sphere could be found, one could hope to find a positive characterization of God's nature without recourse to religious terminology. This could open up a range of data that could be explained by God.[103]

Davis is correct that there is often an inexpressible gulf between religious experience or the perception of God and the ability to articulate it. It is intriguing that Davis used a classical realist, Saint Anselm, to address a theorist, Philips, and a movement, religious nonrealism, which developed after Kant. One was saying that we know the real world, and the other was requiring that we prove we know the real world. The real question is whether our thoughts correspond to the real world and whether the principles by which we know are adapted to reality. The fact that we are sometimes mistaken or deceived about reality does not dismiss all knowledge of it.[104]

---

[102] Ibid., 183-192.
[103] See Edward Schoen, *Religious Explanations: A Model from the Sciences* (Durham, NC: Duke University Press, 1985).
[104] Stephen T. Davis, *God, Reason and Theistic Proofs*, 46-59.

Otto highlighted the idea that language misleads us when we put religious truth into it in a form that tends to stress God's rational attributes. The conclusion is that many words stand for something else that should not be taken literally but should be assumed to have some experiential, subjective meaning.[105]

Wiebe also strongly argued that the language of theology rationalizes religion because its primary explanatory intention is at odds with religious experiential aspirations. He advocated "religious thought" as being unitary head-and-heart thinking that involves poetic and mythopoeic qualities, performing symbolic functions that touch the subjective and affective realms. Wiebe attacked the allegorical, metaphorical, and poetic theology of Louth, McFague, and Wilder for not quite achieving a mode of thought structurally and functionally distinct from rational scientific thought.[106] A key point is that theological language does not provide "religious experiential knowledge"; it only provides rational and conceptual "knowledge about God." Belief involves knowledge that is incompatible at times with rational theology. Religious language has many functions that are often overlooked, including the literal, the metaphorical, and the portrayal of religious experiences that have significance for interpreting life in a religious way. Probably not all religious language or religious claims should be deemed verifiable, falsifiable, or confirmable. Genuine experience may not always be fully expressed in human language, and perhaps this tension between language and thought is

---

[105] Rudolf Otto, *The Idea of the Holy*, 2nd ed. (London: Oxford University Press, 1958), 1-81.
[106] See Donald Wiebe, "The Irony of Theology," *The Irony of Theology and the Nature of Religious Thought* (Montreal: McGill-Queens University Press, 1991), 3-45.

not peculiar to metaphysics and religion. People often find language limited in its ability to describe everyday things such as new technology, unique events, or a human love relationship. Pascal could only find the words "fire, fire" to describe what he identified as an immediate experience with the Holy Spirit. Aquinas could only say that everything he had accomplished was like straw in comparison to his immediate experience with God. Although it is difficult to come up with the right language to convey religious experiences, and language may even be woefully inadequate, the attempt should not be seen as a total failure.

To properly begin to understand biblical language, one must recognize that there is an intimate connection between language and worldviews, that is, the way things are perceived. The biblical worldview is characterized by the understanding that God is known in history. That is, knowledge of God does not come primarily through a mystical experience withdrawn from history but through interpreted events. Therefore, biblical language must be understood in the context of its worldview, in which the aim is to transmit knowledge of God's revelation. Given this worldview, the language we find in the Bible should be seen as complementary and overlapping, not polarized.[107]

Wiebe has created an unsettling dichotomy, proposing the incompatibility of the theological and religious spheres of thought. The biblical concept of creation avoids both a metaphysical dualism and a metaphysical monism. The believing community of the Bible that spoke of "perceiving the beauty of God" came to know God often through an existential,

---

[107] Claude Tresmontant, *The Origins of Christian Philosophy* (New York: Hawthorn, 1963), 19-21.

concrete experience. From their accumulated experiences, believers learned about the nature of God. This history-oriented knowledge is evident throughout the Old and New Testaments. The empirical confrontation in history makes the Bible unique because it is rooted in concrete events and in divinely interpreted experience.

The Bible does not limit itself to just one concrete image when describing a spiritual truth; instead, it often uses multiple images to convey a fuller truth about reality. Being made in the image of God and being endowed with rationality lie behind our ability to think and speak. All language has a particular perspective, and religious and biblical language is only meaningful if it is restricted to its own unique purposes. Biblical literalism, a commitment to demythologizing, and a narrow empiricism or scientific orientation are all inadequate approaches in evaluating biblical language. The variation in biblical language can be accounted for by its comprehensive and coherent worldview. Although Rorty has not delivered us from relativism, he has suggested that we can justify a conception of reality based on what is most reasonable for us.[108]

C. Addressing Religious Experience

Anselm pointed to the fact that God may exist in one's mind and also in reality. An extension of this idea is Swinburne's case that if there is an omnipotent God, then He is everywhere, which would create a greater probability that people could have private and public perceptions of Him. If people have a basic ability to detect how things are, then it is more likely that they may perceive God. Because He upholds all the causal processes in natural law, He could

---

[108] Stumpf, 480.

intervene in their operations and in people's affairs to communicate to people through their perceptions.[109] Certainly this should be qualified by the fact that an infinite God can only be directly perceived to the extent limited perceivers can process.[110]

Swinburne and Alston advocated that the high incidence of experiences such as "perceiving the beauty of God" ought to be taken at face value unless it can be shown that there is good reason to understand them in some other way. When a person believes that God is experientially present, that belief is justified unless there is sufficient reason to suppose it is false.[111]

The assumption that perceptions should be accepted as claimed is based on two principles. The first is the principle of credulity, which advocates, in the absence of special conditions (tenets that defeat and weed out unreasonable claims), that perceptions ought to be taken as genuine. Alston referred to some of these conditions as a system of over-riders or a body of doctrine that can be used to check the acceptability of claims.[112] The second is the principle of testimony, which states, "In the absence of special considerations the experiences of others are probably as they report them." That is, it is very probable that a perception is credible and genuine if it is backed up by positive evidence such as corroborating experiences or a lifestyle change. Swinburne summed up this argument by stating that religious perceptual claims deserve to be taken as seriously as other kinds of perceptual claims, and that the onus of proof against

---

[109] Richard Swinburne, "The Argument from Religious Experience," *The Existence of God*, 244-276.
[110] Phillip H. Wiebe, "Kai Nielsen on Perceiving God," 4.
[111] William Alston, "Perceiving God," *The Journal of Philosophy* LXXXIII (1986): 655-665.
[112] Ibid.

them is on the atheist. If the atheist cannot provide special disqualifying considerations to defeat the theist's case, then the claim of perception stands.[113] Claims of "perceiving the beauty of God" should be considered "innocent until proven guilty." Naturalism has a challenge to explain phenomena such as intersubjective experiences that especially arise in claims of religious experience.

Although the arguments of Swinburne and Alston can be attacked (along the lines of Smart or Nielsen) on the basis that there are other comprehensive and coherent physiological explanations for religious perceptions, those alternative explanations have not been comprehensively proven to be *the* explanation for *all* claims. Those who support William James's views of religious experience should realize that a psychological or physiological explanation of a religious experience could be compatible with God figuring among the causes further back along the causal chain.[114] William James never intended to rule out the proposition that God exists or that He could be empirically associated with religion. Alston made it clear that we are not restricted to certain metaphysical arguments for the existence of God. To require external validation for perceptions of God when this is not always required for causal interactions in the physical realm is to arbitrarily impose a double standard. Various plausible-sounding objections to "perceiving the beauty of God" depend upon the use of a double standard or reflect arbitrary epistemic chauvinism, subjecting such experiences to inappropriate standards.[115] Nielsen's accusation that perceiving God is mostly or always emotional in

---

[113] Richard Swinburne, *The Existence of God,* 244-276.
[114] Alston, "Perceiving God," 655-665.
[115] Ibid.

nature does not match the literature.[116] This begs the question of why the emotions, a human response to cognition, should automatically be suspect. The problem is with a materialistic presupposition that dismisses claims that involve sensory encounters because they cannot be replicated. Nielsen did not have a category for direct experiences that bypass the external and are part of an interior experience.

Plantinga argued that we can be reasonably aware of other true things without direct knowledge, such as the past and other minds, so why can't we be aware of an encounter with God through a nonphysical cognitive experience?[117] Nielsen rigidly conceived of God partly in physical terms and demanded physical observation. This contributed to his inability to come to terms with a concept of God as bodiless and personable, which would make the perception of Him a genuine possibility. Nielsen conceded that "it is not crystal clear that such a Being is imperceptible," but argued that such a Being would be an obscure reality connected to an incoherent conception.[118] Nielsen was correct that every argument for believing in direct awareness of God can be skeptically refuted, but that does not prove that the refutation is objective truth.

Otto called for keeping the nonrational element alive in the heart of the religious experience. In pursuing religion in terms of concepts, we ignore what

---

[116] Swinburne identified a fifth category of claims that fall into perceptions not mediated via any sensations: Swinburne, *The Existence of God,* 251.

[117] Alvin Plantinga, "Reason and Belief in God," in Alvin Plantinga and N. Wolterstorff, eds., *Faith and Rationality: Reason and Belief in God* (South Bend, IN: University of Notre Dame Press, 1983), 90. Plantinga argued (1-91) that belief in God is properly basic (78*, 71-73, 77, 82), just as we can believe in the existence of other things that we don't see, such as the past, the phenomenology of memory, and other minds (17, 39, 59-60, 65-67, 81).

[118] Kai Niilsen, "Perceiving God," 15.

is unique to religious experience. Otto's key point was that religion could not be contained in rational propositions. The "Holy" contains inexpressible elements that cannot be rationally grasped. Otto lamented that Christians tended to emphasize the rational, ethical, and moral language of the Bible while ignoring an "over-plus of meaning." Otto's special term, "numinous," stood for the "Holy" minus the rational propositions. He believed that a numinous state of mind comes from the Spirit and can be evoked and awakened in the mind.[119] Experientially, he was pointing to people sensing God's presence (beauty or glory) or to God's providential encounters with people. There is a nonrational core in the biblical conception of God that is experiential and should not be subjected to imperialistic propositions or rational constructs. Biblical texts and religious experiences both express the incomprehensible, inconceivable, inscrutable, inexpressible, numinous, and mysterious.

Schoen may have been onto something in his attempt to show that certain aspects of religious discourse can be as cognitively respectable as parts of the most rigorous of the sciences. Criteria for determining the reality of religious experience are difficult to establish since we are dealing with singular events that cannot be addressed by explanatory strategies designed for patterns.[120] However, there are ranges of phenomena that may best be explained by the supernatural realm. When we consider the robust volume of data that currently is available regarding people's experiences of perceiving the beauty of God, we should recognize that this represents only a portion of the documented and reported empirical data. The field of religious experience represents a huge amount

---

[119] Otto, 1-81.
[120] Schoen, 59-79.

of unexplored data. The database for religion is continually expanding, but very little has been done to build theory based on research within this database. Wiebe suggested that if enough similar reports of extraordinary kinds of phenomena were collected, they would form a body of information large enough to increase the probability that at least some of them were genuine, thereby convincing skeptics.[121]

Empiricists can be accused of not exploring their empiricism enough by avoiding the places and contexts where religious phenomena are found. If one irrefutable case of a religious experience of "perceiving the beauty of God" could be substantiated, then the whole ladder of materialism would collapse. The bottom line is that the facts are not all in yet. One way to deal with Naturalism is to accumulate enough cases to erode the Naturalists' argument that certain phenomenon do not occur.

The argument for cumulative evidence has been building, especially with semi-experimental data. Cumulative arguments are such that the whole is more than the sum of the parts. Therefore, even if each part is weak, the net effect may not be weak.[122]

Wiebe stated that the most logical place to start in promoting the idea that God can be perceived is to begin with experiences that have intimations of transcendence, for they suggest that another order of reality exists capable of being experienced. [123] Researchers such as Moody, Davis, Hardy, Wiebe, Zimbars-Swartz, and Wilson have pursued this category of religious experience; they have collected many reports that have intimations of transcendence that give credence to the claim that God can be perceived.

---

[121] Phillip H. Wiebe, "Kai Nielsen on Perceiving of God," 1-8.
[122] Ibid.
[123] Ibid., 3.

Moving away from induction and deduction to abduction, to account for postulating unobservables, has shown some promise. Alston pointed out that we know our normal sense experience of perceived objects is confirmed by looking at the strong empirical evidence for it. Similarly, when we look at the data on sense perception, there is increased evidence for the reliability of sense perception. Global data on people's perceptions of God would amount to further empirical evidence. [124] Braude has demonstrated that some phenomena are established well enough to constitute a semi-experimental group. For example the accumulated accounts of over eleven million North Americans who have had near-death experiences has increased the probability and validity of such experiences. [125] Strong bodies of semi-experimental evidence for extraordinary phenomena suggesting an encounter with something transcendent lend credibility to the rest of the nonexperimental evidence, including poorly documented cases.[126]

4. Concluding Comments

Historically, many Christian thinkers have made an argument for perceiving the beauty of God based on natural theology and its rationalistic arguments. This is fraught with problems, leading to debates over the nature of logic and dubious assumptions that probably fail to bring anyone to Christian faith. Indeed, one may question whether the theist's position needs to be boosted by logic drawn from outside Christian revelation and whether the attempt confuses and

---

[124] Alston, "Perceiving God," 655-665.
[125] Stephen Braude, "The Importance of Non-experimental Evidence," *The Limits of Influence: Psychokinesis and the Philosophy of Science* (London: Routledge and Kegan Paul, 1986), 1-58.
[126] Ibid. Phillip H. Wiebe, "Kai Nielson on Perceiving God."

sidetracks the discussion rather than advancing it. Something being logical and it being true can be two different matters. Arguments from natural theology without recourse to revelation and experience—that is, God's disclosure of Himself—perhaps could be viewed as blind alleys. [127] Yet, based on common experience [128] and biblical testimonies, it should still be considered legitimate to speak of a revelation of the beauty of God in nature and a natural awareness of God.

One comment about another aspect of common experience is in order. Ordinary people still commonly use the term "beauty" to refer to scientific theories, math equations, good deeds, nature, and art. Because people seem to recognize various kinds of beauty, it is fair to assume that one can perceive the beauty of God. A philosophical analogy is: "Just as we can perceive another person indirectly by seeing her image in a mirror, so too can we perceive God indirectly through the grandeur of the natural world."[129] Weil's notion of the ability of creation to bring on a religious experience and excite wonder and spiritual longing could be a new starting point for making a case for "perceiving the beauty of God." [130] It is therefore possible that a philosophy of "perceiving the beauty of God" could be worked out on the basis of Christian revelation and the practicing Christian's experience of God. Kierkegaard was onto something when he said that the relationship between God and each individual is a unique experience and that, prior to the actual experience, there is no way to get any knowledge about it.[131] Ultimately, a theist's claim to perceive the beauty

---

[127] Brown, *Philosophy and the Christian Faith*, 271-273.
[128] West and Pelser, 309.
[129] Ibid., 305.
[130] Weil, 103-104.
[131] Stumpf, 489.

of God should come from his experience of God that is in harmony with the Bible, and it should not be made dependent on abstract arguments. The case should be evaluated within its own domain.

My apologetic contains the shortcoming of all apologetics in that it relies on persuasive arguments to change opinions. God has kept Himself invisible enough to leave room for the skeptic. Just because we can explain people's perceptions of the beauty of God without reference to God, it does not mean that we can rule out God.[132] It has been noted that:

> Natural beauty can serve as a natural sign of God. As with other theistic natural signs, the sign embedded in natural beauty is widely accessible, but also easily resisted. Thus, although perceptions of natural beauty may ground knowledge of God, they [may] fail to do so.[133]

I agree with Wiebe that "Christian theology needs to recover the experiential basis that seems to have motivated its original theorizing in order to respond effectively to" the challenge of Naturalism.[134] I am inclined towards the perspective that the beauty of a visible universe and the beauty assessed in immediate experience are two overtures deriving from a single composer, for in them there seems to be a unity and a capacity to spark wordless wonder.

In this discussion regarding the interrelationship between reason and faith, it is reasonable to adhere to

---

[132] See Alexander A. Fingelkurts and Andrew A. Fingelkurts, "Is our brain hardwired to produce God or is our brain hardwired to perceive God? A systematic review on the role of the brain in mediating religious experience," *Cognitive Processing* 10 (November 2009): 293-326. Dean Hamer, *The God Gene: How Faith Is Hardwired into our Genes* (Toronto: Random House of Canada, 2004).
[133] West and Pelser, 312.
[134] Phillip H. Wiebe, "Kai Nielsen on Perceiving God," 8.

religious realism's view that God's existence is completely independent of what any person thinks or believes about God.[135] Smart's metaphysical realism led him to make a wise concession—that "in the end we may agree to disagree, asserting there is an objective truth of the matter, whether or not we can agree on what it is."[136]

---

[135] Stephen T. Davis, *God, Reason and Theistic Proofs*, 46-59.
[136] Smart and Haldane, 77.

CHAPTER 2
Making a Case for the Resurrection from Ground Zero

What does reason have to do with faith when discussing the proposition of a miraculous resurrection? The goal of this chapter is to present a plausible case for the historicity of the resurrection of Jesus Christ and to assert that multiple lines of evidence indicate that a genuine physical resurrection did occur. This assertion will be substantiated by presenting the evidence in the same manner as in a legal trial.

Did Jesus die? Did He rise from the dead? Was the tomb empty? Was He seen later alive? What did the eyewitnesses in the biblical texts mean by a resurrection? How reliable are those texts? How reliable are the eyewitnesses? What is the relative validity of competing interpretations? Did the resurrected Christ have a physical immortal body, or was the resurrection merely the raising of a spiritual body, a resuscitation, or a vision? These are some of the questions that need to be addressed in considering a case for the resurrection.

This is indeed a crucial question. The apostle Paul recognized that if there was no resurrection, then Christianity is nonsense (1 Corinthians 15:14-17). However, if the resurrection did occur, then it confirms the existence of a supernatural reality. If Christ did rise, then it has profound implications, including substantiating Christianity's claim to being the exclusively true and valid belief system, with all other religions being ultimately incomplete. The resurrection hypothesis requires one to assume that God exists, which will certainly conflict with a skeptic's worldview.

This chapter begins by briefly addressing philosophically the probability of the existence of God and then confronts objections to miracles as they are formulated in Hume's and Kant's logic. It then explores some of the core lines of the historical evidence for and the objections to the resurrection of Jesus Christ. Key areas of focus are probability, philosophical assumptions, and known historical facts. The chapter concludes by asking: if the resurrection of Christ is plausible, what might the implications of that be for one's life?

1. The Probability of the Existence of God

Those who object to the probability of the existence of God take on an impossible task. For someone to know, with absolute certainty, that the existence of God is unlikely, that person would have to be in possession of every single fact contained in the universe. If only one fact remains unknown, God's existence and His ability to communicate or to resurrect Jesus cannot rationally or honestly be ruled out, as that one fact might be the key fact that would decide the question. God is a possible fact, and subsequently so is His ability to communicate and to raise Christ from the dead. Therefore, anyone claiming to rule God out of existence is claiming to have infinite knowledge. The probability of God's existence, based on the body of things that we do not know, is very high. This marginalizes the assumption that God is "safely out of range" and increases the probability that one might experience the risen Christ. This points to probable validity but still does not prove that God is personal as He has revealed Himself in the biblical Canon. The argument for probability is only part of a much larger cumulative argument.

Swinburne tried to meet the evidentialist challenge and render plausible his claims about theism by making use of the "probability calculus." Probability becomes greater when many arguments are combined together. Swinburne invoked inductive logic and intricate, technical argumentation to defend the belief that Jesus was resurrected from the dead. He began with the traditional assumption that God exists and that He established the laws of nature. Swinburne then proceeded to weigh the evidence for and against the resurrection, assigning values to factors such as the probability that there is a God. Using a probability formula known as Bayes's theorem, Swinburne calculated the probability of the resurrection to be "a whopping 97 percent."[137] One may find fault with Swinburne for using evidentialist means or for using a model (Bayes's theorem) of learning based on experience,[138] but his case needs to be considered seriously.

Swinburne argued that if God exists, we would expect Him to make a world something like the one we are in, and that is just what we find. Therefore, the

---

[137] In May 2002, Swinburne gave this assessment at a Yale University conference using the tools of probability to quantify his argument. For example, He argued, "Given that e and k are true, h is true if and only if c is true" and that therefore "The probability of h given e and k is .97." Richard Swinburne, *Epistemic Justification* (Oxford: Clarendon Press, 2001), 10-150. See also "Probable First Cause," Editorial, *Christianity Today,* July 8, 2002, 25; Emily Eakin, "So God's Really in the Details?" *New York Times,* Saturday, May 11, 2002.
http://www.selfknowledge.org/resources/pressnyt_eakin.htm
[138] It would seem that Bayes's theorem, which is a model of learning from experience, would accumulate more evidence against the resurrection if Jesus tarries a long time because the long awaited return of Christ continues to not happen.

existence of the world is also reason to think that God exists. Swinburne also felt that religious experience could be evidence of the "thing" that the experience seems to indicate.[139] There is a robust volume of current data available in regard to people's religious experiences with the risen Christ, and these probably represent only a fraction of the empirical data that has been documented and reported. The best explanation for the high percentage of people who feel that they have experienced the risen Christ is Christ Himself. The field of religious experience represents a large area of unexplored data, but very little has been done to build theory based on research within this database. Philip Wiebe has suggested that a "science of spirituality" has not yet gotten off the ground because the data has not been accumulated. If enough similar reports of extraordinary kinds of phenomena are collected, they form a body of information large enough to increase the probability of something being genuine, thereby posing a challenge to skeptics.[140] Empiricists can be accused of not exploring their empiricism enough by avoiding the places and contexts where people claim to have religious experiences associated with Christ. If one irrefutable case can be verified, then the whole ladder of materialism collapses. One way to deal with Naturalism is to accumulate enough cases to erode a Naturalist's argument that phenomenon associated with the risen Christ cannot occur. The cumulative evidence has been building, particularly with semi-experimental data.

Cumulative arguments are such that the whole is greater than the sum of the parts. Therefore, even if

---

[139] Richard Swinburne, *The Existence of God* (Oxford, Clarendon Press, 1991), 116-244.
[140] Philip H. Wiebe, "Kai Nielson on Perceiving God" (unpublished paper presented at Trinity Western University, fall 2001).

each part is weak, the net effect may not be weak.[141] Wiebe stated that the most logical place to start in suggesting that people may experience the risen Christ is to begin with experiences that have "intimations of transcendence," for they suggest that "another order of reality exists capable of being experienced."[142] Braude has discussed strong bodies of semi-experimental evidence for extraordinary phenomena suggestive of an encounter with something transcendent; these lend credibility to other, non-experimental evidence involving experiences with the risen Christ.[143]

2. Addressing Hume's and Kant's Objections to Miracles

The objections of Kant and Hume are in the background of modern skeptics' arguments against the resurrection. We'll address those here.

A. Immanuel Kant

Kant believed that objects conform to the operations of the mind in that the mind brings something to the objects it experiences. He believed that we can only know things as they appear to us and not as they are in themselves; therefore, he saw the mind as an active agent imposing its way of knowing upon experiences and objects. Since thinking involves making judgments about what we experience—the mind imposing its ideas on our experiences—Kant claimed that knowing is limited to the world of experience. His hope was that reason, based on universal regular laws, would help us determine what

---

[141] Ibid., 1-8.
[142] Ibid., 3.
[143] Stephen Braude, *The Limits of Influence: Psychokinesis and the Philosophy of Science* (London: Routledge & Kegan Paul, 1986), 1-58.

was real.[144] The implication is that we cannot have certain knowledge of non-empirical reality; we can only have concrete knowledge of empirical and sensory things that have spatial and temporal form.[145] The problem is that metaphysics is assumed to be non-empirical and therefore, by Kant's definition, an impossible field of knowledge. This Kantian attitude is evident in many contemporary objections to the resurrection.

Kant made some assumptions in affirming that the idea of God is unknowable. Bradley commented:

> The man who is ready to prove that metaphysical knowledge is wholly impossible has himself, perhaps unknowingly, entered the arena [of metaphysics]. He is a brother metaphysician with a rival theory of first principles...to say that reality is such that our knowledge cannot reach it, is a claim to know reality; to urge that our knowledge is of a kind which must fail to transcend appearance, itself implies the transcendence. For, if we had no idea of a beyond, we should assuredly not know how to talk about failure or success. And the test, by which we distinguish them, must obviously be some acquaintance with the nature of the goal.[146]

Kant sometimes sounds contradictory, in the sense that he believed in God yet refused to believe that God's existence could be established by lines of reasonable evidence. He wanted to avoid belief in miracles because he thought that their nature was

---

[144] Samuel Enoch Stumpf, *Socrates to Sartre: A History of Philosophy* (New York: McGraw-Hill, 1994), 306-324.

[145] Immanuel Kant, *Critique of Pure Reason*, trans. Norman Kemp Smith (New York: Saint Martin's Press, 1965), 93.

[146] F.H. Bradley, *Appearance and Reality*, 2nd ed. (Oxford: Clarendon Press, 1930), 1.

unknown. Though Kant felt miracles might be possible, he argued that it would never be rational to believe in them because reason is based on universal laws. Kant had a uniformitarian understanding of the world and advocated that one should live in accord with a universal law of practical reason.[147]

Kant thus assumed that there were no exceptions to natural laws. But why should people assume that everything rigidly comes under a fixed law? Maybe there are singularities, such as the origin of the world and the history of the earth, that defy classification. Maybe there are exceptions to natural law; maybe natural law could be thought of as general and statistical and not necessarily universal. If that is the case, then maybe these laws should not be used as a barrier to the possibility of miracles.[148] In avoiding the miraculous, Kant had to eliminate the miracle accounts from the Christian documents, including the resurrection, without any historical reason for doing so. His unjustified assumption is that whatever occurs must automatically be a natural event having a natural cause.

One does not have to be Kantian to embrace the idea that the most reasonable place to begin looking for explanations would be in empirical causes. Those involved in the field of history would be wise to begin rigorously looking for naturalistic explanations to the events they are investigating. The principle in methodological Naturalism, that one ought to look for naturalistic explanations of events whenever possible, should be imperative for all rational people. However,

---

[147] Immanuel Kant, *Religion within the Limits of Reason Alone,* trans. Theodore Greene and Hoyt Hudson, 2nd ed. (New York: Harper and Row, 1960), 79-80, 82, 100-104, 179.
[148] Terry L. Miethe, *ed., Did Jesus Rise from the Dead? The Resurrection Debate between Gary R. Habermas and Antony G.N. Flew* (San Francisco: Harper and Row, 1987), 15-32.

what do you do when empirical factors cannot account for an event like the resurrection? The insufficiency of empirical factors to account for the event could be pointing to a cause beyond empirical factors. We should be willing to look where the evidence seems to point even if it is outside the margins of our preconceptions.

Methodological principles that help us interpret what is happening do not necessarily lead to metaphysical conclusions such as the assertions that miracles do not happen or God never intervenes in the world.[149] On the other hand, the philosophical assumptions of supernaturalists allow for the possibility of a resurrection. The decision as to whether a miracle such as the resurrection happened depends on whether one believes that miracles are a possibility.

B. David Hume

Hume argued that a miracle was a violation of the laws of nature that are proved unalterable by experience. His presupposition of regularity defined a miracle as a natural impossibility before the evidence was even considered, and even in spite of any evidence. He felt that intelligent people should shape their beliefs on the evidence of uniform experience, which precludes the existence of any miracle.[150] Hume has been foundational in proposing that "historical statements about miracles are the most intrinsically

---

[149] Stephen T. Davis, "The Question of Miracles, Ascension and Anti-Semitism," in Paul Copan and Ronald K. Tacelli, eds., *Jesus' Resurrection Fact or Figment? A Debate between William Craig and Gerd Ludemann* (Downers Grove, IL: InterVarsity Press, 2000), 71-84.

[150] Norman Geisler and Ron Brooks, "Questions about Miracles," *When Skeptics Ask: A Handbook on Christian Evidences* (Wheaton, IL: Victor Books, 1989), 78 ff.

improbable of all historical statements." [151] Hume, Ludemann, and Flew presumed that all possible past, present, and future experience is uniformly against miracles, dismissing out of hand the weight of any past evidence to the contrary and claiming to know in advance that miracles will not occur in the future. Lewis pointed out that such an assertion claims too much:

> We know the experience against [miracles] to be uniform only if we know that *all* reports of them are false. And we can know *all* reports of them to be false only if we know already that miracles have never occurred. In fact, we are arguing in a circle.[152]

Hume had not weighed all the evidence; rather, he equated uniform experience with probability. That amounts to saying that we should not believe in Jesus' resurrection because it does not fit with the principles of regularity and uniformity. Lewis made it clear that the uniformity of nature is a belief that has to be *assumed* because the limited experience of the human race cannot prove all events. [153] Humanity is comfortable with assumed precedence and uncomfortable with unprecedented and unpredictable events.

Hume felt that our impressions are internal subjective states and therefore cannot offer substantial proof of an external reality. Any argument for the perception of a risen Christ could thus be dismissed as an uncertain inference beyond the reach of human experience.[154]

---

[151] C.S. Lewis, "On Probability," *Miracles* (New York: Macmillan, reprint 1978), 101.
[152] Ibid., 105.
[153] Ibid., 101-107.
[154] Stumpf, 280-289.

One of the problems with Hume and those who espouse his views is that they arbitrarily insist that all explanations must be natural ones based on preconceived theories that are closed to supernatural explanations. However, they do not offer any proof for that assumption, which is essentially a blind leap of faith in Naturalism. Flew followed Hume in viewing miracles as questionable because of their non-repeatable nature. However, Flew overlooked the semi-experimental data of the multitudes of people who claim to have experienced miracles. Strict empiricism, which requires repeatable empirical evidence as the only major epistemological test for truth, sets up criteria that are themselves non-empirical and rules out, a priori, vast ranges of reality.[155]

Hume's philosophic views intercept with the critical historical method. That method assumes that historical information can be used as evidence for reconstructing history only if it accords with the laws of nature. That is, these historians presume that the basic regularities of nature held then as they do now. The critical historian is required to use present knowledge of the possible and the probable as criteria for knowing the past.[156]

This recycling of Hume's biased naturalistic argument has hindered the advance of historical study on the question of the resurrection. The assumption of absolute uniformity, without looking at the evidence, has established a prejudice against any supernatural explanation. Hume's theory forces people to shape their beliefs based on an imperialistic view of probability rather than allowing them to reach conclusions based on the facts they find. To require

---

[155] Miethe, 15-32.
[156] Geisler and Brooks, 75-99.

that one always expand the laws of nature to fit a naturalistic explanation reveals a naturalistic prejudice. Building a case on a natural system is faulty if nature is not the supreme reality.[157]

Making the reasonable, probable assumption that an all-powerful God exists, and that He can act in the world, can lead one to a conclusion opposite to that of Hume. Such an assumption can lead to the understanding that a miracle, such as the resurrection, might not be in conflict with any natural law. God might simply have been employing a higher natural law that was expressed in a sovereign act of His supernatural power. The deeper question is: Do we have evidence and reliable testimony by which we can verify the resurrection miracle? This requires looking at texts containing eyewitness accounts by unbelievers and believers in a variety of contexts over the period in question.

C. Some Conclusions

It is very difficult to acknowledge the probability of the existence of God without recognizing the implications. To say that there is a probability of the existence of God is to acknowledge that miracles are also within the range of possibility. The only way to show that miracles are impossible would be to disprove the existence of God. And the only way someone could disprove the existence of God would be for that person to know everything there is to know. For someone to claim to know that all possible experience, past, present, and future, confirms the uniform, regular laws of nature, without exceptions, amounts to that person claiming to know everything, to be omniscient, like God. Such a claim would be hubris, an unsupportable act of pride. Acknowledging

---
[157] Lewis, *Miracles*, 106.

the probability of a "big G" God is to acknowledge that God is able to act in the world.

Because the supernatural is at least a possibility, any claimed evidence of it should be seriously weighed. If there is even the slightest bit of evidence of a supernatural act, it would make a strong claim to be proof that the immutable laws of nature are not immutable after all.[158] If God is a probability, then the origin of the world must be seen in a new light, as having a supernatural cause. This would mean that the natural laws, by which the universe operates, were set in motion by such a God. This would mean in turn that those natural laws could be interrupted, suspended, and overridden by an unusual, unpredictable, and irregular divine intervention, by a special act of the Creator. If an all-powerful God is a possibility, then special acts of God, miracles, are a possibility. If God exists, then God could become the God-man and deliver us in the manner described in the resurrection story. Miracles form the framework of the biblical, historical evidence for Christianity, especially the events surrounding the resurrection and ascension of Jesus Christ. The possibility of the resurrection is a logical implication of the probability of the existence of God, who, by definition, can act in history and in the affairs of humanity.

Paul Little has correctly pointed out that, "It is only people who forbid miracles, for natural laws do not cause, and therefore cannot forbid, anything." The theist works with the presupposition that "God exists and initiated natural law [and] therefore can intervene or supersede it as He pleases."[159] One should seriously question an argument that disallows miracles by using faulty definitions, that assumes the

---

[158] Miethe, 15-32.
[159] Paul E. Little, "Are Miracles Possible?" *Know Why You Believe* (Downers Grove, IL: InterVarsity Press, reprint 2000), 100-111.

evidence before the evidence is heard, and that uses circular argumentation. The question of whether a miracle such as the resurrection is possible hinges on one's worldview and philosophical premises. It depends on whether one espouses Naturalism or supernaturalism.

3. Defining the Term "Resurrection"

There is no shortage of proponents who hold the view that belief in a literal resurrection is outdated and inappropriate in a modern world. Spong used a Jewish literary allegorical method called *midrash* to construct a symbolic interpretation of the resurrection. For Spong, the resurrection was about the presence of transcendent meaning in the midst of defeat. His interpretation of the resurrection was subjective and non-literal. [160] Spong completely ignored the face value of the biographical genre and dismissed the historical nature of the texts he misinterpreted. One would be reluctant to give his spin on the story much attention if it were not for the popular nature of his books.

Wright argued, based on historical data, that Spong created his own interpretation of the resurrection of Jesus out of his own imagination and that this should be resisted based on a rigorous historical assessment. Wright advocated beginning with Jesus in a historical Jewish context, approaching the resurrection and the Gospels as biographical and theological history.[161]

Early Jewish Christians adopted their predominant understanding of the resurrection from orthodox Jewish theology that understood

---

[160] John Shelby Spong, *Resurrection: Myth or Reality?* (San Francisco: HarperCollins, 1995), 1-294.
[161] N.T. Wright, *Who Was Jesus?* (Grand Rapids, MI: Wm. B. Eerdmans, 1993), 1-103.

resurrection in *literal* terms (consider John 11:23-26). Craig pointed out that the very word resurrection (ἀνάστασις, *anastasis)* suggests the transition from a "supine corpse to the standing posture of a live body." [162] Yet many critics argue that Jesus' resurrection, if it happened, was not physical.

A. Allegations that the Resurrection Was of a "Spiritual" Body

Ludemann and Pagels alluded to the Gnostic Gospels' spiritual interpretation and resonated with the symbolic view of the resurrection often proposed by liberal scholarship.[163] Harpur also referred to the resurrection as being "spiritual" and not physical, based on his interpretation of 1 Corinthians 15:53.[164]

Those who believe that the post-resurrection body is immaterial frequently cite texts such as 1 Corinthians 15:44, where Paul referred to the resurrection body as a spiritual body. However, a careful look at 1 Corinthians 15:50 shows that Paul was speaking not of flesh as such but of corruptible flesh, for he added, "nor does the perishable inherit the imperishable." Therefore, Paul was not affirming that the resurrection body will not have flesh but rather that it will not have perishable flesh. Jesus directly demonstrated to the startled disciples that His resurrection body had flesh and was not spirit (Luke 24:37-42). He said, "Look at my hands and my feet. It is I myself! Touch me and see; a ghost does not have

---

[162] Copan and Tacelli, 22. *Who Is This Jesus: Is He Risen?* (Fort Lauderdale, FL: A video presentation by D. James Kennedy and Coral Ridge Ministries, 2001) indicates that Jews believed that the resurrection of the body meant being reanimated.

[163] Elaine Pagels, "The Controversy over Christ's Resurrection: Historical Event or Symbol?" *The Gnostic Gospels* (New York: Vintage Books, 1989), 1-27; Copan and Tacelli, 150.

[164] Tom Harpur, "The Resurrection of Jesus," *For Christ's Sake* (Toronto: McClelland and Stewart, 1993), 97-103.

flesh and bones, as you see I have." A closer look at the context of 1 Corinthians 15:44 indicates that Paul was talking about a body that is directed by the Spirit rather than being under the control of the flesh. In verses 50-58 "spiritual body" does not mean immaterial and invisible but immortal and imperishable. Bauer explained that the words *soma pneumatikos* (σῶμα πνευματικόν) that are translated as "spiritual body" clearly refer to a literal living body that is being divinely directed.[165] "Spiritual" refers to a supernatural body, not one that is non-physical.

A study of Paul's use of the word "spiritual" in other passages demonstrates that it does not just refer to something that is immaterial but is also used to refer to physical objects (see, for example, 1 Corinthians 10:3-4, 2:13-15). Peter said in Acts 2:31 that Jesus' resurrection body was the same body of flesh, now immortal, that went into the tomb and never saw corruption. Paul reaffirmed this truth in Acts 13:35. To hold the view that Jesus' body was merely "spiritual" is to ignore the physical claims recorded in the biblical Canon. If the resurrection had only been spiritual, there would have been no Church, for hostile authorities would have had every reason to parade the body to prove that Jesus had not been resurrected.

B. Allegations that the Resurrection Was a Resuscitation

Scholars point out that a distinction should be made between resuscitations achieved through CPR, biblical resuscitations involving a miracle, and the

---

[165] Walter Bauer, *A Greek-English Lexicon of the New Testament and Other Early Christian Literature* (Chicago: The University of Chicago Press, 1979), 678-679, 799; Wesley Perschbacher, ed., *The New Analytical Greek Lexicon* (Peabody, MA: Hendrickson Publishers, 1990), 399.

resurrection of Christ.[166] Jesus' resurrection was more than the resuscitation or reanimation of a dead body. It is extremely rare to hear about resuscitation after three days when there has been significant physical mutilation.[167] Resuscitated corpses will eventually be conquered by death and die again. Scripture describes Christ's postmortem appearances and ascension before witnesses in His changed state, indicating that His body was immortal, imperishable, and eternal (1 Corinthians 15:54-55; Hebrews 2:14).

C. Allegations that the Resurrection Was a Vision

Theorists such as Ludemann, Goulder, and Flew offer a visionary hypothesis of the resurrection and therefore dismiss a literal bodily resurrection. This view merges into the hallucination theory and refers to something subjective that does not correspond to reality. These theorists support their view by applying contemporary psychoanalytic models to the first-century context. Flew claimed that Paul merely had a vision that was not "sensible to feeling" in the same way that it would have been if he had seen Jesus with his physical sight. Furthermore, Flew denied that the risen Christ was seen by groups but said that there were really only a collection of individual visions or hallucinations.[168]

---

[166] Philip H. Wiebe, "Evidence for a Resurrection" (unpublished article, Trinity Western University, 2002), 4. Maurice S. Rawlings, *To Hell and Back* (Nashville, TN: Thomas Nelson, 1993).

[167] I know of only one man, other than Christ, who rose from the dead after three days, but he was not mutilated and crucified, nor did he demonstrate supernatural powers. Daniel Ekechukwu from Nigeria was resuscitated after three days, but his reanimated dead body will die again. *Raised from the Dead: A 21st Century Resurrection Story* (London, ON: Christ for all Nations video, 2001).

[168] Miethe, 22, 35-36, 52-53, 84, 113-114.

Flew's hypothesis only holds together if the way *all* the disciples experienced the resurrected Christ was no different from Paul's assumed perception of the "heavenly vision."

Goulder presented a detailed argument for the vision theory by discussing the explanatory power of "conversion-visions." Goulder saw psychological forces at work, brought on by a crisis and a sequence of traumatic events. These emotional forces reoriented the disciples, making them liable to delusions and susceptible to a religious conversion-vision. Goulder argued that the circumstances around Christ's crucifixion radically undermined the disciples' world and brought all the emotional forces of their psyches into play. This, in turn, dramatically altered their personalities and direction in life. Such delusions are purported to spread easily among the uneducated, beginning as primary and secondary visions and culminating in collective delusions in mass meetings such as the one with the 500 witnesses documented in 1 Corinthians 15:6. These delusions intertwined with the disciples' expectations, producing what they thought was a real experience.[169]

The basic argument of these scholars is that the resurrection body was invisible and not an observable, historical reality. The problem with this view is that Jesus' disciples claimed they saw Christ's resurrection body with their physical eyes. Appearance accounts use the word ὁράω (*horao*), meaning "to see." Although this word is sometimes used of seeing invisible realities (Luke 1:22) and can refer to both bodily and spiritual appearances, Paul was using terms that refer to ordinary observation.[170]

---

[169] Michael Goulder, "The Explanatory Power of Conversion-Visions," Copan and Tacelli, 86-103.
[170] Miethe, 53, 97-100, 109.

The usual Greek word meaning "vision" is ὅραμα, ατος, τό (*orama*), not *horao* (see Matthew 17:9, Acts 9:10).[171] Visions refer to something invisible such as angels or God. It is interesting to note that John used *horao* when seeing Jesus in His earthly body before the resurrection (John 6:36, 14:9, 19:35) and when seeing Him in His resurrection body (John 20:18,25,29). Since the same word for "body" (σῶμα, ατος, τό, *soma*) is used of Jesus before and after the resurrection (1 Corinthians 15:44, Philippians 3:21), and since the same word for seeing, *horao*, is used of both, there is no reason to believe Jesus' resurrection body was not the same physical body but now immortal.

Various Bible passages (Mark 16:9-14, Luke 24:25-31, 1 Corinthians 15:5-8) report that Jesus let Himself be seen or that He "appeared," translating the Greek word ὤφθη (*ophthe*). However, this refers to the fact that Jesus took the initiative to disclose Himself, not that He was invisible.

Ludemann felt that *ophthe* refers exclusively to visions and that therefore it is reasonable to assume that the other disciples had visions just as Paul had. However, he overlooked the fact that the verb *ophthe* is used in a range of ways. It would be presumptuous to assume that *ophthe* requires all sightings of Jesus to have been visions, because the verb does not rule out substance.[172] To say that *all* the disciples experienced visions imposes the vision hypothesis on the Gospel narratives. This is based on an unwarranted presupposition that overlooks comparative analysis of the language and specific texts. Ludemann posited that there were two

---

[171] Jay Green, ed., *Interlinear Greek-English New Testament* (Grand Rapids, MI: Baker Books, reprint 1996), 56, 395; Perschbacher, 296; Bauer, 678-679.
[172] Copan and Tacelli, 21-22, 25, 61, 116.

traditions, the first of which presented the visionary hypothesis—but then guilt complexes led to a contagious chain reaction of subjective visionary encounters and collective delusion, producing a secondary tradition of a physical resurrection.[173]

This "psychologizing" leads to speculation and fabrication out of keeping with the historical data. To suggest that Paul had a guilt complex that led to a vision or hallucination of the risen Christ would be to stretch the facts. C.S. Lewis, a contemporary writer of myth who affirmed the literal resurrection, pointed out that modern critics were usually wrong when they attempted to read his mind rather than his words.[174] The historical and literary facts favor the bodily resurrection rather than the visionary hypothesis.

As stated before, when English Bibles say "appear," the original Greek word is *ophthe,* which can describe a physical appearance. A look at other biblical passages demonstrates that *ophthe* is used of ocular vision. Since the expression is used in reference to other humans with physical bodies and since Christ is said to have had a body, *soma,* there is no reason to take the expression to refer to anything but a literal, physical body, unless the context demands otherwise.[175] The obvious conclusion is that Jesus' appearances were not simply visions but occurred in reality and were perceived by the natural senses.[176]

It is a flaw in reasoning to assume that because those who were with Paul during his Damascus road experience did not see Christ, then the experience was

---

[173] Ibid., 7-28, 22.
[174] C. S. Lewis, *Christian Reflections,* ed. Walter Hooper (Grand Rapids, MI: Wm. B. Eerdmans, 1967), 161-163.
[175] Perschbacher, 425, 295.
[176] Fritz Rienecker, *Linguistic Key to the Greek New Testament,* ed. Cleon L. Rogers Grand Rapids, MI: Zondervan, 1980), 439; Miethe, "The Continuing Debate," *Did Jesus Rise from the Dead?* 109.

just a vision. The Gospels never describe any resurrection appearance of Christ as a vision, and neither did Paul in his list in 1 Corinthians 15. It is true that in Acts 26:19 Paul said that he "was not disobedient to the vision from heaven," referring to his Damascus road experience, but in 1 Corinthians 15:8 Paul clearly called this event an "appearance."

The word "vision" (ὀπτασία, *optasia*) is never used of a resurrection appearance in the New Testament. It is always used of a purely visionary experience (Luke 1:22, 24:23, 2 Corinthians 12:1). [177] The post-resurrection appearances were described as literal "appearances" (1 Corinthians 15:5-8) and never as visions. Visions are presumed to have no physical manifestations associated with them, whereas appearances do. The resurrection appearances of Jesus were experiences of seeing Christ in His continued, physical form with the natural eye (John 20:10-18, 21:1-25, Matthew 28:1-10, 1 Corinthians 15:5-7, Luke 24:13-35, , Mark 16:14-18, Acts 1:4-8, 9:1-9). Several texts make it clear that the disciples saw Jesus' physical wounds or ate food with Him (Luke 24:13-49, John 20:19-31, John 21, Acts 1:4-8).

Because the resurrection body of Jesus was a supernatural body, one should expect that it could do supernatural things such as appearing in a room with closed doors, but this would not imply that His body was immaterial. Even those in the field of physics would be reluctant to say that it is impossible for a material object to pass through a door, only that it is statistically improbable. If a physical object were to pass through another, it would require the right alignment of the particles in the two physical

---

[177] Kittel, Gerhard, et al., eds., *Theological Dictionary of the New Testament,* abridged in one volume (Grand Rapids, MI: Wm. B. Eerdmans, 1985), 706.

objects.[178] If God is omnipotent, then this is easily explainable.

Because Jesus "appeared in a different form" (Mark 16:12), one should not hastily conclude that this refers to a form other than a real physical body. Without going into the debates over the authenticity of this text, we can compare it with Luke 24:13-32, which says that "they were kept from recognizing him." This would indicate that the miraculous element was not in Jesus' body but in the eyes of the disciples (Luke 24:16,31). Recognition of Jesus was kept from them until their eyes were opened. Whatever "a different form" means, it does not imply a form other than a real, physical body. On this same occasion, Jesus picked up physical food (Luke 24:30). In verses, 38-43 Jesus pointed out that His ability to eat was proof that He was not immaterial.

D. Concluding Thoughts about the Allegations

That Jesus rose from the dead in the same physical body is a foundational proposition and a vital point in orthodox Christian theology. Historic Christianity stands or falls on the historicity and materiality of the bodily resurrection. The Church proclaims the significant facts that the resurrected Jesus was touched by human hands (John 20:27), had flesh and bones (Luke 24:39), ate physical food (Luke 24:30, 41-43), and had visible wounds in His body (John 20:27). Jesus' body was recognized (Matthew 28:7,17), He could be seen and heard (Matthew 28:17), the tomb was empty (Matthew 28:6), the grave clothes were unwrapped (John 20:6-7), and the body that was

---

[178] Adam Archibald, *A Discussion of Quantum Physics & its implications for a serious theory of reality*,
http://www.tardis.ed.uk/~adama/quantum.html, accessed June 28, 2002.

resurrected was recognized as the same one that had died (John 2:21-22, Acts 13:29-31).

Any denial of the physical, bodily resurrection of Christ should be viewed as a serious neglect of eyewitness documentation. The significance of the resurrection has far-reaching implications, and its denial brings into question the authenticity of the salvific experience (Romans 10:9, 1 Corinthians 15:12). The resurrection only substantiates Jesus' claim to be God if He was resurrected in the same literal physical body in which He was crucified. Christianity's legitimacy rests firmly on the bodily resurrection of Jesus. Jesus said that the resurrection would be the proof of His deity (Matthew 12:38-40, John 2:18-22, 10:17-18).

The New Testament teaches that belief in the bodily resurrection of Christ is a key factor in saving faith (Romans 10:9-10, 1 Thessalonians 4:14) and is part of the essence of the gospel itself (1 Corinthians 15:1-5). Because of this, a denial of the physical resurrection of Christ rejects the firsthand testimony of the disciples and undermines the message of salvation. Furthermore, denying the physical resurrection creates a serious problem regarding Christian immortality. If Christ did not rise in the same physical body in which He was crucified, then believers have little to base their hope on. Nor can we assume a postmortem triumph over physical death. Paul indicated that it is only through the physical resurrection that God has "destroyed death and has brought life and immortality to light through the gospel" (2 Timothy 1:10). He told the Corinthians that, "if Christ has not been raised...those who have fallen asleep in Christ are lost" (1 Corinthians 15:17-18).

Those who oppose the view that Jesus rose in a physical body generally do so on the basis of confusing the resurrection body's attributes with its activities. In none of the explicit biblical texts about the resurrection is it stated that Jesus ceased to have a physical body at any point.[179] A second assumption is that because Jesus was said to be unseen at certain times, He was therefore invisible during these periods. This may be confusing perception with reality.

The Bible contains six accounts of the postmortem appearances of Jesus (Matthew 28, Mark 16, Luke 24, John 20-21, Acts 9, and 1 Corinthians 15). These cover a forty-day period in which Jesus was seen by as many as 500 people at one time. We are told about eleven occasions, though John 21:25 implies that there were probably more. Given that some of the witnesses saw the empty tomb and grave clothes, touched Jesus, and saw Him eat, there is reasonable evidence of the physical reality.

We have no biblical basis for believing that Jesus was not raised in the same physical body in which He died. Theorists such as Pagels conclude, because of the Gnostic Gospels' visionary accounts, that the doctrine of a bodily resurrection served a political function. However, orthodox Christianity agrees on the reality of a physical resurrection because the apostolic eyewitnesses disclosed the facts this way.[180]

The proponents of the major arguments and distorted historical reconstructions confronted in this chapter have tried to show that Jesus was raised in an invisible and immaterial body. However, it is clear that they have misrepresented and misinterpreted the biblical texts and ignored the clear meaning of the Greek language in which the New Testament was written. Their arguments do not stand up to the overwhelming textual evidence and rigorous historical

---

[179] Murray Harris, *From Grave to Glory* (Grand Rapids, MI: Zondervan, 1990), 390.
[180] Pagels, 1-27.

assessment that the resurrection body was the real physical body Jesus said it was.

4. Making a Case for the Historicity of the Resurrection

Christians base their faith on historical facts, not on fideism (which is defined as "reliance on faith rather than reason in pursuit of religious truth"[181]). Scripture supports the use of reason (Isaiah 1:18, Matthew 22:36-37). God is a rational being and created us as rational beings. That means we should have a sufficient reason for our beliefs because faith needs some factual basis. One difference between orthodox Christian faith and existential theologies is that facts are the foundation for an orthodox faith commitment.

A. Addressing the Legendary Hypothesis

Many, such as John Dominic Crossan of the Jesus Seminar, have questioned the historicity of the resurrection, claiming that a mythologizing process is evident in the biblical texts. Templeton, Harpur, Spong, and Pagels questioned the isolated mention in Matthew's Gospel of the veil torn, the major earthquake, the guard at the tomb, and the mass resuscitations of an abundant number of people who were dead and long buried in tombs.[182] Templeton asked, "Why are none of these resurrected men and women named?" and "Why is there no other mention of them in the New Testament?" Flew and Ludemann

---

[181] *Merriam-Webster's Collegiate Dictionary,* 11th ed. (Springfield, MA: Merriam-Webster, 2004), 465.
[182] Charles Templeton, "The Resurrection," *Farewell To God: My reasons for rejecting the Christian faith* (Toronto: McClelland and Stewart, 1996), 121; Harpur, 101-102; Spong, 3-27; *Who is this Jesus, Is He Risen?*

described aspects of the resurrection story as serendipitous hearsay and embellishment.[183]

Many events around the cross and resurrection have been classified as legend and myth and therefore not historical. Gundry claimed that some texts resist harmonization and show traces of development and progression, especially in the resurrection narratives; he argued, for example, that Joseph of Arimathea progresses in character. Although this evidence must not be ignored, it should also be pointed out that development does not necessarily mean distortion.[184]

Theorists such as Craig, Habermas, and Morison have dismissed the legendary-development theory, pointing out that a legend cannot tell anyone how it originated. They also point out that the Gospel accounts lack the mythical tendencies that are so obvious in much of ancient literature and demonstrate that the historicity and authenticity of the texts are defensible.[185] Morison stated:

> If Christianity began by proclaiming merely the survival of Jesus and progressed by slow stages of legendary accretion to belief in the physical vacancy of the tomb, the oldest and most primitive documents ought to be the least emphatic. It is not so, It is precisely the Matthean and Marcan documents, which by universal consent reach back furthest towards the lost origins, that are sharply cut in their outlines and describe the vacant tomb with the coldest objectivity.[186]

---

[183] Copan and Tacelli, 16; Miethe, 134.
[184] Robert Gundry, "Trimming the Debate," Copan and Tacelli, 20, 105-106.
[185] Copan and Tacelli, 168-171. Gary Habermas, "Resurrection Claims in Non-Christian Religions," *Religious Studies* 25 (1989), 24. Frank Morison, *Who Moved the Stone?* (Grand Rapids, MI: Zondervan, reprint 2002), 138, 168-169.
[186] Morison, 138.

The miracle events around the resurrection are surrounded by references to real people, places, and times. A scrutiny of these geographical, political, and archeological details establishes their historical reliability. In addition to the Gospels, there are twenty different non-Christian sources containing sixty-five facts about the life, death, and resurrection of Jesus.[187] The New Testament documents and witnesses are too early, too numerous, and too accurate to be accused of being legends.

Science is all about causes and effects, whether it involves establishing the reality of dinosaurs by studying fossils, diagnosing diseases by looking at symptoms, or solving crimes by analyzing evidence. In the same way, if it can be established that Jesus died on the cross, that there was an empty tomb, and that He later appeared to people, then we have made the case for the resurrection.[188] There are good historical grounds for affirming the facts of the resurrection and the disciples' belief in it.

This does not mean that there are no historical gaps. Indeed, there are. Scholars such as Blanchard and Pannenberg recognize that there are gaps that do not allow the Gospels to be considered reliable historical sources in terms of providing the full story. However, they do view the resurrection texts as solid historical documents.[189]

Philip Wiebe has also indicated that proponents of orthodox Christianity seldom realize that the New

---

[187] Habermas, 106; *Who Is This Jesus: Is He Risen?*
[188] Lee Strobel, "Researching the Resurrection: The Evidence of Appearances," *The Case for Christ: A Journalist's Personal Investigation of the Evidence for Jesus* (Grand Rapids, MI: Zondervan, 1998), 225-245; Philip H. Wiebe, "Evidence for a Resurrection," 1-36.
[189] John Blanchard, *Does God Believe in Atheists?* (Darlington, England: Evangelical Press, 2000), 581; Wolfhart Pannenberg, "Response to the Debate," in Miethe, 132.

Testament documents do not have as much historical concreteness as they assume. They often claim there is more evidence than they are able to present, and they seldom examine what is necessary to prove conclusively that the resurrection happened. Wiebe said many orthodox Christians are talking out of both sides of their mouth when they insist there is ample evidence for the resurrection but then say that the resurrection comes down to faith. It would not be necessary to appeal to faith if the claim was highly probable on New Testament evidence alone. Wiebe's point is that the resurrection claim can be enhanced by additional historical evidence, including the Shroud of Turin (as per Ian Wilson's latest research findings noted in Section 5E of this chapter) and examples of religious experience with the risen Christ. Wiebe argued that these additional types of evidence supplement the New Testament appearance stories.[190]

Other scholars argue that the evidence demands assent to the historicity of the resurrection. Using standard critical historical methodologies, their investigations have led them to conclude that the best explanation for the given historical facts is that the resurrection is a reality and that in this instance God directly intervened in history.[191]

B. Addressing the Authority of the Biblical Canon

One quickly recognizes that critics attack the resurrection texts with the accusation that the biblical Canon is filled with errors and therefore not authoritative or definitive. Some have felt that the historicity and authority of Scripture has rested on

---

[190] Philip H. Wiebe, "Evidence for a Resurrection," 1-36; Philip H. Wiebe, "Christic Appearances and Visions in the New Testament," *Visions of Jesus* (New York: Oxford University Press, 1997), 119-121.

[191] Copan and Tacelli, 15, 37; Craig in Miethe, 19-28.

unreliable and insecure foundations because the Christian Church has taught differing things throughout its history or because of perceived unpalatable elements in the texts such as slavery, patriarchy, character defects, sin, anti-Semitism, and so forth. [192] One manifestation of this is the interpretative attacks on the historicity of the Bible through higher criticism.

One of the definitions of God's character is that He is perfect. If God cannot make a mistake and the Bible is the inspired Word of God, then the Bible must be an accurate report. This means that errors in interpretation, in translation, or in transcription are human errors, not errors of the divine Author.

The authority of Scripture is grounded in assertions about its origins. It is not the intention of this chapter to elaborate on or to diffuse the controversy around the authority of Scripture, but it should be acknowledged that this is an issue and it deserves to be treated more fully in the defense of the veracity of the resurrection.

5. Primary Arguments for the Historicity of the Resurrection

Critical investigations using standard historical methodologies confirm a list of events that scholars agree are part of knowable history. These can be categorized as primary, secondary, and peripheral arguments for the resurrection. In this section, we will look at the primary arguments.

---

[192] Stephen T. Davis, "The Question of Miracles, Ascension and Anti-Semitism," Copan and Tacelli, 19, 60-61; Morison, 9-12, 185.

A. Jesus Died because of the Severity of Crucifixion.

Scholars cite a number of points of evidence to prove that Jesus was dead and did not survive the cross. There is no textual evidence to suggest that Jesus was drugged. The heavy loss of blood makes death highly probable. The best evidence suggests that when His side was pierced, it ensured death. There was no doubt in the minds of the Roman executioners that Jesus died a death by asphyxiation. A Roman soldier would have been unwilling to risk his own life by mistakenly allowing Jesus to survive. Jesus was executed in a way that would have ensured death, and one should not overlook the deadly character of the wounds inflicted.[193] It is highly unlikely that Jesus would have been able to unwrap Himself from His grave clothes and thirty-four to forty-five kilograms of spices, and even if He did, His appearance would have been more that of a resuscitated wretch than a resurrected Savior. Also, Pilate had asked for assurances that Jesus was truly dead before releasing the body.[194]

Scholars point to the clear details of torture and agony on the cross—that most likely included hematidrosis (sweating blood as a result of ruptured blood vessels due to extreme physical or emotional stress), hypovolemic shock (loss of a fifth of the body's blood or fluid supply), crushed nerves, dislocated shoulders, and asphyxiation. Given these details, scholars argue that death could not be faked or eluded.[195]

---

[193] Strobel, "The Medical Evidence," *The Case for Christ*, 191-204; Morison, 96.
[194] Geisler and Brooks, "Questions about Jesus Christ," *When Skeptics Ask*, 118-128.
[195] Strobel, "The Medical Evidence," 191-204.

World famous specialists in the area of medical education and research at the Mayo Clinic [196] conducted an interdisciplinary investigation into the circumstances of the crucifixion. Drawing from a range of historical Christian and non-Christian source material, and a knowledge of both anatomy and ancient crucifixion practices, the authors reconstructed the probable medical details of the slow process of execution by crucifixion. They also provided a plausible medical commentary on Christ's extreme suffering in Gethsemane and during His trials leading up to His crucifixion. Based on their research, they concluded that the weight of historical and medical evidence indicates that Jesus was dead before the wound to His side was inflicted. Interpretations that assume Jesus did not die on the cross contradict modern medical knowledge.[197]

B. Jesus Was Buried in a Dignified Tomb.

The four Canonical Gospels attest to the fact that Jesus was not simply buried in a common grave, as was the custom with the condemned,[198] but buried in Joseph of Arimathea's tomb (Matthew 27:57-61, Mark 15:42-47, Luke 23:50-56, John 19:38-42).

---

[196] The Mayo Clinic is a nonprofit medical practice and medical research group based in Rochester, Minnesota. It employs more than 4,500 physicians and scientists and 57,100 allied health staff. The practice specializes in treating difficult cases through tertiary care. It spends millions of dollars each year on research. In 2016-17, Mayo Clinic, Rochester, was ranked as the number one overall hospital in the United States by the *U.S. News & World Report.*

[197] William D. Edwards et al., "On the Physical Death of Jesus Christ," *The Journal of the American Medical Association* 255, no. 11 (March 21, 1986): 1455-1463.

[198] Strobel, "The Evidence of the Missing Body," *The Case for Christ,* 208-9.

C. Jesus' Death Caused the Disciples to Despair and Lose Hope.

All four Gospels attest to the fact that the disciples became disheartened and discouraged after the crucifixion. All of the disciples deserted Jesus and fled (Matthew 26:56, Mark 14:52). Judas fell into remorse and became suicidal (Matthew 27:3-5, John 18:15-18, 25-27). Peter turned his back on Christ (Matthew 26:69-75, Mark 14:66-72, Luke 22:54-62). Those who didn't run away in despair watched gloomily from a distance (Matthew 27:55-56, Mark 15:40, John 19:25-27). They went about with "faces downcast" and expressed that what they had previously hoped for was gone (Luke 24:17,21). We even find some behaving neurotically outside the tomb, crying and weeping (John 20:11-15).

D. Jesus Was Buried in a Tomb that Was Discovered to Be Empty Just a Few Days Later.

Isaiah 53:9 and Psalm 16:10 indicate that the Christ was to be buried in a rich man's tomb and the Holy One would not "see decay" of the body. All four Gospels attest to the empty tomb (Matthew 28:1-7, Mark 16:1-8, Luke 24:1-12, John 20:1-9). That the tomb was empty does not necessarily mean that there was a resurrection; there must also be evidence that no remains exist.[199] When a dead body goes missing in a morgue, people do not automatically conclude that a resurrection has occurred. More is needed to establish that fact. However, if there was a resurrection, there would definitely be an empty tomb—and that is precisely what there was. Pannenberg made it clear that the argument for a literal resurrection depends on the convergence of the appearance reports and the

---

[199] Philip H. Wiebe, "Evidence for a Resurrection," 5-6; Strobel, "The Evidence of Appearances," *The Case for Christ,* 225.

empty tomb; these two lines of evidence gain their full weight together.[200]

Most deniers of the resurrection, including Flew,[201] do not object to the idea of the empty tomb in itself, but they object to the implication that the empty tomb helps build a case for the resurrection. What is really at issue here is that in the world of our ordinary experience, dead people do not rise. Wilson, Spong, and Pagels claimed that the tomb was either still full or it was empty for alternative, naturally explainable reasons.[202] Harpur suggested that because God merely raised Jesus from the dead spiritually, the tomb still had a body in it.[203] Goulder did not believe that a miracle was needed to explain the empty tomb because he was convinced that the resurrection story developed in relation to tensions in the Church thirty to seventy years after Christ's death. He concluded that the empty tomb should not be taken seriously because of the discrepancies, contradictions, and differences in the Gospel accounts concerning issues such as the number and names of people at the tomb.[204]

Ludemann thought it ludicrous to suggest that a decaying corpse could be made alive again, stating, "The tomb of Jesus was not empty, but full, and his

---

[200] Wolfhart Pannenberg, "Response to the Debate," Miethe, 130-131.

[201] Flew avoided any consideration of the empty tomb. He took issue with the fact that the early eyewitnesses cannot be cross-examined, stated that there are no current valid naturalistic theories to account for this event, and concluded that we do not have all the information needed to make a judgment: *Miethe*, 72, 75, 91.

[202] Wright, 39-92.

[203] Harpur, 97-103; Pagels, 1-27.

[204] Michael Goulder, "The Explanatory Power of Conversion-Visions," 19, 100-101.

body did not disappear but rotted away."[205] Ludemann attacked the empty tomb tradition by claiming that it was not part of the earliest tradition and was not known by Paul. His view was that the empty tomb reports were motivated by religious enthusiasm, which was not open to reason or objections, and that the story became embellished over time.[206] Gundry believed that the empty tomb reports were made up because subjective visions were thought to imply a physical resurrection.[207]

All of the above represent complex objections that cannot be exhaustively dealt with in this chapter. What can be stated at this point is the affirmative evidence for an empty tomb that demonstrates it was a historical fact. The empty tomb is implicit in the very early creed found in 1 Corinthians 15.[208] It is widely agreed that the site of Jesus' tomb was known to Christians, Jews, and the Roman authorities.[209] The Gospel of Mark, which contains the story, is considered an early source, too early for legend to have corrupted it. There is an absence of a fictional narrative style such as is common in the apocryphal accounts.[210] Further, the unanimous testimony that the empty tomb was discovered by women points to the authenticity of the story; a made-up story would have had men as the witnesses.[211] No one in the context of the first-century event was claiming that the tomb still contained Jesus' body; the assumption that the tomb was empty was universal.[212] Scholars who support the

---

[205] Copan and Tacelli, 8, 15.
[206] Ibid., 23, 150.
[207] Gundry, "Trimming the Debate," 21.
[208] Copan and Tacelli, 15; Strobel, "The Evidence of the Missing Body," *The Case for Christ*, 220.
[209] Strobel, 220.
[210] Ibid.
[211] Ibid.
[212] Ibid.; Morison, 111-112, 116; Blanchard, 579.

idea of the empty tomb have pointed out that because Jesus' enemies buried him and knew the tomb's location, they would have had every reason to expose Jesus' remains if they could—but they could not. An occupied tomb would have silenced the disciples' preaching, but the authorities could not produce a body. Even Ludemann finally conceded that the burial site was probably known and that one would have to be arbitrarily selective to not acknowledge this fact.[213]

At least five people who visited the tomb claimed the body was gone on Sunday morning (Mark 16:1-8, John 20:1-9). It must be acknowledged that the discovery of the empty tomb is described differently in the various Gospels. Some feel that such discrepancies undermine credibility. Many of the discrepancies can be minimized by obtaining some background knowledge and thinking through the issues with an open mind. It is important to note that in the secondary details there is a historical core. Craig has attempted to reconcile the seemingly incompatible texts of the women at the empty tomb to prove that they are mutually reinforcing. He argued that the Gospel narratives only diverge after the discovery of the empty tomb, which points towards authentic historicity.[214]

Morison saw no inconsistency in the first visits to the empty tomb because comparative study would suggest that Mary was simply in the company of others.[215] Morison had no explanation for why the women visited the tomb when they knew that it was probably securely sealed.

---

[213] Blanchard, 579; Copan and Tacelli, 15, 114, 164.
[214] Copan and Tacelli, 24, 173.
[215] Morison, 72-76.

E. Implications of the Shroud of Turin

Because the traditional argument contains gaps (the period of incomplete documentation between the closed tomb and the open tomb) and sketchy details, the Shroud of Turin holds potentially strong evidential value for the otherwise unwitnessed and private event of Christ's resurrection moment.

Critical scholars such as Hoover have referred to the missing textual evidence of the private event as an absent link that debilitates the argument for the resurrection.[216] Although some contemporary scholars such as Flew have objected to the use of the Shroud to substantiate Jesus' resurrection, its potential validity is immense. Habermas has stated that no scientist holds to the "fraud" thesis in reference to its image.[217] Scholars such as Ian Wilson have ripped apart the flawed 1988 radiocarbon dating tests of the Shroud that branded it a medieval fake. Forensic science provides plenty of evidence in favor of the Shroud's authenticity.[218]

The Shroud displays evidence of all the wounds associated with Jesus' death (scalp lacerations, beating marks, contusions on the knees and shoulders, nail wounds in the wrists and feet, postmortem blood flow from a chest wound, and so forth). Medical professionals have concluded that it did once wrap a body that had undergone a real-life crucifixion.[219] Its image has been identified as that of a Semite based on the evidence from the coins over the eyes, pollens of a

---

[216] Roy W. Hoover, "A Contest between Orthodoxy and Veracity," Copan and Tacelli, 22.
[217] Miethe, 119-120.
[218] Ian Wilson, *The Blood and the Shroud* (New York: Touchstone, 1998).
[219] Edwards, 1455-1463; Ian Wilson, "And is it a genuinely crucified human body?" *The Blood and the Shroud*, 30-61.

Mediterranean origin, and the Shroud's historical genealogy.

Because there is no evidence of paints, dyes, or pigments on the fibrils, and because the three-dimensionality, superficiality, and nondirectionality of the image are otherwise unexplainable in scientific and naturalistic terms, scholars believe that this is not a forgery but an authentic relic.[220] There is no evidence of bodily decomposition on the shroud, indicating that the body exited quickly from the cloth. The condition of the bloodstains indicates that it is unlikely the body was unwrapped. The probable cause of the image on the cloth seems to be a light or heat scorch from the dead body; the cloth acted as a type of photographic negative, capturing an image of the body leaving the cloth without being unwrapped.

Philip Wiebe believes that the complex, cumulative evidence associated with the Shroud offers strong support for the theory that a person dematerialized within it and can provide another line of defense for the resurrection.[221] However, not all theologians agree. J.I. Packer believes that bringing in the topic of the Shroud prematurely does not strengthen the case for the resurrection. In his view, the Shroud should only be introduced once the resurrection has been established on other grounds; otherwise, it is not evidence for anything. However, once those historical grounds have been established, then it makes sense to ask whether the marks on the Shroud might have been made by the rising process and then speculate on the likelihood of this being Jesus' burial cloth.[222]

---

[220] Miethe, 27-28.
[221] Philip H. Wiebe, "Evidence for a Resurrection," 1-36; Philip H. Wiebe, "Christic Appearances and Visions in the New Testament," *Visions of Jesus*, 111-149.
[222] J.I. Packer, "Response to the Debate," Miethe, 149-150.

6. Attacks against the Historicity of the Empty Tomb from Naturalistic Theories

This section will identify a few of the most popular naturalistic hypotheses and explanations for the central facts. These alternative theories have been almost universally rejected by the majority of contemporary scholarship. Naturalistic theories fail to explain away this event mainly because they are disproved by the known historical facts.

A. The Fraud (Body-snatching) Theory

Matthew 28:11-15 states that the chief priests paid the soldiers to lie about how the tomb became empty while they were guarding it. The lie was that the disciples came during the night and stole the body from the tomb. There are many problems with this claim. The first is that it is not in keeping with the moral character of the disciples. These were honest men. Moreover, if they had lied, it is unlikely that they would have been willing to trade their lives for a hoax when it came to facing martyrdom. Instead, they stuck to their beliefs and statements about the resurrection even when it meant that they themselves would be killed. Before the resurrection, Scripture indicates that the disciples did not understand the prophecies Jesus had made about rising from the dead, and therefore they would have had no reason to seek to make them come true.

Scripture indicates that the tomb was made secure by these guards and by a Roman seal. One would have to believe that the group of fearful and unarmed disciples somehow decided to face a detachment of highly trained soldiers in order to commit a criminal act and steal the body. Or one would have to believe that all these soldiers fell asleep on the job—which was punishable by death—and yet still knew what was going on while they were sleeping. One would also have to believe that the disciples could have quietly moved the huge stone without waking up any of the guards.[223]

B. The Theory that the Authorities (Jewish or Roman) Removed the Body

The enemies of Jesus had no reason to remove the body, and it would have been to their advantage to let the body remain where it was. Pilate was primarily concerned about keeping the peace. If the Romans or the Jewish council had the body, then why were they senselessly accusing the Christians of stealing it? If these adversaries of Christianity had moved the body and knew where it was, then why didn't they bring it out in order to stop the resurrection story? Instead, what we see is that the authorities were endlessly resisting the disciples' teaching on the resurrection but were unable to refute or disprove the message.[224] Ludemann's rebuttal to this is that forty days after the death, Jesus' decomposing body would have been too unrecognizable to disprove the resurrection.[225] However, the authorities could still have produced the decomposing evidence—but they did not!

Joseph of Arimathea, a member of the Sanhedrin, is also often implicated in taking the body. The problems with suggesting that a devout Jew, who also was a follower of Christ (Luke 23:50-51), would break the Sabbath and fool the guards, are multiple. Theorists can offer no motive, no opportunity, and no plausible method to support this accusation.

---

[223] Geisler and Brooks, 124; Strobel, 211-213; Blanchard, 578-584; Little, 47-57.
[224] Morison, 94-96; Geisler and Brooks, 124.
[225] Copan and Tacelli, 61.

C. The Unconscious/Swoon Theory

This dated theory claims that when Jesus was taken off the cross, He was still alive and was later revived by the effects of the spices and/or the cool air in the tomb. The problem with this is that several professional executioners had signed off on the fact that Jesus was dead. Death on the cross was death by asphyxiation. Then a spear was thrust into Jesus' side and into the heart, ensuring that He was dead. It is preposterous to believe that, after receiving no medical attention, food, or warmth for three days, Jesus could loose himself from yards of grave clothes full of thirty-four to forty-five kilograms of spices (John 19:39) and roll away a stone that would normally take several people to move. And He would have had to have done this without disturbing the sleeping Roman guards, or He would have had to fight off the Roman guards, and then walked miles on wounded feet. Even if all of this had been possible, His wretched condition probably would have invoked pity or sympathy from the disciples. It certainly wouldn't have inspired the kind of radical change in the disciples that the narrative passages indicate occurred. The texts portray the disciples' response to an active, radiant Lord of Life and Conqueror of Death![226]

D. The Wrong Empty Tomb Theory

Some critics have claimed that the disciples simply went to the wrong tomb. The problem with this claim is that it assumes that people did not know where the right tomb was. However, if the disciples or the women had gone to the wrong tomb, the authorities could simply have gone to the right one and shown people the body. This would have quickly disproved any

---

[226] Morison, 96ff.; *Who Is This Jesus: Is He Risen?*

resurrection claims. To say that nobody knew where the right tomb was is ludicrous, for the soldiers had been there, this was Joseph of Arimathea's personal tomb, and this was in a location easily accessible to the authorities.[227] One obvious observation in the Gospels is that Jesus' tomb was a busy place on Easter morning; there were guards, women, and men such as Mark, John, and Peter. It is unconvincing to say that they were all at the wrong tomb.

E. The Theory that Faith Generated the Empty Tomb Stories

This accusation of "faith in unfounded beliefs," shared by Ludemann, does not explain the resurrection appearances, the immediate radical transformation of the disciples, or the mass conversions of people only days and weeks later in the same city where the resurrection happened.

7. Secondary Arguments for the Historicity of the Resurrection

While not direct proofs of the resurrection itself, these arguments provide strong secondary support for the fact that the resurrection happened.

A. Something Clearly Happened.

Scholars concede that something happened and that the disciples had real experiences which they believed were literal appearances of the risen Christ.

Scripture indicates that there were eleven (Paul Little says there were only ten, while Geisler claims there were twelve) [228] post-resurrection physical

---

[227] Morison, 97-102; Geisler and Brooks, 125.
[228] Little, 53; Geisler and Brooks, 125. These authors make a serious error by stating that Jesus "was seen by more than 500 people on twelve different occasions." They also tend to confuse

appearances of Jesus which involved seeing, hearing, touching, and/or eating. The witnesses included: Mary Magdalene (Mark 16:9-11, John 20:11-18), the women returning from the tomb (Matthew 28:8-10), Cleopas and a friend on the Emmaus Road (Mark 16:12, Luke 24:13-35), Peter (1 Corinthians 15:5), the ten disciples in Jerusalem (Luke 24:36-49, John 20:19-25, Acts 1:3-5), and the eleven disciples (John 20:26-31, 1 Corinthians 15:5). Then there were the seven disciples in Galilee (John 21:1-25), the apostles and over 500 brethren (Matthew 28:16-20, 1 Corinthians 15:6-8), James (1 Corinthians 15:7), the apostles on the Mount of Olives (Acts 1:6-12, 1 Corinthians 15:7), and Paul at his conversion (Acts 9:3-8,17, 22:6-15, 26:12-19, 1 Corinthians 9:1, 15:8).

These appearances happened on various occasions, both indoors and outdoors, at different times and places, with people of different dispositions, including skeptics, unbelievers, and the unwilling. When there are six independent testimonies, three by eyewitnesses, telling of eleven separate appearances over forty days, a visionary or hallucination theory simply cannot account for the event.[229]

The evidence on the literal appearances is not without its problems, some of which have been mentioned in the earlier section on "Defining the Term 'Resurrection.'" Many find the one mention of the 500 witnesses problematic.[230] Others focus on problems with the idea of a literal ascension, which supposedly depends on an outdated three-story cosmology. Others point to seeming contradictions in the texts—Luke

---

later visions of Christ with appearances during the forty-day period.
[229] Blanchard, 581; Little, 53-56; Gundry, "Trimming the Debate," 109.
[230] Strobel, "The Evidence of Appearances," *The Case for Christ*, 225-245; Flew in Miethe, 53.

24:51 implies the ascension happened on Easter Sunday, three days after Good Friday, near Bethany, while Acts 1 says it happened forty days later from the Mount of Olives.[231] Templeton attacked the story of the literal ascension as an attempt to give a happy ending to a tragic story and questioned why the details of Christ's words were not meticulously recorded just prior to the ascension.[232]

Davis argued that the supposed absurdities of the ascension story do not undermine belief in Jesus' literal, bodily resurrection. He suggested that the New Testament writers used the three-story universe as a metaphor rather than a literal description. They would have understood that God could not be contained in the heavens—the ascension was thus primarily a symbolic act for the sake of the disciples, indicating a change of state rather than a change of location.[233] Some also take issue with the permanent continuity of Christ's personal identity and current form.[234]

Flew attacked the claims of literal appearances by dismissing the creed in 1 Corinthians 15, arguing that it contradicts the descriptions of the first appearances in the Gospels. In his view, 1 Corinthians 15 was based on unreliable, late, secondhand information, which cannot be used to reconstruct the original testimony nor provide sufficient evidence of what happened. He believed that Paul was referring to visions rather than a real body and refused to believe that the eleven claimed to have simultaneously seen Christ at the

---

[231] Ludemann in Copan and Tacelli, 154-155.
[232] Templeton, "The Resurrection," *Farewell to God*, 123.
[233] Davis, "The Question of Miracles, Ascension and Anti-Semitism," Copan and Tacellui, 71-84.
[234] Philip H. Wiebe, "Evidence for a Resurrection," 9-10; John P. Newport, "The Question of Death and Life Beyond," *Life's Ultimate Questions* (Dallas: Word Publishing, 1989), 297-306.

same time. Flew argued that "what we have is Paul *saying* the disciples *told him,* this is different from having an account from the people themselves." Because Christians cannot even specify the year Easter happened with any precision, he refused to recognize it as a historical event.[235]

Habermas addressed these attacks by stating that 1 Corinthians 15:1-9 was part of an early pre-Pauline creed transmitted with care from the eyewitnesses three to eight years after the crucifixion; 1 Corinthians 15 reveals three stages of transmission—the facts, the disciples' formulation of them, and Paul's receiving of them. Paul's point is that there were other eyewitnesses who were testifying about their own sightings of the risen Christ (1 Corinthians 15:11 and who were included in the "we" in 1 Corinthians 15:14-15).[236]

The distinction between appearances and visions in the New Testament is perhaps too sketchy to allow for definite interpretation. As well, we do not know what bearing the apostle's statement in John 21:25 might have on expanding the number of reports about the resurrection. The result is that we are left with a lot of gaps that did not exist in the first century, when more information was likely available.

B. The Disciples Were Transformed.

Scholars also concede that the disciples were transformed from doubters who were afraid to identify themselves with Jesus to bold announcers of His death and resurrection, even in the face of death. What experience other than the actual resurrection of Jesus could have radically changed this whole group of followers? Scholars recognize that the transformation

---

[235] Flew in Miethe, 10-11, 34ff., 53, 75.
[236] Miethe, 23, 42, 83-86.

was sudden and that something radical must have happened to change a group of depressed, fearful disciples into a band of fearless martyrs who would maintain their testimony to the point of their own grim deaths. Ten disciples would be martyred for their refusal to recant their testimony, suffering severe abuse, including decapitation, crucifixion, and stabbing. A crucified messiah is a failed messiah. Myths do not make martyrs. Something real must have happened to account for such a radical change.

C. The Resurrection Message Was Central in the Preaching of the Early Church.

A few select Scriptures are sufficient to demonstrate this point: Acts 2:36, 5:20,29-32, 7:52-56, 10:39-42, 17:31). The 21st-century Church would do well to reacquaint itself with the fact that the message of the cross should be accompanied by the message of the resurrection.

D. The Resurrection Message Was Proclaimed in Jerusalem.

It is significant that the message of the resurrection was proclaimed *in Jerusalem*, where Jesus had died shortly before. Further, the message was repeated over and over again in confrontations with the authorities.

Some theorists have claimed that the resurrection message was a late Christian idea, developed long after Jesus' death. They have argued that the idea did not begin circulating until much later and was not mentioned in any secular history of the time.[237] The rebuttal to this is that, as recorded in the historical book of Acts, the disciples remained in Jerusalem and

---

[237] Hoover, "A Contest between Orthodoxy and Veracity," Copan and Tacelli, 140; Templeton, 118-119.

continued to proclaim the message of the resurrection there. What they preached and wrote was within the living memory of the eyewitnesses. The growth of the Church began in Jerusalem, where it would least have been able to start if Jesus' body was still there in the tomb. The women proclaimed the message very early (Matthew 28:8-10). The facts about the burial, the empty tomb, and the postmortem appearances of Jesus were well known in the area and could have been checked out with people such as Joseph of Arimathea, the gardener, and the apostles. It would seem that the site of the burial and resurrection was widely known but the authorities never demanded that people visit the grave. Instead, they used threats and violence to silence the local preachers (Acts 4:21, 5:40). In Acts 7, Stephen was given no response other than rage and stoning.[238] The question remains as to why the authorities in Jerusalem didn't simply parade the body to stop the preaching of the resurrection. The conclusion is that there wasn't one to parade.

E. The Birth and Rapid Growth of the Church

Theorists such as Ludemann have argued that there are parallel accounts of authentic faith experiences that take place outside of Christianity. However, one has to come to terms with the fact that the disciples would have had no reason to believe that Jesus had risen from the dead if He had not actually done so. Why would they have concluded that Jesus had been raised if they had only seen a vision of Him and not experienced the reality of the resurrection?[239]

It is true that other religions have spread in short periods of time and even become official state

---

[238] Strobel, "The Evidence of the Missing Body," 205-223; Geisler and Brooks, 123-125; Morison, 167-185; Blanchard, 578-584; Craig in Copan and Tacelli, 24-25.
[239] Ludemann and Craig in Copan and Tacelli, 17, 25.

religions. However, many are convinced that the existence of the worldwide Church is evidence of the truth of the resurrection. The first converts to Christianity were monotheistic, law-abiding Jews, firm in their beliefs and reluctant to make a change. Yet Acts 4:4 mentions that there were about 5,000 male believers. From this Morison calculated "that over three persons had been converted every day (including Sabbaths) for four years."[240] It is recognized that the Church grew quickly in just four years, and within twenty years it had spread all over Galilee and throughout the Roman Empire. Within fifty years, it threatened the Pax Romana, and by the fourth century it had become the official religion of the Roman Empire. [241] Clearly, the resurrection message had turned the first-century world upside down (Acts 17:6). How can one explain this rapid expansion of the Church, in the face of a hostile reception, without the resurrection?

F. Monumental Changes in Religious Practice

Without the resurrection, it is impossible to explain how Sunday became the primary day of worship for Christian Jews and why the sacraments/observances took on a whole new dimension of meaning. Christianity revolutionized many key social and religious structures, including the sacrificial system, the law, the notion of monotheism, the concept of the Messiah, and the Sabbath.[242] One needs to consider how large a change it was for a Jew to establish Sunday, the Lord's

---

[240] Morison, 110.
[241] Morison, 115; Little, 49; Newport, 297-306; Strobel, "The Circumstantial Evidence," *The Case for Christ*, 244-257; Blanchard, 578-584.
[242] Strobel, "The Circumstantial Evidence", 244- 257; Newport, 297-306; Little, 49.

resurrection day, as the primary day of worship, rather than Saturday, the traditional Sabbath (Acts 20:7). Furthermore, the symbolism behind communion and baptism would be described in the New Testament, by independent eyewitnesses, as pointing to the celebration of the resurrection of Christ.

G. Many Skeptics Were Persuaded against Their Will to Become Converts.

Shortly after the resurrection, why did so many normal people, with diverse beliefs, suddenly switch over and become completely convinced that Jesus had risen from the grave? The cumulative conversion of such a diverse group suggests that there was something powerful going on. Many would be persuaded against their wills, such as Thomas and Mary, who didn't expect the miraculous and resisted belief at first. Others reacted in fear and disbelief when Jesus first appeared (Luke 24:36-43). Yet thousands of Jews were persuaded to abandon key social and religious structures that they held dear.[243]

Wilson claimed that Jesus stayed dead but His brother James, who resembled Him, was mistaken for Jesus and that Paul would later invent a new religion based loosely on the idea of resurrection.[244] The problem with this theory is that it doesn't explain Josephus' historical report that James went to martyrdom for his beliefs.[245] People rarely die for a trick or hoax. If James had formerly opposed Jesus'

---

[243] Strobel, "The Circumstantial Evidence," 244-257; Blanchard, 583; Little, 55; Morison, 104; Harpur, 97.
[244] Wright, 39, 61.
[245] *Josephus' Antiquities, Nicene and Post-Nicene Fathers*, vol. 1, 2nd series, 2, 8, 3; and Hegesippus, quoted by Eusebius, *Ecclesiastical History, Nicene and Post-Nicene Fathers*, vol. 1, 2nd series, 125, http://apostlesrec.com/wilderness/saints/jmsjrslm.htm, accessed July 8, 2002; Morison, 126, 129-131; Craig, Copan and Tacelli, 25.

religious activities (Mark 3:31-33, 6:2-4), then why would James be chosen as a Messianic replacement? The real question is what led to James ultimately becoming a prominent leader in the Jerusalem church? The answer is that James, the brother of Jesus and a pronounced skeptic, was converted to the faith when he believed that he also saw the resurrected Jesus (1 Corinthians 15:7).

Why would a tough man like Paul, a man of sound mind and deep learning, be uprooted in an instant from his precious beliefs? Why would one of the greatest intellects be brought over from one perspective of dogmatic belief to another? Paul's indoctrination in a Pharisaical worldview would require an entire reorientation of his presuppositions. He would have viewed Christians as heretics, deceivers, and blasphemers. Yet, if the authorities knew there was no body, then so did Paul—and a few years later, Paul. the persecutor of Christians, was also converted by an experience he believed to be an appearance of the risen Christ (Acts 9:3-8,17, 22:6-15, 26:12-19, 1 Corinthians 9:1, 15:8). When Paul was really convinced that he had seen the risen Christ, the significance of the empty tomb may have brought him to the conclusion that the disciples were right.[246]

8. Additional Peripheral Arguments for the Historicity of the Resurrection

A. The New Testament

Within the New Testament are prophecies that Jesus made about His own deity, death, and pending resurrection (Matthew 16:21-23, 17:22-23, 20:17-19, Mark 8:31-33, 9:30-32, 10:32-34, Luke 9:22,43-45,

---

[246] Morison, "The Evidence of the Man from Tarsus," *Who Moved the Stone?* 133-145; Strobel, "The Circumstantial Evidence," 244-257.

18:31-34, John 2:19-22). A case could be made for the existence and survival of the New Testament as being evidence for the historicity of the resurrection.[247]

B. Old Testament Predictions

Nearly three hundred Old Testament Messianic prophecies were fulfilled in Jesus' short lifetime (e.g., Isaiah 53, Zechariah 13:6, Proverbs 30:4, Psalm 16:10, 22:16, 31:5, 34:20, 35:1, Daniel 9:25). Twenty-nine were fulfilled in the last period of His life, leading scholars to conclude that Jesus is the "melodic line to the Old Testament."[248] Again, we have a cumulative argument here that provokes the question: What is the probability that one person's brief life would meet all the criteria in hundreds of centuries-old Messianic prophecies?

C. Religious Experience

There are many categories of religious experience that point to the reality of a supernatural worldview. Ludemann observed that the Church has suppressed reports of later appearances of Christ throughout the ages.[249] However, Philip Wiebe made the case that historical and contemporary phenomena (such as visions), through which individuals have encountered the living Christ, could provide supplementary evidential data, supplementing the New Testament appearance stories, for those who want to defend a traditional interpretation of the resurrection.[250]

---

[247] Newport, 297-306.
[248] Geisler and Brooks, 118-119; *Who is this Jesus: Is He Risen?*; Habermas in Miethe, 40.
[249] Ludemann in Copan and Tacelli, 55.
[250] Philip H. Wiebe, "Evidence for a Resurrection," 1-36; Philip H. Wiebe, *Visions of Jesus,* 111-149.

D. Contemporary 21st-Century Testimony

Perhaps most people have never had the opportunity, time, or training to conduct a historical investigation of the evidence for the resurrection, yet millions believe because of their religious experience with Jesus. Millions of Christians could testify that they have been transformed by the risen Lord.[251] Craig suggested that there are indeed two ways one may come to a knowledge of the resurrection, one via the historical path, and the other via the personal path.[252]

9. Some Conclusions on the Historical Facts

The sections above have discussed some of the known historical facts. Any conclusion concerning the historicity of the resurrection should therefore properly account for the primary, secondary, and peripheral data outlined there. How do we explain these facts? The most plausible explanation for the facts, in my opinion, is that God raised Jesus from the dead.

McCullagh has outlined six tests used by historians to determine the best explanation for given historical facts. A hypothesis must: provide great explanatory scope; have great explanatory power; be plausible; not be ad hoc or contrived; be in accord with accepted beliefs (such as that people don't naturally rise from the dead); and outstrip any other rival theory in meeting the mentioned conditions.[253] A key point in this chapter is that because the historical facts have been established by critical and historical procedures,

---

[251] Reinhard Bonnke's five-day evangelistic crusade of 2001 in Nigeria hosted 3.4 million attendees resulting in the staggering figure of about one million people converting to Christ, all of whom could testify to experiencing transformation by the risen Christ. Cited in *Raised from the Dead* (video).
[252] Copan and Tacelli, 63-65; Little, 56-57.
[253] C. Behan McCullagh, *Justifying Historical Descriptions* (Cambridge: Cambridge University Press, 1984), 19.

their factual basis is strong enough to show that Jesus' resurrection is by far the best historical explanation.

Four core historical facts have been cited as being accepted by historians of international reputation who attest that the text of the New Testament supports the resurrection. They are: the change in the disciples' faith; the ancient uncontaminated eyewitness creed (1 Corinthians 15:3-7); the early material concerning the resurrection appearances (e.g., Luke 24:34); and the lack of a mythical tendency in the documents.[254]

Philip Wiebe suggested that all that is needed to defend the reality of a resurrection are three pieces of evidence: an empty grave, evidence that no remains of a corpse exist, and postmortem appearances. These requirements are met. The known historical facts are sufficient to support the claim that Jesus was raised from the dead.

Each opposing hypothesis is fraught with inconsistencies. The pieces of evidence that corroborate the historical and literal nature of the resurrection provide a strong case for the historicity of Jesus' resurrection—because each line of evidence is based on known historical facts.

10. Things Left Untidy

In engaging with the topic of the resurrection, one must address perceived inconsistencies, variations in the narratives, and discrepancies in the Gospel reports. The facts that the resurrection was a private event, that two different locations are mentioned for the ascension, that the 500 witnesses are only mentioned once, that the women were going to a securely sealed tomb, and that we cannot retrieve any

---

[254] Habermas in Miethe, 23-25, 116; Strobel, 225-245.

pre-Markian narratives [255] (or Q source) [256] indicate that there are some "untidy bits" in the Gospel accounts.

One should expect of authentic independent testimony that, like real life, eyewitnesses will see the same events from various perspectives, providing various accounts that may not fit together smoothly. If the texts were perfectly harmonious, one could suspect collusion. When it comes to eyewitness claims, in many legal cases, only one is needed to establish certainty; two to three would be sufficient. There are many more for the resurrection of Jesus

Simon Greenleaf, a famous Harvard law professor and convert to Christianity, made a careful legal examination of the Gospels. He concluded that the four Gospels would have been received as evidence in any court of justice without any hesitation.[257]

11. The Conclusion of the Matter

When scholars assume naturalistic theories in the face of such contrary evidence as is provided by the resurrection, they are guilty of prejudiced and biased reasoning. Western history writers have embraced a methodology that insists on explaining everything in terms of naturalistic regularities and dismisses other categories of explanation. Given the many positive evidences for the resurrection, the established historical facts, the complex evidence of the Shroud of Turin, the fact that a supernatural act is at least

---

[255] Copan and Tacelli, 99, 165.
[256] Q is the designation for a Gospel that no longer exists, but many theologians think must have existed at one time. In fact, even though no copy of this Gospel has survived independently, some 19th-century scholars found fragments of such an early Christian composition embedded in the Gospels of Matthew and Luke.
[257] Simon Greenleaf, *The Testimony of the Evangelists* (Grand Rapids, MI: Baker Books, reprint 1984), 9-10.

possible,[258] and the failure of naturalistic theories in this sphere, *the evidence points to a literal resurrection as the best explanation for the facts.*

It is obvious that the issue is not merely historical, but also philosophical. The deepest source of division is the philosophical assumptions brought to the issue rather than the available historical evidence. One thing that the evidential arguments for the resurrection often demonstrate is that unbelief is frequently unreasonable and based on a prejudice against Christian tenets. J.I Packer summed up the situation by saying that:

> Arguments alone do not make Christians. Without prevenient grace no one recognizes the full force of God-given evidence about Jesus so as to come to the knowledge of God's saving truth.[259]

12. What Are the Implications of a Resurrected Christ for One's Life?

Ludemann, in opposing the historical orthodox view on the resurrection, sarcastically asked, "What picture of God do we project when we say he sent his Son to die for us?"[260] Indeed, it is a picture of love for humanity beyond comprehension. Without personal application, one can remain aloof from the implications of the resurrection. However, the historical, biblical evidences for the resurrection of Jesus should compel anyone one with an open mind and heart to place an active trust in Him as God. Based on a careful examination of the historical facts, it can be concluded that putting faith in Christ is not wholly a *blind leap of faith.*

---

[258] Antony Flew, "The Continuing Debate," Miethe, 75.
[259] J.I. Packer, "Response to the Debate," Miethe, 143-150.
[260] Copan and Tacelli, 67.

If it is conceded that the resurrection has been proved, then it authenticates the inspiration, accuracy, and prophetic power of the Bible. It validates the teaching of Jesus Christ, including His deity, and substantiates the completion of His work of atonement for sin. The resurrection makes Christianity what it is (1 Corinthians 15:12-32). It provides the basis for an ethic that should govern how our present life ought to be lived and inspires hope for the future.

The resurrection has also been referred to as a source of joy. C.S. Lewis tried to capture this in his book *The Lion, The Witch and The Wardrobe*.[261] The story is about four children who end up in a fictitious land called Narnia via a wardrobe closet. Aslan, a lion and a symbol of Christ (who is referred to in Scripture as "the lion of Judah"), discovers that one of the children, Edmund, has lost control of his life, becoming subject to evil entities. This is going to cost Edmund his life. Therefore, Aslan bargains with the wicked authorities to exchange his life for the boy's. Aslan is sacrificed brutally on a stone table in the exchange. Every demonic creature imaginable is present to abuse him, tie him up and then put a knife through his heart. In the morning, two children, Lucy and Susan, return to find the stone altar broken in two. Aslan (symbolic of Jesus) is no longer on the altar (symbolic of the cross). The story continues to unfold:

> "Who's done it?" said Susan. "What does it mean? Is it magic?" "Yes!" said a great voice behind their backs. "It is more magic." They looked round. There, shining in the sunrise, larger than they had seen him before...stood Aslan himself. "Oh Aslan!" cried both the

---

[261] C.S. Lewis, *The Lion, The Witch and The Wardrobe* (UK: William Collins, Sons, reprint 1990), 135-141, 144ff.

children, staring up at him, almost as much frightened as they were glad. "Aren't you dead then, dear Aslan?" said Lucy. "Not now," said Aslan. "You're not—not a—?" asked Susan in a shaky voice. She couldn't bring herself to say the word *ghost*. Aslan stooped his golden head and licked her forehead. The warmth of his breath and rich sort of smell that seemed to hang about his hair came all over her. "Do I look it?" he said. "Oh, you're real, you're real! Oh, Aslan," cried Lucy, and both girls flung themselves upon him and covered him with kisses. "But what does it all mean?" "It means," said Aslan, "that when a willing victim who had committed no treachery was killed in a traitor's stead, the Table would crack and Death itself would start working backwards". "And now—"

"Oh yes. Now?" said Lucy, jumping up and clapping her hands. "Oh children," said the lion, "I feel my strength coming back to me, catch me if you can!" He stood for a second, his eyes very bright, his limbs quivering, lashing himself with his tail. Then he made a leap high over their heads and landed on the other side of the Table. Laughing, though she didn't know why, Lucy scrambled over to reach him. Aslan leaped again. A mad chase began. Round and round the hill-top he led them, now hopelessly out of their reach, now letting them almost catch his tail, now diving between them, now tossing them in the air with his huge and beautifully velvety paws and catching them again, and now stopping unexpectedly so that all three of them rolled over together in a happy laughing heap of fur and arms and legs. It was such a romp as no one has ever had except in Narnia.[262]

Lewis was trying to capture the Christian's indescribable response to the resurrection as joy. When something is so wonderful, perhaps the only response is to laugh. How else can we respond when confronted with Christ's words that "All power is given unto me in heaven and in earth" (Matthew 28:18 KJV)? Reason only takes us to the bridge of faith. Some say that to go further requires "a leap of faith" (believing outside the boundaries of reason). Faith can be stirred by the evidences explored in this chapter, yet to see the full truth manifested requires a response similar to that of the apostle Thomas when he blurted out his confession: "My Lord and my God!"

---

[262] Ibid., 147-149.

CHAPTER 3
The Potential for Christian Fantasy Literature to Promote Enchantment and Religious Experience

This chapter investigates the value and function of Christian fantasy literature and its ability to facilitate "enchantment" or a "sense of the numinous," a religious experience of something awe-inspiring and mysterious. The chapter argues that this literary genre is an expression of the Christian imagination, which is rooted in the *imago dei*, the image of God in human beings. How can we speak of fantasy, enchantment, and existential faith in the same sentence as reason? What does reason have to do with faith in a discussion of mythic and allegorical fiction?

1. Introduction

Growing up, many people associate "enchantment" with things such as mystical feelings, love, or perhaps fairy tales. Some have had bookshelves full of enchanting classics such as Hans Christian Andersen's fairy tales, L. Frank Baum's *The Wonderful Wizard of Oz*, the Brothers Grimm's "The Old Man Made Young Again," Carlo Collodi's *The Adventures of Pinocchio*, Kenneth Grahame's *The Wind in the Willows*, Charles Dickens's *A Christmas Carol*, and Andrew Lang's *The Blue Fairy Book*. Reading these books could be comparable to Lewis Carroll's Alice stepping through the looking glass into another reality.

The modern celebration of Christmas has also provided children with a sense of enchantment, with its claims of flying reindeer, spying elves, and a Santa who is mysteriously watching what children do. Many children perceive Santa to be more real than God. They have been told that he knows all their faults but on Christmas morning he will confirm his love for them by providing presents personally addressed to them.

As we get older, Christmas may still cause us to feel, in some quiet way, a touch of that distant enchantment, but for many, Christmas and life have lost their former magic. The problem for many adults is that we don't know how to awaken the experience of enchantment felt in childhood. We often don't know how to revive our capacity for wonder and our sense of the numinous. Our childhood experience of wonder has been overwhelmed by the challenges, philosophies, and complexities of adulthood. Too often life is diminished by the exclusive utilitarian, pragmatic way of processing reality. This article explores the potential for Christian fantasy literature to promote enchantment and religious experience among people of all ages. What makes Christian fantasy literature [263] unusual is that it presents a whole other world that is enchanted. What makes fantasy literature Christian is that it is informed by a Christian worldview.

2. Objections and Obstacles to Christian Fantasy Literature

A. Historical Roots

Over the last two millennia, the Christian

---

[263] From this point forward the term "fantasy literature," unless otherwise stipulated, refers to Christian fantasy literature.

Church's attitude towards the arts has been uneven, deeply impacted by secular practices, renewal and philosophical movements, and hermeneutics. Two things should be stated at the outset. First, the Church's attitudes towards the arts have not been conceived in a vacuum. Second, as C.S. Lewis has pointed out, "When Christian activities have been directed toward this present world...the arts have tended to flourish."[264] Historically, the Church has nurtured some highpoints in literary art, but it has also experienced philosophical shifts that have produced a wasteland void of Christian fantasy literature.

Christianity's rapid growth began in a largely Hellenistic world, and therefore it embraced many classical ideas, including some Platonic ideas: "Platonic principles were finding new meaning in the Christian context" for the purpose of explaining faith.[265] This was bound to have a negative impact on the Church's attitude towards some arts, as Plato felt that art "had the effect of distorting knowledge because it was removed several steps from reality."[266] Plato considered "imagining as the most superficial form of mental activity and the lowest form of knowing" and therefore "subject to illusion."[267] Images fashioned by the literary artist and poet were considered to be "deceptive." (It should be noted that, although Platonism led many in the Church to depreciate some forms of literary art and consider them an unworthy focus of activity, some, including later writers Dante Alighieri and Geoffrey Chaucer,

---

[264] Wayne Martindale and Jerry Root, eds., *The Quotable Lewis* (Wheaton, IL: Tyndale, 1989), 97.
[265] Samuel Enoch Stumpf, "Aristotle," *Socrates to Sartre: A History of Philosophy* (New York: McGraw-Hill, 1994), 106.
[266] Ibid., 55.
[267] Ibid., 55.

drew some inspiration for their art from this stream.) The Ancient Church was a foundational period in which fundamental attitudes were established, including attitudes towards fantasy literature. Some of these attitudes fossilized, and they continue to reverberate down to the present.

Platonic traditions would precipitate the Renaissance. One characteristic of the Renaissance was the desire to portray nature and life realistically. This was more holistic in the sense that art was no longer limited to religious subjects but could now include secular subjects. This blurring of the historical division between the sacred and secular encouraged the development of fantasy literature because deeper meanings could now be seen in mundane things. The Renaissance thus allowed people to consider mystery and wonder in art forms that were not explicitly religious. However, the Church also embraced Greek humanistic ideas about art and imagination, and this resulted in a dangerous exaltation of the arts and the artist.

The Reformation, in part, was an attempt to free Christianity from the entanglements of philosophy, which had played a role in religious abuses, including some that touched on art. Reformation leaders such as Martin Luther recognized that Thomas Aquinas had led the Church into accepting a synthesis of Christian theology with Aristotelianism, which had resulted in an incomplete definition of the fall of humanity and reason when seen through the lens of the Bible. Luther felt that reason that was not kept subservient to the Scriptures would lead to abuses.[268]

Although Luther was eager that all the arts be used in the service of God, other Reformers, including

---

[268] Paul Grime, "The Changing Tempo," *Christian History* XIL, no. 3 (1993): 1.

Ulrich Zwingli and John Calvin, raised philosophical questions as to the place of art in the Christian's life, seeing it as a distraction and an impious pursuit of pleasure. As a result, many forms of art were not considered to be vindicated vehicles of communication. These negative attitudes persisted even as literacy rates continued to advance. Many of the Reformers contributed to splitting life into sacred and secular spheres, with art relegated to the secular sphere. Later in history, this was a contributing factor to many religious circles abandoning the production of Christian fantasy literature.

A split opened between "high" churches and "low" churches (those derived from separatist, Free Church traditions, including Puritanism and Pietism). The high churches affirmed many categories of art, while the low churches tended to scorn them. European high and low churches exported their attitudes abroad, perpetuating assumptions about the boundaries of literary and other art.

At this stage of history, there was a dearth of Christian fantasy literature, its potential for a high purpose remaining largely unexplored.

In this same period, modern science would begin to be elevated to the status of an idol. Rationalism and empiricism influenced the Church with their emphasis on human reason as "the source of truth."[269] This emphasis would cast doubt on the idea that fantasy literature could contain meaning and point to reality. Cairns suggests that a "formalism" and a "cold intellectual expression" appeared in pockets of Christianity.[270] Descartes, reflecting on art, proposed that only things science can detect and measure, "only those things one can understand rationally, clearly

---

[269] Stumpf, 235.
[270] Earle E. Cairns, *Christianity through the Centuries* (Grand Rapids, MI: Zondervan, 1981), 373.

and distinctly, are real and important."[271] Producing fantasy fiction to point to a transcendent truth would automatically be challenged by this cold, rationalistic view. Thus, rationalism impacted many in the Church, stunting literary creativity as a means of knowing and communicating God. Since the Renaissance perception of literary art as a secular occupation was still in force, Pascal charged that the arts were pursued "so men could keep their minds off themselves" or so they could escape into pleasure and entertainment.[272] Kant promoted the notions of "disinterested contemplation" and "art for art's sake," which further isolated art from the activity of "everyday life."[273] Hume said literary artists were liars by profession.[274] Philosophy in this era thus weakened the "ties between beauty and eternal reality" by positing that literary art existed primarily "to give pleasure and not inform truth."[275] Relegating art to being subjective diminished its claim of pointing to purpose and order in the world. Many people were influenced to believe that if science was true, then art must just be an expression of emotion.

The all-out attack from rationalists and scientific imperialists put artists on the defensive, and they reacted by also relegating art to a separate world. They began to claim that imagination, not scientific reason, was most godlike. Furthermore, they insisted that literary art finds its highest form, not in

---

[271] H.R. Rookmaaker, "Background to a Dilemma," *Art Needs No Justification* (Downers Grove, IL: InterVarsity Press, 1978), 9.
[272] Colin Brown, *Philosophy and the Christian Faith* (London: InterVarsity Press, 1973), 59-60.
[273] Jeremy S. Begbie, *Voicing Creation's Praise: Towards a Theology of the Arts* (Edinburgh: T. & T. Clark, 1991), 192-194, 199, 207; Nicholas Wolterstorff, *Art in Action* (Grand Rapids, MI: Wm. B. Eerdmans, 1980), 58.
[274] Begbie, 250.
[275] Ibid., 188.

representing reality, but in creating something new and imaginary.[276]

Nineteenth-century Romanticism further idolized the idea of the literary artist, elevating him/her to a prophetic status and emphasizing that art was just for special, gifted people. In the literary arts, Romanticism emphasized "passion, imagination, and inspiration" over reason.[277] It favored a full expression of the emotions and stressed freedom for the artist rather than restraint. Romanticism influenced many writers, including some Christians, to use their art to seek sensation and emotion for their own sake, which provided an excuse for self-indulgence. Romanticism contributed to the attitude that the artist was "not responsible to society" and was free to "retreat into her own subjective fancies."[278] Wolterstorff pointed out that Romantic notions about literary art arose in the nominal Christian West after the "collapse of religion."[279] Many people in the Church accepted the cultural perspective that art was "not for meaningful purposes but for satisfaction in contemplation."[280]

Not all Romantic insights were negative. George MacDonald was deeply influenced by the Romantic writers and their doctrines of mysticism and creativity. His fantasy fiction was based on a synthesis of Calvinism and the Romantic idea of desiring God in all His beauty.[281] A small number of medieval, Puritan, and later Christian authors (including Dante, Chaucer, Edmund Spenser, John Bunyan, John

---

[276] Chuck Colson and Nancy Pearcey, *How Now Shall We Live?* (Grand Rapids, MI: Wm. B. Eerdmans, 2000), 446.
[277] Stumpf, 290-298.
[278] D.W. Gotshalk, "Art and Social Living," *Art and the Social Order* (New York: Dover Publishing, 1962), 230-235.
[279] Wolterstorff, 57.
[280] Ibid., 35, 38, 48.
[281] D. Bruce Hindmarsh, *The Faith of George MacDonald*, (Vancouver: Regent College, 1989), iii, iv, 174.

Milton, Jonathan Swift, Nikolai Gogol, and Fyodor Dostoevsky) pioneered the use of symbol, fiction, and the novel. They provided a foundation for future authors such as George MacDonald and the Inklings (a group including C.S. Lewis and J.R.R. Tolkien) to explore how theological points of reference could be weaved into the fantasy genre. Twenty-first-century evangelical authors such as John White and Stephen Lawhead have tried to keep this tradition alive.

Throughout its history, the Church has been impacted by many philosophical perspectives that have influenced its attitude towards the production of fantasy literature. In many cases, the Church embraced these philosophical perspectives without subjecting them to critical theological analysis. As a result, the Church has displayed several different attitudes toward fantasy literature. Some in the Church assume that such art is "an end in itself." Others have adopted the "enlightenment conviction that artistic creation is like unto creating as God."[282] Another large group would devalue all fantasy literature in an attempt to resist idolatry.

B. The Impact of Modernity

Enchantment has not disappeared from the modern world; it has just been pushed aside. C.S. Lewis, in his book *The Discarded Image*, discussed the medieval model of the universe. Although there were some obvious flaws with the medieval worldview, to its credit, there was an enchanted realm alive with a sense of the presence of God. That worldview has been largely discarded and replaced by the modern worldview—and the impact of this has reverberated down to those who have ventured into writing Christian fiction. Lewis stated that,

---

[282] Wolterstorff, 67.

> In every period the model of the universe helps to provide a backcloth for the arts...and makes some appeal to imagination. No model is a catalogue of ultimate realities and none is mere fantasy. Each is a serious attempt to get in all the phenomena known at a given time.[283]

The rational and scientific worldview that prevails in Western culture is seldom questioned and is presumed to be self-evident. But fantasy literature challenges this worldview and attempts to recover the sense of enchantment. The rational model otherwise tends to bridle and regulate fiction so that it makes a point, serves as an illustration of a rational concept, or teaches a moral lesson. In pushing aside the medieval model, the modern model has "thrown out the baby with the bathwater" because it leaves no room for mystery, the inscrutable, and the limitations of reason. Fantasy literature lets loose the enchantment, opening up a world of risk and danger. There is terror, fear, pathology, and a wildness that stimulates the imagination to soar in the presence of the sacred or the dark.

According to Tolkien, fantasy starts out with an advantage, an arresting strangeness. But that advantage has been turned against it and has contributed to its contemporary disrepute. Many people dislike being "arrested" or having their familiar primary worldview meddled with. Hence fantasy may be maliciously confounded with dreaming, delusion, and hallucinations rather than art.[284] Many moderns see the fantasy genre as insulting reason and blunting perception, leading to unreal expectations and

---

[283] C.S. Lewis, *The Discarded Image* (Cambridge: Cambridge University Press, reprint 1998), 14, 222.
[284] C.S. Lewis, ed., *Essays Presented to Charles Williams* (Grand Rapids, MI: Wm. B. Eerdmans, 1981), 67ff.

longings which cannot be fulfilled. In particular, many moderns are hostile to any attempt to smuggle theology into fiction. C.S. Lewis became unpopular in some secular circles for doing exactly this.

Bruno Bettelheim stated that fantasy literature has been subject to severe criticism following the development of psychoanalysis, child psychology, and the Freudian theory of literature. These revealed just how violent, anxious, destructive, and even sadistic a child's imagination can be.[285] Freud spoke of fantasy fiction as representing a lack of fulfillment in the author.[286] Those who accuse enchantment literature of being infantile or a product of pathological regression fail to see that often behind the story the author is tapping into some universal truths.

Some Christians object to reading this genre because they feel that it is an attempt to satisfy a vacuum that reading the biblical Canon is intended to fill. Others feel it can only be useful for the *missio Dei* (the mission of God, particularly outreach and evangelism). Classic fairy tales of the Victorian era and Walt Disney productions seem to have also contributed to the modern idea that fantasy is "just for kids." The fact that many adults feel too old for it was viewed as unfortunate by Tolkien, who suggested that the fantastic can give people experiences they have never had and help them throw off irrelevancies.[287] Bettelheim added that "understanding the meaning of one's life is not suddenly acquired at a particular age."[288]

---

[285] Bruno Bettelheim, *The Uses of Enchantment* (New York: Vintage Books, 1989), 120.
[286] Peter Gay, *Freud: A Life for Our Time* (New York: Doubleday Books, 1988), 307-308.
[287] Joseph Pearce, *Tolkien: Man and Myth* (San Francisco: Ignatius Press, 1998), 131.
[288] Bettelheim, 3.

There was some discussion by Jung and Campbell about fantasy literature using preexisting myths. Depth psychology indicates that human sensory experiences and perceptions are structured by universal patterns. Some treat enchantment literature as an exploration of Jungian archetypes and myths.[289] But fantasy does not simply explore myth; it explodes myth in order to clarify the real subject. Lewis fundamentally disagreed with modernists such as Rudolf Bultmann because they removed the numinous element from literature and the biblical Canon, which led to a denial of the possibility of the supernatural. This, in Lewis's view, resulted in a descent to a lower level of reality. Lewis and other fantasy authors attempted to demonstrate that the realities of the Canon can be transported into a fictional world without distorting or detracting from God's message of the Good News.[290]

C. The Contemporary Picture

In the Church, there have been a few lonely voices which have endeavored to promote an understanding of how a Christian worldview can be integrated into fantasy literature. They have had to address the Church's traditional distrust of certain literary arts.

Bettelheim has suggested that the Church has largely accepted the popular idea that enchantment literature does not "render truthful pictures of life as it is" and that an over-rich fantasy life interferes with healthy, successful coping with reality.[291] The idea that "fantasy aims to avoid truth" seems to have roots

---

[289] Christopher Monte, "Carl G. Jung: Analytical psychology," *Beneath the Mask* (Chicago: Holt, Rinehart and Winston, 1991), 317-323.
[290] Mark E. Freshwater, *C.S. Lewis and the Truth of Myth* (Boston: University Press of America, 1988), 122-126.
[291] Bettelheim, 116, 119.

back in Plato.[292] Fantasy literature is perceived by many as "breathing a lie through silver."[293] Those who enjoy the genre have been accused of engaging in a form of escapism.[294] Some in the Christian community feel that there is a danger of drifting into idle fantasy or frivolous thought through the misuse of the power of imagination. There is a concern over what philosophers call "solipsism"—the danger of becoming self-absorbed and lost in a subjective world that cannot be shared by others.

However, C.S. Lewis saw nothing wrong with "escape"; for him, writing fantasy stories was a way to "break out of the narrow, cramped, 'real' world into the spacious, and just as real, world of the imagination."[295] He believed that Christianity presented "incarnated myth":

> Incarnated myth [was] an idea introduced to Lewis by J.R.R. Tolkien...It means that the Christian story of God descending, dying and rising again, while it shares many similarities with myths of other cultures (particularly Greek and Norse myths) has the added quality of being true.[296]

For Tolkien, the fullness of reality was to be found beyond the physical in the supernatural, and writing fantasy literature captured this.

Postmodern thought has been steadily attacking the idea that language and the literary arts can be bearers of divine meaning. Perhaps, in this

---

[292] "Fantasy and Imagination," in David E. Cooper and Robert Hopkins, eds., *A Companion to Aesthetics* (Malden, MA: Blackwell Publishers, reprint 1997), 215.
[293] Lewis, *Essays Presented to Charles Williams*, 38-90, 71.
[294] Pearce, 144-146; Beatrice Gormley, *C.S. Lewis: Christian and Storyteller* (Grand Rapids, MI: Wm. B. Eerdmans, 1998), 119.
[295] Gormley, 119.
[296] Anderson Todd, "Transposition of Joy in C.S. Lewis" (MA thesis, University of Waterloo, 2014), 47.

postmodern era, there is a poorer understanding of what once were commonly held symbols, symbols that fantasy literature has made use of.

D. The Fear of Magic and the Occult in Fantasy Literature

There has existed in the Church a puritanical distrust of fantasy literature on the basis of Scriptures such as Leviticus 19:26, which says, "Ye shall not...use enchantment" (KJV). Some Christians have been fearful that fantasy literature has the potential for spiritual deception. They have questioned the use of satyrs, witches, centaurs, goblins, fairies, and other mythical figures in Christian fantasy literature. Looking at the fairy queen in MacDonald's *Phantastes* or the wizard Gandalf in Tolkien's *Lord of the Rings* or the powerful talking creatures in Lewis's Narnia series, they ask: Should the Church be promoting literature that elevates supernatural powers? They fear that such literature dilutes Christianity with pagan elements and contributes to it uncritically assimilating into the realm of myth.

Some ideas from the New Age movement have also contributed to the contemporary confusion over the value of Christian fantasy literature because the New Age movement also draws on mythical figures and tales from paganism's past. There is a concern that younger generations might confuse the world of fantasy with the world of the biblical Canon and ordinary life.

There is also an expressed allegation that fantasy literature might be condoning occult practices such as white magic as long as it is used for good purposes. The conclusion is that literature that elevates beings with supernatural abilities is inappropriate reading. However, it is misunderstood that while white magic in the real world may be associated with demonic forces, the basis for supernatural power for the authors of Christian fantasy literature is the Triune God. In the fantasy worlds of authors such as Sayers, Williams, Lewis, and Tolkien, there is a good Supreme Being who defeats evil, lesser supernatural beings.[297] The motivation behind this literature is to "honor and promote values associated with the attributes of the God found in Scripture, such as love, justice, truth, and faith in a trustworthy object."[298] White magic has a different purpose and objective.

Some critics fail to see the religious dimension in Christian fantasy literature and look for meaning in the wrong places. Others have assumed there is no meaning at all. A failure to understand the deeper meaning can result in the assumption that the fantasy story makes no real connections. This is because the fantasy genre can be a more difficult form of literature to produce and to read and understand. It takes significant talent to produce it, and the evangelical Christian subculture historically has not provided much support for the intellectual life. Ultraconservative habits of thought have inflicted significant damage on the intellectual life in general.[299] Many Christians have been poorly equipped to appreciate the Christian fantasy genre and often cannot differentiate between it and eschatological fantasy books such as Tim LaHaye's Left Behind series and Frank Peretti's *This Present Darkness* and the like. They seem willing to accept LaHaye's and Peretti's books literally, but are often not sure how to process other Christian fantasy literature.

That the Christian community is still trying to sort

---

[297] Ibid., 190-194.
[298] Ibid.
[299] Mark Noll, *The Scandal of the Evangelical Mind* (Grand Rapids, MI: Wm. B. Eerdmans, 1994), 38, 137.

out its understanding of the use of enchantment in fantasy literature was evidenced by its divided opinions of the Harry Potter books published between 1997 and 2007. Author J.K. Rowling introduced a new generation to the possibility that we live in an enchanted universe, where goodness triumphs and evil will be overcome. However, many Christians felt threatened by her fantasy world and fantasy characters and her use of elements of magic. Although she was trying to convey some positive moral values, including justice, fairness, and hope, segments of the Church felt she was trying to use mystery, magic, and enchantment to expose youth to witchcraft. What is clear is that Rowling tapped into a powerful medium, the fantasy genre, stimulating the imagination with a mix of myth, mystery, and riddles.

Many Christian communities tend to be utilitarian and pragmatic, a modern characteristic, in their reading. This makes Christian publishers justifiably hesitant to publish fantasy literature. [300] The staunchly practical will have little time for this genre. However, it would not be accurate to say that the Church has lost a sense of the high dignity and purpose of fantasy literature. You need to have something before you can lose it. There is not a large body of Christian fiction authors, in comparison to the secular market, to begin with. The subcategory of Christian fantasy fiction has a very short history, and only a limited number of writers have been producing it. The Church has yet to explore the full scope of this genre's potential to promote enchantment and religious experience. There is a lot of uncharted territory here.

---

[300] My comments here are based on interviews with those who market Christian books.

3. The Potential for Christian Fantasy Literature to Promote Enchantment and Religious Experience

Theists who try to communicate the numinous through fantasy fiction do so in the spirit of Rudolf Otto's *The Idea of the Holy*. The heightened awareness of the ethereal, supernal, and holy aroused by fantasy fiction can elicit awe and fascination. One may instinctively want to run from what controls life and death or to be joined with it. The religious experience of perceiving that realm of mystery and magic is called enchantment. It is an existential place where people may seek to join themselves with the sacred. Lewis introduced his readers to an experience of the "beauty of holiness" in *That Hideous Strength* when the character Jane experienced something invisible and intolerably huge that was approaching and pressing on her. She felt herself shrinking, suffocated, and emptied of all strength. The room she was in became a tiny place, like a mouse's hole, as if the mass and splendor of this formless hugeness had changed everything. In leaving Saint Anne's hilltop home, Jane realized she had experienced a state of joy, and everything, from cows to rabbits, now seemed more beautiful.[301] Here Lewis attempted to illuminate real life through this imagined world.

Otto argued that many in the Christian community try to conceptualize God in rational terms and make belief possible on the basis of a rational description of God's attributes. But Otto pointed out that it is an erroneous assumption that Deity can be completely and exhaustively defined in rational terms. Otto noted that language misleads us because when we put religious truth into language, we put it in a

---

[301] C.S. Lewis, *That Hideous Strength* (New York: MacMillan, 1965), 150-152.

form that tends to stress God's rational attributes. Otto wanted readers to realize that we cannot fully comprehend God's essence through descriptive language.[302] The gravitation of authors to utilizing the fantasy genre is a reaction against the bias towards rationalism that prevails in so much of Christian literature and is therefore an attempt to keep the nonrational element alive in the heart of religious experience. It is an acknowledgement of the nonrational core of the biblical Canon's conception of God and an attempt to protect that conception from excessive rationalization. Fantasy literature conveys that religion cannot be contained in sensible assertions, and it uses a genre that points to inexpressible elements that cannot be rationally grasped. Fantasy literature is unique in that it does not emphasize reasonable, ethical, and moral behavioral elements at the expense of mystery and the inscrutable. Fantasy attempts to awaken a numinous consciousness, starting the reader on a journey to sense God's intangible presence and to experience the mysterious. It is a genre suited to expressing the incomprehensible, inconceivable, inexpressible, mysterious, and numinous. There is a potential for fantasy literature to affect lives on a deeper level by evoking emotional responses such as awe, enchantment, and inspiration. In awakening the imagination, fantasy literature can transport the reader into a heightened reality that is only dimly discernible in the partial reality in which we live. Stories can shape the reader and lead the reader closer to ultimate truth, which is found in God. Tolkien and Freshwater felt that the highest function of fantasy

---

[302] Rudolf Otto, *The Idea of the Holy,* 2nd ed. (London: Oxford University Press, 1958). Freshwater stated that C.S. Lewis was deeply influenced in his fiction writing by Otto's book and the notion of "experiencing the numinous" (Freshwater, 15).

literature was to give a clear view of reality by providing "a bridge between the infinite realm of Absolute Reality and the finite realm of abstract propositional truth."[303]

There are further aspects to this ability of Christian fantasy literature to promote enchantment and religious experience.

A. Connecting to Human Need

Bettelheim felt that one general purpose of enchantment literature was to emotionally and psychologically satisfy readers by addressing the inner pressures and anxieties they experience. Enchantment literature frequently speaks directly to the struggle against the severe difficulties, unexpected calamities, and unjust hardships that are an intrinsic part of human existence. It often addresses an existential dilemma, such as the need to be loved; the fear that one is worthless; the fear of death; or the wish to live eternally. It presents this deep inner conflict in a way that readers can come to grips with. In this sense, it can be therapeutic. Good and evil are given bodily form through the actions of some figures. Evil is recognized as having some deceptive attractions.[304]

B. Providing Hope for the Future

Bettelheim also spoke of enchantment literature as being optimistically future-oriented and as providing guidance by offering alternative solutions. The reader is provided with heroes and models for human behavior that give meaning and value to life. Enchantment literature often reassures and gives hope for the future by holding out the promise of a

---

[303] Freshwater, 37-39. Pearce, 146-7, 166, 170.
[304] Bettelheim, 3-12, 25.

joyful ending. Lewis worked this idea into a number of his books because he came to realize that joy does not point to itself[305] but is "a sign post directing [people] to focus [their] attention on God."[306]

C. Discovering Identity

Enchantment literature also may help people to discover their identity and calling by teaching concepts of origin and purpose. It may suggest experiences that are needed in order to develop and transform character and to move beyond a principal pursuit of pleasure to a principal pursuit of reality. Enchantment literature speaks to us in the language of symbol and therefore is a carrier of deep meaning.[307]

Some things are different and some things overlap in the secular and Christian use of enchantment that Bettelheim has described. Pearce noted that the escapism in secular fantasy is based in scientific reality and offers escape from ourselves, a distancing of ourselves from the real world. In contrast, Christian fantasy offers an escape into ourselves, and beyond ourselves, in a quest to rediscover who we are in the midst of life's distractions.[308]

Tolkien wrote that certain elements were necessary in any good enchanting story. The first element is fantasy, magical and fantastic elements that engage the imagination. Second, enchanting stories include elements of recovery—from pride, from deep despair, or from lack of a clear perspective. Such stories free us from the blur of familiarity so we can see things as we were meant to see them. Tolkien said that:

Because creative fantasy is mainly trying to

---

[305] Todd, 50.
[306] Ibid., 49.
[307] Ibid., 24, 26, 35-38, 41, 66.
[308] Pearce, 126-152.

make something new, it may open your hoard and let all the locked things fly away like cage-birds. The gems all turn into flowers or flames, and you will be warned that all you had or knew was dangerous and potent, not effectively chained, free and wild; no more yours than they were you.[309]

Third, enchanting stories include elements of escape—from danger, hunger, thirst, poverty, pain, sorrow, injustice, weaknesses, entrapment, and death. Escape may also include the desire to travel, to glimpse other worlds and splendors, or to talk with animals and other forms of creation. Fourth, enchanting stories also include consolation, the joy of the happy ending. When the wild and dreadful adventure looks like it is going to end in sorrow, failure, and defeat, consolation is a sudden, miraculous, unexpected grace. Consolation gives a fleeting glimpse of joy that is beyond the walls of the world.[310]

When we consider the elements of an enchanting story, it's easy to recognize that the biblical Canon contains a story that has many of the features of enchantment literature. It is full of fantastic, miraculous, and marvelous elements that engage the imagination. It deals with the grand issue of recovery, allowing us to see things as we were meant to see them. It communicates through a variety of literary art forms, including images, stories, symbols, metaphors, and allegories, that speak to the whole person. Jesus' parables were fictional stories, a subcategory of the fantasy genre. When we consider Scripture's use of literary art forms such as the apocalyptic, narrative, and poetry, we can see an affirmation of, and love for, beauty. Also, like

---

[309] Lewis, *Essays Presented to Charles Williams*, 75.
[310] Bettelheim, 143-150; Lewis, *Essays Presented to Charles Williams*, 63, 72-84.

enchantment literature, Scripture contains the element of escape—escape from the enemy of our soul, the tyranny of sin, and the effects of living among a sinful community; escape from meaninglessness and from living in a spiritual wasteland. Our earthly life is a period of trial and tribulation, where there are many physical, moral, and spiritual threats. It is a period when inner growth happens, often through misfortune. Scripture also contains the element of consolation, in which the right order of the world is eventually restored and the evildoer is punished. Things may look bad, but the grace of God will turn things around. Scripture begins and ends in joy and looks forward to joy in the eschaton (the end time). It provides a taste of joy beyond the grave where there is a happy ending. In this regard, Lewis recognized that a direct pursuit of joy is vain. To follow the glimmers and trace the feeling in the senses and imagination is a distraction from the real purpose of the longings, which is to direct attention to God. Moreover, Lewis suggested that joy symbolically directs attention to God, just as the wine and bread of communion are generally not about eating and drinking but symbolically represent the body and blood of Christ sacrificed for humanity.[311]

In enchantment, the wonderful happens, the lover is recognized, and the spell of misfortune is broken. Perhaps there is a parallel between the Cinderella story and the Christ story. They share the same message that transformation to a new state is effected by the perfect love of one for another. Jeffrey argued that the reason we see a connection between Western fantasy literature and Scripture is that the biblical Canon has informed our thinking about texts. We tend to look at texts of fantasy and fiction with the

---

[311] Todd, 51.

assumption that they may contain meaning. Western fantasy fiction thus has its roots in Christian literary history.[312] Postmodern theories have posed a threat to this because of their arbitrary notions of story and truth.

D. Encouraging Spiritual Development

Christian authors of fantasy use this genre because of its potential ability to touch the whole person, encouraging spiritual development at a deeper level than just the intellect. They encourage "enchantment" in the sense that the enchanted world is only visible by faith. The stories they create possess a healing and redemptive quality because they "bear the potential of showing us something of the actual world" and give us permission to emotionally connect with its hidden mysteries.[313] As well, some Christian authors have adopted this art form because analogies and symbols are the language of faith—fantasy draws from a repository of symbols from God's creation. It is based on a recognition that art can express truth about the human condition and not simply emotion. Those claims to express truth "find the test of acceptance or rejection in our own inventory of experiences."[314] For example, in J.R.R. Tolkien's *The Hobbit*, Bilbo Baggins experiences many human feelings, including fear, anger, joy, an appreciation for simple things, the struggle with good and evil, a sense of destiny, and even a sense of Providence.[315] Weitz affirmed that through such literature we can also learn about "the

---

[312] David Lyle Jeffrey, *People of the Book: Christian Identity and Literary Culture* (Grand Rapids, MI: Wm. B. Eerdmans, 1996).
[313] Begbie, 252.
[314] Morris Weitz, "Truth in Literature" in John Hospers, ed., *Introductory Readings in Aesthetics* (New York, The Free Press, 1969), 219.
[315] J.R.R. Tolkien, *The Hobbit* (UK: HarperCollins, reprint 1991).

behavior of disenchanted men as a lesson."[316]

E. Enabling Fresh Vision

Morgan agreed with Weitz in saying that "fantasy can lead us back to our own world to see the world anew with intensified awareness."[317] This is precisely what George MacDonald attempted to accomplish in *Phantastes* and *The Princess and the Goblin* and C.S. Lewis attempted to accomplish in the *Chronicles of Narnia*. They sought to put readers in touch with the wonder and mystery of their own world. In Lewis's *The Lion, The Witch and The Wardrobe,* the wardrobe opens into a strange new country. But there is a sense that what Lewis is really doing is helping his readers re-enter their own world with a child's sense of enchantment and recognize that that world is infused with Immanence.

Christian fantasy literature generally tries to help readers see the world anew. In presenting the metaphysical, invisible, and unobservable, authors encourage readers to open themselves up to truths they have forgotten or refuse to see in their own world. In *Phantastes*, MacDonald described the adventures of Anodos, which means "aimless," in Fairyland. At the beginning of the book, Anodos is dominated by a rationalistic and utilitarian perspective, and the spiritual and imaginative side of his life has been suppressed. Through suffering, he dies to his own desires to control and possess, changes from being self-focused to being other focused, and discovers the grace and forgiveness of God. In following the life of Anodos, readers discover that God may also save them from themselves through unpleasant experiences. MacDonald pointed to joy in eternity by stating that

---

[316] Weitz, 219.
[317] Douglas Morgan, "Must Art Tell the Truth?" in Hospers, 24.

"a great good is coming."[318]

Williams picked up this idea that a "terrible good" is coming and made clear that the good contains the terror rather than the terror containing the good. People often want the good so badly that they take the illusory good rather than the terrible good. In *Descent into Hell*, Williams leads the reader through an exploration of power and free will, demonstrating that self-absorption is the way of isolation and hell. The idea that Pauline's ancestor could pray for her opens up the idea that prayer is not limited by time but can be futuristic or retroactive. Williams's fantasy also illustrates that substitution and exchange are possible in unequal relationships, opening up an understanding of Christ's relationship to the believer. The "city" is portrayed positively as a kind of Zion and as a place of exchange, where people practice community and mutuality.

Williams's fantasy is full of symbolism. For example, he mentioned a place called Battle Hill, which seems to point to Calvary. Williams also borrowed heavily from Dante's *Divine Comedy* for some narrative sections. When he speaks of the way of Gomorrah or Zion, there is a sense that he is contrasting two spiritual roads. Williams leaves the reader with the understanding that love requires being transported out of selfishness.[319] His preoccupation with the in-breaking of the supernatural dimension into our world is conveyed through a variety of bizarre occurrences, numinous revelations, and intense spiritual experiences.

Lewis's fantasies also contain the idea that every person is destined for eternal life, with every moment

---

[318] George MacDonald, *Phantastes* (Grand Rapids, MI: Wm. B. Eerdmans, reprint 1994), 185.
[319] Charles Williams, *Descent into Hell* (Grand Rapids, MI: Wm. B. Eerdmans, reprint 1996), 51, 64, 65, 68-9, 115, 174, 207, 220.

of life being a preparation for that condition. In *Till We Have Faces* and *The Great Divorce*, he presented the point that humans' real identity lies ahead and that there is a beauty in choosing God.

In her *Time* fantasies, Madeleine L'Engle had her characters delve into important, ultimate questions such as "Are we alone in the universe or not?"[320]

F. Satisfying Human Longing

At the heart of Christian enchantment literature is the desire to encourage authentic spirituality. Some authors try to bring readers into touch with deep longings that have not been satisfied and point them to the idea that these longings are from God and that only God can satisfy them. In his "journey to understand Joy [Lewis came to] the recognition that the long sought after object was Christ...the longing for God is hidden in longings for friends, family, *Fairyland*, fame, and many other experiences." [321] Enchantment literature can thus promote a hunger for God. In *Till We Have Faces*, Lewis demonstrated that we substitute many things for God instead of falling down before God to say what has been at the center of our soul for years:

> I saw well why the gods do not speak to us openly, nor let us answer. Till that word can be dug out of us, why should they hear the babble that we think we mean? How can they meet us face to face till we have faces?[322]

Here people, who have longed for God, are confronted with the fact that they have prayed many empty prayers they didn't really mean and that this could be the reason for these prayers not being answered. If

---

[320] Madeleine L'Engle. *A Wrinkle in Time* (New York: Bantam Doubleday Dell Books, reprint 1989).
[321] Todd, 1.
[322] C.S. Lewis, *Till We Have Faces* (UK: HarperCollins, 1991), 305.

they have a longing for reality and a touch of the supernatural in their lives, then then they need to realize that the only valid relationship they can have with God requires them to change and discover the cure for their facelessness—there is a need for a death and rebirth. Lewis thus attempted to tap into people's "*Sehnsucht*" or sense of longing for ultimate fulfillment.[323]

G. Revealing the Beauty of God

Fantasy literature can also attract readers to the beauty of the love of God. It can provide a new understanding by conveying truths that enable the heart to make amendments. For example, in Lewis's *Prince Caspian*, Aslan, the Christ symbol, offers some soldiers the opportunity to go through a door into another world where there is abundance, adventure, and peace. Despite great apprehension among the men, one soldier steps forward and says, "I'll take the offer." Aslan responds:

> "Go through it my son", bending towards him and touching the man's nose with his own. As soon as the Lion's breath came about him, a new look came into the man's eyes—startled, but not unhappy—as if he were trying to remember something. Then he squared his shoulders and walked into the Door.[324]

This represents taking steps of faith into an unknown future on the basis of God's promises. The willing soldier's transformation can help readers understand that some things must be done in faith and that certain knowledge only comes by experiencing faith choices.

---

[323] Freshwater, 128.
[324] C.S. Lewis, *Prince Caspian* (UK: William Collins, Sons, reprint, 1990), 186.

H. Promoting Humility

Fantasy literature can promote humility by helping readers realize their spiritual limitations. Humility, perhaps a result of grace, is crucial for risking a vulnerable imaginative journey. Humility involves asking primary questions such as, "Who am I to God?" It can help us to transcend ourselves, taking us beyond our reason to admit our limitations. Tolkien's Frodo and Bilbo Baggins have a humble approach to living. These characters invite the reader to join them in admitting that they don't know it all.

I. Promoting Reverence

Fantasy literature can promote a reverence of the Divine. In one of Lewis's Narnia books, Mr. Beaver tells Lucy that Aslan, a Christ symbol, is not a safe lion but that he is good and a King.[325] This refutes the false idea that God is just an old, benevolent, kindly, tame Supreme Being. Fantasy can help readers see their real situation and understand the invitation and approaches towards God that are available.

False spirituality can lead to a blind contentment based on the assumption that people already know enough about God and have no need to go any deeper. If they read with an open mind, enchantment literature can point readers towards the values of surrender, listening, patience, and facing life's tests and suffering with perseverance. It can teach them that there is a transcendent quality to the narratives of their own lives.

Many modern religious fiction authors have tried to resist a totally rational representation of reality by insisting on the reality of the supernatural. They have challenged readers to abandon the hegemony of

---

[325] C.S. Lewis, *The Lion, The Witch and The Wardrobe* (UK: William Collins, Sons, reprint, 1990), 75.

secular assumptions. Many, including Flannery O'Connor, experienced frustration over the problem of communicating faith through fiction because Christian readers often expect a realistic genre that mimics secular life. As a result, some prominent Christian writers abandoned the novel in favor of writing theological fantasies.[326] They recognized that the fantasy genre promotes enchantment and helps readers accept the reality of the supernatural. The fantasy genre also conveys that peace and happiness can only exist on some conditions.[327]

According to Markos, Lewis saw a need for a revival of humans' capacity for wonder and a renewed awe before the mystery of God and His creation. Lewis used fantasy fiction to expose the presuppositions upon which modernism stands. He reacted against modernism's narrow focus on the material world and used fiction to show that the things on earth are a shadow of higher things in heaven.[328] He believed that one of the functions of the natural world was to provide symbols that point to this spiritual reality.

Lewis was convinced that the part of us that yearns for myths could be channeled properly. He understood that Christ didn't come to put an end to myth but to take all that was most essential in myth up into Himself and make it real. Lewis felt that a mythical radiance rested on the gospel and that if God chose to be "mythopoeic," then humans should not refuse to be mythopoeic either.[329]

---

[326] Barbara Pell, *Faith and Fiction* (Waterloo, ON: Wilfrid Laurier University Press, 1998), 1-8.
[327] Iona and Peter Opie, *The Classic Fairy Tales* (New York: Oxford University Press, 1974), 13-36.
[328] Louise Markos, "Myth Matters," *Christianity Today* 45, no. 6 (April 23, 2001), 36-39.
[329] Ibid., 32-39. Also see Gormley, 95-96; Lewis, *Essays Presented to Charles Williams,* 83.

4. Christian Fantasy Literature Stems from the Christian Imagination, Which Is Rooted in Humans Being Made in the Image of God.

Psalm 19:1 (ESV) states that "The heavens declare the glory of God and the sky above proclaims his handiwork." Nature proves that God is interested in aesthetics. Art is rooted in the orderly structure and harmony of what God has created. When God created the world, He made it beautiful and called it good. In nature, we can see something of the character of God, yet the mystery remains. Since God made humans in His image, He gave us our capacity for artistic creation and enjoyment. An engaging fantasy story can incite aesthetic pleasure, cause us to meditate on the beauty of God's world, and provoke a consideration of the eternal beauty of God. One of the characteristics common to God and humans is the desire and ability to make things. The obvious difference is that God creates *ex nihilo* (from nothing). The closest the literary artist can get to this experience of creating out of nothing is to realize that God created the world by imagination. Like procreation, using their creative imaginations is one of the few ways humans have to capture an understanding of the concept of creation presented in the biblical Canon.[330]

God has invited humanity to share in the process of co-creating with Him. Rooted in the cultural mandate found in Genesis 1:26-27, God has allowed humans to take elements of His creation and make new arrangements with them. This explains why creating fantasy literature can be so fulfilling to authors. There is an invitation to those of the *imago Dei* (those made in God's image) to exercise their creative capacities to the fullest extent. Being fallen

---

[330] Dorothy Sayers, *The Mind of the Maker* (San Francisco: Harper Collins, reprint 1987), 19-33.

creatures as well as bearers of the divine image, humans may produce works of inferior or extraordinary quality. Yet, through fantasy literature, literary artists can express a Christian understanding of the world and humans' place in it under God. God has created us in His own image so that we can, in a sense, show the world what God looks like. In this sense, humans' creative work can be seen as the fulfillment of the Creator's secret will. We are intended to bring creation with us in our redemption, and this could include encouraging good fantasy literature, restoring it to its proper place, and encouraging authors to use it to renew, inspire, or renovate culture.

What does reason have to do with faith? In Christian fantasy, universal truths can be engaged that are difficult for the intellect to grasp—because they need to be imaginatively experienced—and conveyed in a way the imagination can comprehend. Christian fantasy contains meaning, not to those who insist on literal truth, but to those who have spiritual eyes to see and ears to hear the truth conveyed through imaginative forms of story, including myths, symbols, analogies, and abstractions. A theological understanding of the dominion of Christ involves all of culture, including imagination and creativity. Fantasy literature, therefore, should not be marginalized but recognized as having a legitimate place. An author can use this genre to steward the creation of beauty. Noll has noted that when we study something, we learn about the thing, but we learn even more about the one who made that thing. The problem is that many Christians have not pursued comprehensive thinking or a mind shaped to its furthest reaches by Christian perspectives. The effort to do this is an effort to take seriously the sovereignty of God over everything in His world. In this sense, the search for a Christian imagination is ultimately a search for God.[331]

---

[331] Noll, 4, 50, 253.

CHAPTER 4
Why Is God Good to All People?

That all people know some of the good in life is a reasonable understanding of universal experience; that those good things come to us from a Transcendent Source is a matter of faith. Psalm 145:9 says, "The Lord is good to all; he has compassion on all he has made." One insight in life is the observation that non-Christians have often been abundantly blessed with talents, skills, vocational and artistic predispositions, and financial prosperity. The bystander may ask: "Why is God so good in bestowing such gifts, talents, and capacities on people who reject Him?" The question, of course, assumes that God exists and has willed all people into existence. Some Christians may also ask, "If we are part of God's family, then why doesn't God bless us in greater measure in the areas of talents, gifting, mastery, expertise, and prosperity?"

1. Two Kinds of Grace

It may be theologically helpful for us to recognize that we can see the expression of God's grace in two ways: saving grace and common grace. Common grace is God giving people blessings (goods, giftings, talents, dispositions) that are apart from the salvation of the soul. "Common" means such grace is not limited to believers. One of the primary ways all humans experience common grace is through God's provision of the things they need pertaining to their physical existence, for instance, through such things as the harvests of the earth. (This can be explored in biblical texts such as Acts 14:16-17 and Psalm 145:9,15-16.) God has lavished upon all humanity a good creation (Psalm 8:3-4, 139:14).

I am always amazed at the extent of the common grace that God has given to people in the secular arts community. Some of the greatest creativity, skills, and artistic achievements I have witnessed have been in the secular sphere in the lives of non-believers. Christians can enjoy some of these creative artistic presentations because the source of these good gifts ultimately is God (James 1:17: "Every good and perfect gift is from above").

The Reformer John Calvin acknowledged that the reason everyone is disposed to have a "talent" is that God has given natural gifts to the "pious and the impious as a particular grace," as well as the wherewithal to creatively develop, "perfect, and polish" these gifts.[332] Because of total depravity, humans' natural gifts are tainted. However, the sparks that gleam in degrees of artistic achievements are dependent on God's enablement and grace.[333]

Common grace is given to humanity in all dimensions of life that require natural gifts and abilities, along with the accompanying "virtues, graces, wisdom, understanding," capacities, and ethical discernment. The granting of "temporary permissive rights" and benefits in common grace is a

---

[332] John Calvin, *Institutes of Christian Religion*, ed. John T. McNeil (Philadelphia: The Westminster Press, 1960), vol. 1, 273. Christians may find it hard to understand how the unsaved may be abundantly talented. Madeleine L'Engle explained: "God is no respecter of persons...he lavishly gives enormous talents to [individuals that some] people would consider unworthy...he chooses [people to bestow talents and gifting upon] with as calm a disregard of surface moral qualifications as he chooses his saints." Madeleine L'Engle, *Walking on Water: Reflections on Faith and Art* (Wheaton, IL: Harold Shaw Publishers, 1980), 30-31.
[333] Calvin, vol. 1, 270, 276.

reflection of God's love, longsuffering, mercy (Psalm 145:9), kindness, righteousness, and preservation (Matthew 5:45). Theologians view common grace as functioning to preserve order and decency, restrain and moderate the effects of sin, enable civic good, bless, refresh, and promote the good, including in the aesthetic dimension.

This simply means that without common grace life would be even more malevolent and chaotic than it is. God restrains evil through common grace by influencing the human conscience (Romans 2:14-15). Out of a sense of right and wrong, communities establish laws and customs that in many cases reflect biblical moral standards. The collective expression of common grace is also seen in the societal realm (Romans 13:1,4) through various organizations that provide a degree of good (the institution of the family, the institution of government, educational institutions, corporate institutions, nonprofit institutions, etc.).

The Bible indicates that a human may be endowed with a special capacity—of skill, ability, knowledge, or wisdom—by which that person is fitted to serve God's purpose while still remaining in the common state of human depravity (Exodus 31:3, 1 Kings 4:30-31). Calvin believed that all have received their "competence from the same Spirit who fills, moves, and quickens all things according to the character he bestowed upon each kind by the law of creation."

Even in the intellectual domain, God's common grace is at work. The academic enterprise demands integrity in order for the results to be dependable. Grudem noted:

> All science and technology carried out by non-Christians is a result of common grace, allowing them to make incredible discoveries and inventions, to develop the earth's

resources into many material goods, to produce and distribute those resources, and to have skill in their productive work.[334]

God is good to *all* people in *some ways* (common grace) and to *some* people in *all* ways (common grace plus saving grace).

2. How Should We Understand God's Goodness to the Unbeliever?

God is good to all people to the point that such goodness might lead them to ask questions about the source of life's goodness; it sets them on a pathway that can lead to contrition and saving grace (2 Peter 3:9, Romans 2:4). This means that Christians should consider referring to "the good in life" (note that I did not say "the good life") in their missional initiatives. Furthermore, common grace is evidence that God wants to show His undeserved goodness and mercy to all people (Psalm 145:9). He uses every loving measure to draw people into a saving grace that will bless them ultimately in every way eternally. Although common grace may open people to a spiritually transcendent awareness, those people still must invite Christ into their hearts and lives (Romans 10:9-10). Without Christ, the unbeliever remains under a guilty verdict and at enmity with God (Romans 5:10, Matthew 12:30, Ephesians 2:3). What might perplex a few high-principled people about seeing common grace lavished on unbelievers is that they equate that with God *favoring* some people more. Grudem commented:

> [U]nbelievers often receive more common grace than believers—they may be more skillful, harder working, more intelligent, more creative, or have more of the material

---

[334] Wayne Grudem, *Systematic Theology* (Grand Rapids, MI: Zondervan, 1994), 659.

benefits of this life to enjoy. This in no way indicates that they are more favored by God in an absolute sense or that they will gain any share in eternal salvation, but only that God distributes the blessing of common grace in various ways, often granting very significant blessings to unbelievers.[335]

Common grace is one of God's amazing means of blessing the entire human family. People can be thankful for the common grace that God has given to some non-Christian engineers since it allows them to build good bridges which will be a safe means of transportation for the benefit of all. Similarly, people don't have to be suspicious of using the services of an unbelieving surgeon who is a specialist in her field. Common grace helps people see the good that functions in the world through the lives of the unregenerate. Common grace should facilitate openness in the way we Christians relate to the unbelievers around us. Their gifts, virtues, insights, expertise, forms of mastery, skills, talents, and so forth come ultimately from God. Our response should be thankfulness to God and receptivity to the gifts they steward.

Christians share in both common grace and the potential of their talents and gifts to be enhanced by saving grace. Pneumatologically understood, salvation enhances gifts and callings and enables expanded expressions of gifts in the Church, the community, and the marketplace. Scripture reveals a variety of gifts given to the Church (Romans 12:3-8, 1 Corinthians 12:4-11); these lists are not exhaustive, but they do indicate that some gifts are natural talents transformed by the work of the Holy Spirit for "the common good" (1 Corinthians 12:7). God inspires

---

[335] Ibid., 663.

special activities in accordance with each person's calling (Judges 6:34, 1 Samuel 10:6,10,26). Recognizing common grace is the domain of reason; acknowledging that we are given such gifts as a form of stewardship is an act of faith.

CHAPTER 5
Conversations with Cultured Pagans: The God Question

Isaiah 1:18 (NASB) begins: "Come now, and let us reason together." When engaging in a conversation on the God question, we again come back to our central question: what does reason have to do with faith? Perhaps one starting place in a discussion of the God question would be to define a worldview. What is a worldview? It is a fixed point of reference that helps us know where we are and where we are going. For example: if you were to go to Vancouver or Montreal and had never been there before, you would definitely notice the Living Shangri-La (at sixty-two stories, Vancouver's highest building) or Mount Royal (which can be seen from anywhere in Montreal's downtown area). So, wherever you went in the city, you could look around and find one of those fixed points of reference. You could see it towering above almost everything. If you should get lost, you could reference one of those fixed points and figure out where you were. This would keep you from wandering in circles.

That's what a worldview is. One key thing about a fixed reference is that it cannot be you. It has to be bigger than you and outside of you. It can't move. If you can carry it, it's not a fixed point of reference capable of keeping you oriented.

There is a battle over worldviews today in which the key question is: if there is a God, who is God? The answer to that question shapes our worldview. It is the beginning point for how we understand the meaning of life.

Today, people in the West face what people in the East have had to cope with for centuries—a wide variety of religious worldviews (pluralism) that have little in common with Christianity. The world's major religions—Hinduism, Buddhism, and Islam—as well as cults, New Age philosophies, occult beliefs, and neo-pagan views all have growing numbers of adherents in the North American context. How do we navigate in a world that knows or cares so little about the key principles of the worldview that is near and dear to us?

The apostle Paul left behind one model on how to engage in discussions with people who don't share our worldview. The occasion was when he visited the then world center of pagan philosophy and religion—Athens. Paul's letters in the biblical Canon offer ample evidence that Paul was well versed in Greek philosophy. Consider Galatians 2:16-22, where Paul argued against a Platonic approach to the faith life. Throughout Paul's epistles, he often engaged with Greek philosophy in presenting his theology. It is reasonable to assume that Gamaliel (a chief representative of the Pharisaic school under whom Paul studied) taught his students Greek philosophy so that they could engage with the Greek-speaking world of their time. Paul had grown up in the city of Tarsus, which had a first class philosophical academy. The Greek geographer Strabo noted that the Tarsus academy excelled the academies of Athens and Alexandria. [336] We cannot be sure that Paul had academic training in philosophy, but it is almost unthinkable that in a Hellenistic context (a culture

---

[336] Thomas Stackhouse, *A History of the Holy Bible: From the beginning of the world to the establishment of Christianity,* ed. George Gleig (Longman, Hurst, Rees, Orme, and Brown, University of Iowa, 1817), vol. 1, 405.

dominated by a Greek philosophical worldview) Paul would not have been aware of some of the debates and dialogues going on around him.

The intention of this chapter is to explore how Paul addressed the question: Who is God? It should be acknowledged that Paul began with an a priori assumption that there is a Divine Entity. This is significant because not all worldview belief systems start there. In Acts 17, Luke (the author of the book of Acts) portrayed Paul as a kind of Socrates as he engaged a group of educated philosophers. It will be instructive for us to observe how Paul built bridges with those who held dissimilar worldviews. His approach was echoed by the apostle Peter in 1 Peter 3:15: "Always be prepared to give an answer to everyone who asks you to give the reason for the hope that you have. But do this with gentleness and respect." In other words the Christian tradition advocates that Christians pursue intelligent cultural engagement, not segregation or hostility. As a basis for the discussion in this chapter, I will use the narrative of Paul's visit to the city of Athens recorded in Acts 17.

1. The Setting (Acts 17:16-21)

Verse 16 describes how Paul entered the proud city of Athens in Ancient Greece, where a colossal collision between radically different worldviews would occur. He had left Berea and made the 200-mile trip south to Athens unaccompanied. While waiting for Timothy and Silas (two fellow Jews who served with Paul) to join him, he was walking around the streets of this famous city, the cradle of democracy, the glorious home of Plato, Socrates, Aristotle, and Zeno. Athens was the world center of culture, religion, and philosophy. It boasted remarkable works of art, magnificent architecture, a refined pagan culture, and one of the greatest universities in the world. It was the equivalent of a modern Ivy League university such as Harvard, a cluster of sharply educated minds. Athens had been conquered by the Romans 200 years before, and though it remained the academic center of the world, it was a city living on the glory of former days. It was stuck in the nostalgic eddies of its past.

Paul clearly had some extra time on his hands and wandered around the city. It is easy to relate to his experience of being a sightseer in a new city and being struck by what stands out. When I visited Istanbul, I couldn't miss the large number of mosques. In Paul's case, he was disturbed to see that the city was full of sculpted images of gods (idols). Some historians have commented that there were more statues of gods and goddesses than there were people in Athens, which then had a population of 10,000. The art of Athens was a reflection of its worship. We could say that this is a contemporary touchpoint. Generally, we can see what holds preeminence in people's lives through where they put their focus, and often the arts (paintings, sculptures, movies, and music) help make that very clear.

Acts 17:17 describes how Paul began introducing the Athenian intelligentsia to his own worldview—apparently, he couldn't wait until Timothy and Silas joined him. Paul seems to have recognized that he needed to build some bridges and touchpoints with the assorted worldviews of those he was talking to. The lesson for us is that, in order for us to build relationships with people who hold diverse worldviews, it is wise to begin by learning where we share common ground. Paul "reasoned in the synagogue with both Jews and God-fearing Greeks, as well as in the marketplace...with those who happened to be there."

Verse 18 reports that:

> A group of Epicurean and Stoic philosophers began to dispute with him. Some of them asked, "What is this babbler trying to say?" Others said, "He seems to be advocating foreign gods." They said this because Paul was preaching the Good News about Jesus and the resurrection.

The concern about advocating foreign gods is that it could be perceived as a threat to the patron gods of the Athens community. One observation that could be made about this interaction is that people with differing worldviews often misunderstand each other. One lesson we can learn from this is that stereotyping Muslims, Hindus, Sikhs, Free Thinkers, those who hold to a First Nations spirituality, and so forth won't help us build relationships based on our shared humanity. Bridging the gap between worldviews takes patience and intentional work.

In this context, it would be helpful to consider details of the worldviews that Paul was engaging with.

The Epicureans believed that life was random and that humans were free to make of it whatever they could. Since there was no afterlife or immortality of the soul, their goal was to grab all the fun they could get, pack their lives with as much happiness and pleasure as possible. The gods were uninvolved, uninterested, and distant, and human affairs were not governed by Providence. Therefore, the supreme good was to "pamper the flesh," to indulge their desires, to eat, drink, and be merry.

The Stoics were pantheistic, regarding God as the "world-soul." (A contemporary version of this might be: "May the Force be with you.") In their view, whatever happened was fate, determined by the gods. However, God's providence was flawed because he didn't rule the world with wisdom, justice, and power. As a result, people had to resign themselves to the fact that what was going to happen had already been determined and there was no point in trying to do anything to change things. We might call this a form of apathy and fatalism. Stoics emphasized duty, self-discipline, self-sufficiency, living in harmony with nature and reason, and developing their own power to handle whatever came.

It is very obvious that Paul was engaging in a cultural context where a variety of worldviews were already colliding. But there were very fundamental differences between Paul's Judeo-Christian worldview and the Athenian worldviews. Paul attempted to communicate knowledge about the God who wanted to have a personal connection with human beings. The Athenians insulted Paul and called him a "babbler" (σπερμολόγος), which means "a seed picker," one who picks up secondhand scraps of knowledge that have not been thought through and tries to pass them off as his own—we might call that plagiarizing. In contemporary terms, it was alleged that Paul was someone with half-baked ideas, not sophisticated enough to be taken seriously.

Yet verse 19 reveals that the Athenians were curious enough to take Paul to a meeting of the Areopagus. This was a sort of philosophic review board responsible for safeguarding the intellectual and moral quality of the city. This philosophic review board had authority over who was allowed to lecture in the city. These elite intellectuals met at a place called Mars Hill, a sophisticated intellectual environment similar to a university. Paul would have looked up from Mars Hill to see the incredible edifice of the Parthenon perched atop the Acropolis. Here Paul's worldview would be examined by the experts in philosophy and religion: "they said to him, 'May we know what this new teaching is that you are presenting? You are bringing some strange ideas to our ears, and we would like to know what they mean'" (Acts 17:19-20). Acts 17:21 says that these men "spent their time doing nothing but talking about and listening to the latest ideas." Their practice of getting together every day to "shoot the breeze" might be compared to one long Oprah Winfrey show, talking about the latest trends in a culture of pluralism. One thing I've witnessed in my university journey has been that intellectuals delight in relieving their boredom by exploring new ideas in hopes of discovering something novel. We might call this a pointless talk fest designed to show off their intellectual talents.

2. Paul's Speech (Acts 17:22-31)

Acts 17:22 reports that Paul then stood up and launched into a presentation: "'People of Athens! I see that in every way you are very religious." Paul created a friendly atmosphere by first complimenting his audience; he commended them for demonstrating open-mindedness and an inquisitive attitude. They seemed to recognize the necessity of keeping an open mind when trying to make sense out of life. Some would say that when you give all your energies to making something supreme and look to it to give you meaning and comfort in life, you might want to be sure that you're getting it right. So the Greeks in Acts 17 agreed to hear what this Jew had to say.

In Acts 17:23 Paul pointed out that the Athenians claimed to know the names and identities of thousands of gods but had also erected an idol to one they called an unknown god. Paul then asked them if they would like to know that "god" they thought was unknowable. For the Greeks to have identified that there was an unknown god was to admit that they were living with some uncertainty. (Perhaps today we would call this agnosticism.) Then Paul began to answer the big question: Who is God? Note that Paul didn't have to establish reasonable grounds for believing that a God exists; that was already a given for the Athenians. In the contest of worldviews, the key question is: Who is God? The answer to this question shapes our understanding of the meaning of life.

3. Paul's Judeo-Christian Answer to the Question: Who Is God? (Acts 17:24-31)

A. God is the Origin of the Entire Universe.

The starting place of any worldview is the question: Why does anything exist at all? On a personal level, we might ask: "Where did I come from?", "Why am I here?" and "Where am I going?"

Paul attempted to build bridges in his discussion by appealing to the Athenians' cultural-traditional knowledge of the natural order, what we would call general revelation. This resonates with Ecclesiastes 3:11, which indicates that there is an innate human intuition of a greater mystery to life because God has "set eternity in the human heart." I remember that my grandfather had a dog named Suzie. It looked like a large rat with hair. I'd see the dog lying in the family room and wonder, "What is he thinking?" I doubt that he ever had any deep thoughts, pondering questions such as "Where did I come from?" The unique thing about human beings is that we ask ourselves those kinds of questions, even if we never verbalize them.

So, Paul started to answer the question, "Who is God?" He stated that "God...made the world and everything in it" (Acts 17:24) and "He himself gives everyone life and breath and everything else" (Acts 17:25). It will be helpful for us to remember that the Epicureans believed that there was no God and that everything was random. In contrast, the Stoics believed that everything was god. Paul opposed the

Greek idea that the universe was eternal and that the Demiurge had shaped things out of preexistent materials. Paul was telling the Athenians that the stuff (the natural order, the substance of creation) that they could see around them was not God but that it was made by God, *ex nihilo*, out of nothing. Paul also stated that God "does not live in temples built by human hands." He was telling the Athenians that God is not contained in creation (or kept in a box, a temple, or a statue made by humans); He exists apart from it.

Modern readers might think, "Worshiping creation—that is so primitive!" However, that is exactly what modern people do when they look for the definitive meaning of their lives in the material stuff of this world. When we look for ultimate happiness and well-being in the material things of this world, we are implying that this world is our everything. However, a reminder that our lives have a shelf life brings us back to the God question. So, the first part of Paul's answer to that question is that God is the origin of all things.

B. God is the Authority over Everything.

Paul then said in Acts 17:24 that God "is the Lord of heaven and earth." That's what rubs some people the wrong way, being presented with the idea of a transcendent authority higher than them. But Paul said this God of origins is also sovereign—He is in control! He has established the physical, moral, and metaphysical ways in which the world functions, and He sustains it. Humanity has an innate sense that this moral order exists, and this allows our intersubjective understanding (our collective conscience) to establish the conventions by which society operates. The majority of people know that a healthy society can only function when there is a standard, where rules operate to provide the greatest good for the greatest number of people—it is the basis of our laws. We know that there are better ways to live, and the explanation for that, according to Paul, is the God who created us and everything around us.

C. God Exists Independently of His Creation.

Paul then stated that God "does not live in temples built by human hands. And he is not served by human hands, as if he needed anything. Rather, he himself gives everyone life and breath and everything else" (Acts 17:24-25). Then he added in verse 29: "Therefore since we are God's offspring, we should not think that the divine being is like gold or silver or stone—an image made by human design and skill." In contrast, here is how many Greeks looked at things. They would decide, "We're going to create our own god today." So they would get a rock, set it down, and think about what kind of god they wanted. They would say, "I think we want our god to be fierce." So they would put a fierce face and big muscles on the image. They would say, "I think our god should know all things." So they would put eyeballs all over it. They would say, "We want our god to be virile and productive." So they would give the god some naughty bits. And then they would bow down and worship the god they had created. In essence, they were really just worshiping thin air. Paul pointed out that God doesn't need us to make images of Him. He doesn't need to be taken care of. He does not depend on us to meet His needs. The God of the Bible is self-existent and self-sufficient. It is human beings who are finite and dependent.

D. God Created Every Person with a Purpose.

Then, in Acts 17:26, Paul stated: "From one man he made all the nations, that they should inhabit the whole earth; and he marked out their appointed times in history and the boundaries of their lands." The first part of this statement hit at the Greeks' ethnocentrism because Greeks viewed themselves as cultured and all other people as barbarian. The second half of the statement declared that the Athenians' lives were providential rather than accidental. In other words, Paul invited the Athenians to think about the purpose of their lives and why God had given them life. Paul was saying that God (whom he had defined as the Originator, the Authority, and the Self-existent One) had willed humanity into existence. He knew where and when each of the Athenians had been born—and why. Remember that some of these Athenians (the Epicureans) believed that life wasn't going anywhere and that they should make decisions based on maximizing their pleasure and minimizing their pain in the here and now. In contrast, Paul presented the Christian worldview that said that God had created each of the Athenians for a purpose and that they had a destiny.

The same question faces us today. Naturalism posits that human beings are here due to a random cosmic accident. We have no reason for being here, no meaning, no purpose. We are merely a bundle of meaningless molecules that came together by chance in a process that started billions of years ago. The dust and gases of the galaxy floated around for who knows how long until they collided and became an organic, gooey, slimy primal soup. Out of that an animal emerged, grew legs, climbed onto land, grew feathers and fur, became a monkey, and then eventually became the hairless apes called homo sapiens. The logical conclusion of that is that the universe won't mind a bit if human beings die and become a heap of compost. For that reason, Paul's articulation of the biblical worldview is just as relevant to us as it was to the Athenians. Paul declared that God had made humanity and we are all here for a reason.

E. God Desires a Relationship with All People.
Paul then expanded the envelope of the biblical worldview a little further. In Acts 17:27, he said, "God did this so that [people] would seek him and perhaps reach out for him and find him, though he is not far from any one of us." Paul was stating that God desires to have an intimate relationship with humanity—He is available. God willed us into existence in such a way that we would instinctively yearn for the explanation for our life and would "seek him and perhaps reach out for him." The image is of a blind person groping about in the darkness, reaching for something to hold on to. Paul was saying that, since God is real, if we are riding high enjoying success, health, prosperity, and a sense of self-sufficiency but don't know God, then something is missing. And when we mess up, when we experience loneliness, when life's load seems heavy, when we face failure and loss, then God is only a prayer and a breath away.

Paul's was pointing out that if God remains "unknown," it is not because He desires to be that way. He is a communicating God. Paul commented in Romans 1:19-20 that God communicates through the natural order, demonstrating clearly that there is an Intelligent Designer behind it. Psalm 19:1 declared: "The heavens declare the glory of God; the skies proclaim the work of his hands." When we find a watch in the desert or a painting in a gallery, we conclude that they didn't just happen but that there must have been a designer. That there is design behind the natural order, that there is a moral order to human existence, and that there is a first cause to everything—all of this is intended to provoke humanity to reflection and inquiry.

F. God Holds People Accountable for What They Do with Christ.

Perhaps the most challenging aspect of Paul's worldview was expressed in Acts 17:30: "In the past God overlooked such ignorance, but now he commands all people everywhere to repent." Paul recognized that the Athenians knew how to paint, sculpt, and talk philosophy, but when it came to God, he said they were ignorant. In many ways, Paul's observation is also very relevant to contemporary society. Paul's message was that God does not want people to be ignorant of His existence and that He is giving people an invitation and opportunity to approach Him and abandon the errors of their former lives based on an incomplete and erroneous worldview. Paul continued in verse 31: "For he has set a day when he will judge the world with justice by the man he has appointed. He has given proof of this to everyone by raising him from the dead." The assumption that Paul was making is that the resurrection of Christ is a miracle, a profound piece of evidence that validates the Christian worldview, and that it is another way that God has revealed Himself.

At this point, Paul had put forward the claim that God is the origin of all things, including human existence, and that, by implication, human beings are made for friendship with God. This raises the next question: What might a relationship with this God look like?

4. Who Is God? The Answer Is Found in Jesus Christ.

Now we come to the most debated and offensive part of the discussion for many people—the incarnation and the proposition that human lives will face a final evaluation. In John 14:9, Jesus declared: "Anyone who has seen me has seen the Father." Now here in Acts 17:31, Paul declared that God is the universal judge of all persons and that the basis for His judgment will be what we do with His Son Jesus.

Paul further stated that God has given proof of this assertion by raising Jesus from the dead. Paul here presented the resurrection—a fact completely contrary to our observation of the way the laws of nature work. In nature, things die, death is death. Paul could have simply confined his discussion to arguing for theism or monotheism, but he made the astounding claim of the resurrection of Christ. (A more detailed discussion of this topic is found in Chapter 2 of this book, "Making a Case for the Resurrection from Ground Zero.") In the beginning of the discussion with the Greeks, Paul had appealed to reason and observation of the natural world. But now Paul found it necessary to move the conversation onto the topic of specific revelation (the biblical Canon), faith, and religious experience.

In moving the discussion into the personal religious realm, Paul was making the point that what the Athenians chose to do with Christ would determine the quality of their present and their future. His presentation called for a response. Acts 17:32-33 describes three types of response to Paul's presentation.

A. Rejection

Some Athenians mocked Paul's presentation. They considered themselves too sophisticated to accept the resurrection of a physical body. The resurrection was incompatible with Greek philosophy. The Greeks wanted to get rid of their bodies, not take them on again, since the body was considered evil (a dualistic view derived from Platonic thought).

B. Reluctance

Others wanted more information. They were not yet thoroughly persuaded, but they were willing to dialogue further. Their position was still in process. We might compare their position to some contemporary deists and agnostics.

C. Acceptance

Some were persuaded and became Christians. One of these was Dionysius, a man who evidently belonged to the cream of Athenian society.

Critics have pointed out that no mention is made of the formation of a church in Athens, nor is there any record of a later visit by Paul to this city. Some feel that this indicates he failed in his mission at Athens. They argue that this was because he compromised his message, offering a philosophical presentation instead of his usual straightforward clear-cut gospel message. Proof of this, they say, is the small number of converts and Paul's mood of discouragement as he went on to Corinth. (1 Corinthians 2:2: "I resolved to know nothing while I was with you except Jesus Christ and him crucified.") Paul's own assessment of his experience at Athens may be found in 1 Corinthians 1:21: "The world through its wisdom did not know [God]."

In light of this, perhaps a defense of Paul's method is in order. To begin with, we should recognize that Acts 17 contains only a summary of Paul's dialogue with these cultured pagans. Furthermore, if Paul won even a small number of converts from this highly intellectual audience, it should be considered a fruitful and successful dialogue. If we look more carefully at the historical record, we may see a different picture. Eusebius (AD 170) was told by the bishop of Corinth that Dionysius became the first bishop of Athens. And let us remember that in the twenty-first century, 98 percent of Athenians are adherents of the Greek Orthodox Church. This is quite astounding considering that things seemed to be a bit rough for Paul in Acts 17 back in the first century.

5. Seven Ways in Which Paul Engaged Alternative Worldviews

In Paul's dialogue with the Athenians, we can find some great pointers on how to engage people who embrace another worldview.

A. Paul Looked for Ways to Find Common Ground (Acts 17:22-23).

Paul went where people were geographically and began where they were at intellectually. He used idols (sculpted images of gods) and poetry as points of contact. He started building a case from examples they understood (not the biblical Canon) in order to establish common ground and bridge into introducing a theistic worldview. He then moved the discussion toward an explanation of the Christian worldview that called for a decision to be made on Christ's claim. What Paul was attempting to do was contextualize, adapt his presentation to the Athenian context. A contemporary parallel might be engaging in a discussion utilizing philosophy.

B. Paul Attempted to Portray an Alternative View of God (Acts 17:24-26).

Paul gently but firmly exposed what he perceived to be the flawed views of the Athenians. He began with their confessed ignorance about God and put forth the proposition that there is a knowable God.

C. Paul Attempted to Nurture the Longing in People to Explore Ultimate Reality (Acts 17:27).

Common to human experience is the instinctive sense of mystery behind our existence. Alvin Plantinga has suggested that the belief that there is a God is "properly basic" to human beings—there is a *sensus divinitatis*, an innate sense of the Divine.[337] Paul attempted to tap into that sense, that longing, and push people to explore ultimate reality, even if that led to knowing an Ultimate Being in a personal way.

D. Paul Was Cross-culturally Astute (Acts 17:28-30).

Paul was a student of culture, which helped him to articulate his beliefs clearly and persuasively, even quoting from authors the Athenians admired. In Acts 17:28, Paul quoted a line from "Phaenomena," a poem by the Greek poet Aratus: "In Him we live and move and have our being." Paul connected this Greek line with the biblical ideas that existence is a gift of God (John 1:4: "that life was the light of all mankind") and that we subsist in God (Genesis 1:27: "God created mankind in his own image"). In Acts 17:28, Paul also quoted Epimenides the Cretan poet: "We are his offspring"—in the sense that human beings are created by God. Paul quoted from the popular Greek playwright Menander (in 1 Corinthians 15:33) and again from Epimenides (in Titus 1:12). He was familiar enough with Hellenistic culture to build bridges into it. That means that Paul had to have been a diligent student of the worldview he embraced but

---

[337] Alvin Plantinga, "Is Belief in God Rational?" in C.F. Delaney, ed., *Rationality and Religious Belief* (Notre Dame, IN: University of Notre Dame Press, 1979), 7-27. See also Alvin Plantinga, "Is Belief in God Properly Basic?" *Noûs* 15:1 (March 1981), 41-51.

that he had also taken the time to understand other cultural worldviews. As a result, Paul was able to respectfully engage people who held other worldviews. This is the antithesis of Christians segregating themselves in some kind of holy huddle that avoids engagement with culture, philosophy, and the arts.

E. Paul Did Not Shy Away from What He Deemed to Be a Profound Proof of Christianity—The Resurrection (Acts 17:31).

Christ's resurrection was the focal point of Paul's faith. He knew that if the resurrection was true, it proved the central theme of Christianity. On the other hand, without the resurrection, Christianity is just metaphysics (1 Corinthians 15:13-14).

F. Paul Made Clear That Each Person Is Accountable for the Choices They Make in Regards to Christ (Acts 17:30-31).

Paul began with courtesy, sensitivity, and restraint. But he didn't candy-coat how he understood the truth. He made very clear that there comes a time when a final audit of people's lives will be done by Jesus Christ. C.S. Lewis put it this way:

> I am trying here to prevent anyone saying the really foolish thing that people often say about him: I'm ready to accept Jesus as a great moral teacher, but I don't accept his claim to be God. That is the one thing we must not say. A man who was merely a man and said the sort of things Jesus said would not be a great moral teacher. He would either be a lunatic—on the level with the man who says he is a poached egg—or else he would be the Devil of Hell. You must make your choice. Either this man was, and is, the Son of God, or else a madman or something worse. You

can shut him up for a fool, you can spit at him and kill him as a demon or you can fall at his feet and call him Lord and God, but let us not come with any patronizing nonsense about his being a great human teacher. He has not left that open to us. He did not intend to.[338]

G. Paul Understood That There Will Be a Great Variety of Responses to a Presentation of the Christian Worldview (Acts 17:5-9,13,18-20,32-34).

Paul received varied responses to his preaching in Athens—mockery, rejection, agnosticism, and a willingness to accept the Christian worldview. Paul's story in Acts 17 has a contemporary ring and finds its urgency in the *missio Dei* (the mission of God). So, what does reason have to do with faith when having a conversation about the God question? Paul demonstrated that if Christians don't start out making some reasonable linkages with other people's existential worldviews, it will be harder to engage in meaningful dialogue and parachute a Christian metaphysic into the contemporary context.

---

[338] C.S. Lewis, *Mere Christianity* (New York: Macmillan, 1960), 55-56.

CHAPTER 6
Saint Augustine's Philosophy of Time:
The Enduring Contemporary Debate

Many of us struggle with the interface of reason and faith when trying to understand time and the mystery behind its past, present, and future. Augustine was struck by the importance of time and its puzzling and elusive character. In Book Eleven of *The Confessions*, he attempted to unravel its secrets by addressing problems that continue to be debated by modern philosophers and philosopher-theologians. Although the problems raised by Augustine are often dismissed by Naturalists and empiricists because of his theistic worldview, rarely do the objectors admit to their own assumptions. To borrow from Husserl's words, "The crisis of modern humanity is to insist that the realm of knowing must be understood after the assumptions and methods of the natural sciences."[339]

Philosopher-theologians are divided as to how we should best understand time and God's relationship with our time-bound universe. Does God experience each moment of time in succession or are all times present to God? How we think about God and time has implications for our understanding of the nature of time, the creation of the universe, God's knowledge of the future, His interactions with His creation, and the

---

[339] Samuel Enoch Stumpf, "Edmund Husserl," *Socrates to Sartre: A History of Philosophy* (New York: McGraw-Hill, 1994), 493-495.

fullness of God's life.

The starting point for this chapter is Augustine's proposition of "divine eternity," sometimes called "God's timelessness" or "eternalism." This will be compared with the contemporary philosophical position of "divine temporality." The chapter will then propose a way forward out of the impasse of this controversial and challenging area of philosophical theology.

Problem #1: What Is Time?

Philosopher-theologians have debated whether time is change, movement, succession, a substance, transitory presence, and so forth. The issue Augustine raised about the nature of time is whether the "now" exists independently of our experience or it is our own subjective construct created by our own understanding of the world. There are a broad number of theories on time, but just a few will be presented in this section.

A. Time as Subjective Reality

Augustine introduced the subjective notion of time by suggesting that it is a distention of the mind. Augustine was aware that "We perceive definite periods of time and we compare them with each other indicating some are longer and others are shorter," but he posited that what we are actually measuring is "time by our perception of it."[340]

Our perception of the passage of time can change with the blink of an eye. Time may seem to stand still or be fleeting. We may find ourselves saying things such as, "Where did time go?" or "I just need a little more time!" Sometimes time seems to drag on forever.

---

[340] Augustine, *The Confessions,* trans. Rex Warner (New York: Mentor Books, 1963), 270, 281.

In sudden accidents, some people report that their whole life flashed before their eyes in detail in what was probably only a few seconds on the clock. At night, a dream that seems to last many hours of time is shown by REM (Rapid Eye Movement) sleep patterns to actually take only minutes of elapsed time.[341]

Subjective time, the appearance of time to our consciousness, varies widely and cannot be measured by a stopwatch. Sartre said that "it is impossible for a man to transcend human subjectivity, subjectivity must be the human starting point."[342] Heidegger felt that our subjective consciousness is a phenomenon of *Da-sein* ("being there," our existential existence) and therefore should not be used, as Augustine tried to do, to prove God's existence or an "immediate" consciousness of God.[343]

A further problem arises over our consciousness of change. Many people recall how time seemed to move very slowly during their youth. Intervals of time between holidays or periods of boredom in certain contexts seemed to last an eternity. However, adults often look back on those same years and reflect that those decades seem to have passed rapidly.

Given a "subjective perception" of past, present, and future time, Augustine questioned whether there

---

[341] Rod Plutnick and Sandra Mollenauer, "Altered States of Consciousness," *Introduction to Psychology* (New York: Random House, 1986), 137-143. Testimonies of near-death experiences often provide extensive time-related detail coming out of a condensed time frame.

[342] Jean-Paul Sartre, "Existentialism is a Humanism," in Forrest E. Baird and Walter Kaufman, eds. *Twentieth-Century Philosophy* (Upper Saddle River, NJ: Prentice-Hall, vol. 5, reprint 2000), 206-238.

[343] Martin Heidegger, "Temporality and within-timeness as the origin of the vulgar concept of time," *Being and Time*, trans. Joan Stambaugh (Albany: State University of New York Press, 1996), 248-249.

really are three times, stating, "If the future and past exist, I want to know where they are."[344] His conclusion was that these three times exist in the mind in terms of memory, immediate experience, and expectation. Time for Augustine is "a kind of extension of the mind itself" because sensory things, after they no longer exist, are measured in our memory, which remains fixed. It is in this way that the mind measures time. "As things pass [through the mind] they leave an impression that remains," and this impression is measured in the present when time is measured.[345]

Augustine identified that the concept of time seems to contain a couple of distinct ideas fused into one. First, there is the idea of succession, in which individual moments are realized one after the other. Second, the march of time seems to know neither a pause nor an interruption. It is difficult to imagine ceasing to grow older, or that "moment" would cease to be followed by the next "moment."

Augustine was not alone in offering a subjective view of time. Kant also suggested that time, one of the structuring principles of experience, is a creation of the knowing subject. He viewed time as a feature of the "phenomenal" world (that world known through our senses) and not of "things-in-themselves." He felt that both the outer experience of physical objects and the inner experience of psychological states were framed in the format of the temporal intuitive structure.[346] Leibniz said that time was an "order of successions," or a relation between things that follow one another, that is purely mental.[347] Husserl was

---

[344] Ibid., 271.
[345] Ibid., 279-281.
[346] J.J. Smart, ed., *Problems of Space and Time* (New York: Macmillan, 2nd printing, 1968), 124-125.
[347] Gottfried Wilhelm Leibniz, *"Space and Time,"* http://www.philosophypages.com/ph/leib.htm, accessed November

convinced that the natural sciences had developed a faulty attitude regarding what the world is like and how best to understand it. He posited that there is a mystery regarding the connection of experiences and consciousness, where description should include our perception and reflection along with empiricism.[348]

Sartre was opposed to associating eternal values or God with one's subjective temporal experience of being and time. He said all truth begins with this:

> I think, therefore I exist. There we have the absolute truth of consciousness becoming aware of itself. Every theory that takes man out of the moment in which he becomes aware of himself is, at its very beginning, a theory that confounds truth...for outside the Cartesian cogito, all views are only probable.[349]

For Sartre, "existence precedes essence" such that "life has no meaning a priori." Sartre said, "Before you come alive life is nothing" and it is people who choose its value and meaning. Man is thrust into existence and is "at the start a plan which is aware of itself [as one] who hurls himself toward a future." There is nothing in heaven, no a priori Good, Infinite, or Perfect Consciousness. "Being-in-itself" has no purpose or meaning, yet "being-for-itself" is the consciousness that at every temporal moment one is choosing the future.[350] People believe what they believe because they choose to believe such things. The meanings people create—for example, about "time"—create the way they see the world they live in. In Sartre's words,

---

20, 2002.
[348] Edmund Husserl, "The Crisis of European Science and Transcendental Phenomenology," in Baird and Kaufman, 12-21.
[349] Jean-Paul Sartre, "Existentialism is a Humanism," in Baird and Kaufman, 233-234.
[350] Ibid., 227-229, 206-238.

"Things will be as man decides they are to be." Sartre felt that it was cowardly to relinquish one's freedom to choose by succumbing to religious dogma.[351]

B. Time as Reality outside Our Minds

Many materialists and Naturalists represent time as something that has its reality outside of the mind. Some regard time as being independent of all created things and capable of surviving the destruction of them all. Infinite in its extension, it is portrayed as the receptacle in which all events of this world are enclosed. Often it is portrayed as permeating all things, regulating their course, and preserving in the uninterrupted flow of its parts an absolutely regular mode of succession.[352] Supporters of this view assert that time has an external concrete reality and that the mind's representation of time is only a copy of that reality. These "objective" views tend to present time as: possessing the property of being; being irreversible; having linking parts that manifest an unchangeable order of succession and a past time that does not come back.

Newton published the first mathematical model of time in his *Principia Mathematica*, in which he advocated that time was separate from space or matter. Time was considered to be linear and infinite in both directions.[353] This premise could shed light on Augustine's other question of "What [was] God doing before He created the universe?"[354] A difficult question to answer is whether time is a feature of God's existence. Hawking speculatively interpreted

---

[351] Ibid., 232-233, 237, 206-238.
[352] Stephen Hawking and Roger Penrose, *The Nature of Space and Time* (Princeton, NJ: Princeton University Press, 1996), 1-36.
[353] Stephen Hawking, "The Shape of Time," *The Universe in a Nutshell* (New York: Bantam Books, 2001), 29-65.
[354] Augustine, *The Confessions*, 264.

Augustine as meaning that before God made heaven and earth, He did not make anything at all. [355] Augustine can also be interpreted as saying that creation was not done in time but with time.[356] The idea that God was not doing anything (acting, creating) before He created the world and was simply being God is difficult to reconcile with the definition of God as being omnipotent and creative. An alternative explanation is that time was itself a creation of God that could have preceded His creating of heaven and earth. Augustine was reflecting on the world as temporal and changing, concluding that there must be an eternal and unchanging Being.[357]

Naturalism tends to see time as a linear stream of events, proceeding in a straight line, linked by cause and effect, with no predetermined goal or overarching purpose. Evolution is credited with producing self-conscious humans who construct human history. But when human history disappears, it is assumed that natural history will go on its way alone.[358]

Russell blamed Augustine's preoccupation with a "sense of sin" for leading him into excessive subjectivity so that he substituted subjective time for the objective time of history and physics. [359] Furthermore, Russell criticized Kant at length for not concluding that the past and future are infinite, with no overarching meaning. [360]

Kant was challenged by the idea that "if the

---

[355] Hawking, "The shape of Time," 35.
[356] Augustine, *The Confessions*, 265-266.
[357] Ibid., 265: "Behold the heavens and earth are; they proclaim that they were created; for they change and vary. They proclaim also that they made not themselves."
[358] James Sire, *The Universe Next Door* (Downers Grove, IL: InterVarsity Press, 1988), 68-70.
[359] Roland J. Teske, *Paradoxes of Time in Saint Augustine* (Milwaukee, WI: Marquette University Press, 1996), 39.
[360] Smart, *Problems of Space and Time*, 145-167.

universe had been created, why had there been an infinite wait before creation?" Furthermore, "if the universe had existed forever, why hadn't everything that was going to happen already concluded with history being finished?" Perhaps the reason why there seemed to be a contradiction was that these questions were associated with the context of a Newtonian mathematical model in which time was an infinite line.[361]

Heidegger felt that for one to say that "time is endless in both directions is only possible on the basis of an orientation toward an unattached 'in-itself' of a course of 'nows' covered over with regard to 'datability, spannedness, and publicness of Da-sein', so that it has dwindled to an unrecognizable fragment."[362]

Russell did not feel that there was enough evidence to introduce God into any notion and dismissed any meaning to the universe by stating, "It's just there."[363] He viewed "the self as a bundle of sense impressions" that goes from one moment to the next with the "I" entangled in the sense datum (the input from our senses).[364] Time is a notion that we construct from temporal relations that are sense given.

The general approach among theoretical physicists and positivists has been to classify time as being

---

[361] Hawking, "The shape of Time," 29-65. Calvin felt that it was inappropriate to raise questions about God and time and a waste of time asking the incomprehensible question of "Why did God delay?" For him, this lay in the realm of God's hidden purposes. John Calvin, *Institutes of the Christian Religion,* ed. John T. McNeill (Philadelphia: The Westminster Press, 1960), vol. 1, 160-161.
[362] Heidegger, "Temporality and within-timeness as the origin of the vulgar concept of time," 388.
[363] John Blanchard, *Does God Believe in Atheists?* (Darlington, England: Evangelical Press, 2000), 275, 311.
[364] Bertrand Russell, "Knowledge by Acquaintance and Knowledge by Description," in Baird and Kaufman, 59.

infinite in both directions. This allowed them to skirt around any awkward questions about the creation of the universe, which, it was assumed, should be relegated to the realm of metaphysics. Scientific theories of time were required to be based on the most workable philosophy of science, particularly a positivist approach. Positivists generally try not to say what time actually is, but rather try to describe what has been found to be a good model for time.

Although Russell wanted to advocate that there are some categories of knowledge "that enable us to pass beyond the limits of our private experience," he did not seem to go far enough in admitting how mysterious some knowledge really is.[365] It is not hard to agree with Russell that one of the values of philosophy is that it "is able to keep alive a sense of wonder with familiar things" and "help us enlarge our thoughts," but one cannot help but feel disappointed that such great promises are confined to the limitations of reason.[366] Russell's presuppositions did not allow him to seriously engage the question of "what lies beyond human reason?"

Ayer also disassociated himself from any metaphysical proposition that would try to connect ideas such as God and time. He stated, "It cannot be asserted that there is a non-empirical world or that there is a transcendent God."[367] Ayer's commitment to reason and sense-experience would not allow him to believe that "knowledge of a reality transcending the world" is possible. For Ayer, "One way of attacking the metaphysician who claims to have knowledge of a reality which transcends the phenomenal world is to

---

[365] Ibid., 63.
[366] Bertrand Russel, "The Value of Philosophy," in Baird and Kaufman, 63-64.
[367] A.J. Ayer, "Language, Truth and Logic," in Baird and Kaufman, 169-170.

enquire [about] the premises that the propositions were deduced."[368]

This argument can also be turned the other way, as one can question a Naturalist's faith premises in things such as the uniformity of nature and the preeminence of reason as the only way of knowing. Many cumulative arguments can be constructed as to why one may embrace the idea of a transcendent reality.[369] Ayer's radical empiricism and commitment to the scientific method require that verification be either conclusive or probable. His assumption was that the process of "verification" always works and is unbiased. Because he assumed that God cannot be verified, observed, or fit into empirical or logical categories, he felt comfortable in claiming that the subject of "God" can be classified as "nonsense."[370] This approach resulted in questions about the meaning of life, the existence of God, and theistic perspectives on time being "lopped off" or discreetly ignored.

Pragmatists such as Dewey almost never address eschatological issues, nor do they affirm notions of transcendent truth. Dewey embraced Naturalism as a means to achieving progress, assuming that that also meant the supernatural needed to be eliminated. But given the fact that the latest developments in cosmology indicate a starting point, pragmatists are now faced with a why question as to the cause of the universe. An implication of their denial of absolutes in the realm of truth leaves pragmatists vulnerable to

---

[368] A.J. Ayer, "The Elimination of Metaphysics," in Baird and Kaufman, 170-171, 173.
[369] Some examples are a cumulative argument for the probability of the existence of God, semi-experimental data on religious experience, general or specific revelation, and especially the historicity of God showing up in time. One wonders why Ayer cannot see that these are theoretically conceivable.
[370] A.J. Ayer, "Language, Truth and Logic," in Baird and Kaufman, 169-177.

the accusation that they are inadvertently claiming that they have a non-relative (that is absolutely objective) vantage point from which to view all truth.[371] If God exists, whether timeless or temporal, then there are absolutes.

Rorty also rejected the idea that there is an essence to reality or some reality eternally "out there," which for some reason is inaccurately represented to the mind. He rejected the idea that there might be timeless truth with an intended purpose. He argued that to assume that there is a fixed stable reality, such as a timeless God who has a relationship with time, is to allow oneself to be "bound by inherited language." Rorty believed that the language of Plato, theologians, and Kant has imposed labels and descriptions upon our consciousness which purport to be absolutely true descriptions but are not. He advocated that we can create ourselves by giving meaning to our own life and telling our own story.[372]

Quine recognized that treating time on par with space is not new to natural science; however, he realized that the distinction between analytic and synthetic is not that straightforward. [373] Even empiricists cannot avoid resorting to abstract theories and speculations to try to explain sense datum and to provide theories for subjects such as time. Quine remained optimistic that synthetic categories might one day be verified, and he recognized that synthetic categories can be utilized in trying to make sense of the datum.

Serious issues with the datum and the theory of a

---

[371] John Dewey, "The Quest for Certainty." in Baird and Kaufman, 25-40.
[372] "Analytic Philosophy,"in Stumpf, *Socrates to Sartre*, 475-479.
[373] "Quine on Time," in Smart, *Problems of Space and Time*, 370, 372; Willard Van Orman Quine, "Two Dogmas of Empiricism," in Baird and Kaufman, 269-271.

time-dependent universe were already evident in the 1920s when many scientists believed in a cosmological constant, that the universe came from nothing—which is sometimes called the "steady state theory." This was an unverified theory that seemed to violate a fundamental law of science, the law of causality. Up to that point in history Einstein figured that the idea of a uniformly expanding universe would break down if one followed the motions of the galaxies back in time.[374]

Theorists have tried to propose an infinite number of universes, [375] or a number of completely self-contained universes with no beginning, where time is an inclusive factor. However, they seem stumped as to the issue of existence. Whether time had a beginning or has always existed, we are faced with a profound question: What explains the *existence* of space and time? One problem with the idea of "infinite regression" is that there are human limitations in the retrieval of knowledge related to ultimate reality.

Atkins attempted to answer the question by positing the "quantum fluctuation hypothesis" that implies that "space-time generates its own dust in the process of its own self-assembly."[376] Atkins suggested that time, space, and matter are produced by a "quantum flutter" that sparks them all off and before we know it there are a hundred billion galaxies pulled out of the "quantum hat." Atkins went so far as to say, "We can even discern how the universe could come from absolutely nothing as time induced, by chance,

---

[374] Stephen Hawking, "A Brief History of Relativity," *The Universe in a Nutshell*, 3-27.
[375] J.J.C. Smart and J.J. Haldane, *Atheism and Theism* (Oxford: Blackwell Publishers, 1996), 46*; see also 16-23.
[376] Peter Atkins, *Creation Revisited* (Harmondsworth, UK: Penguin, 1994), 143.

its own existence.[377]

The existence of the entire matter-energy, space-time package is problematic for the atheist. In partial agreement with Augustine, Craig stated that,

> Since everything that began to exist has a cause of its existence, and since the universe began to exist, we conclude, therefore, that the universe has a cause of existence. We ought to ponder long and hard over this conclusion, for it means that transcending the entire universe there exists a cause that brought the universe into being ex nihilo.[378]

Einstein's theory of relativity gave time shape.[379] It implied that the universe began in a singularity called the Big Bang and that therefore time had a beginning. He redefined the universe by saying that energy and matter are interrelated and that, in an expanding universe, time, space, and matter are all part of the expanding singularity. In this theory, time was not considered to be some kind of passive background, but intricately bound up with space and matter. Einstein's theory also predicted that time would come to an end.[380]

Jastrow, director of NASA's space studies, has summarized the evidence for Einstein's theory as including the motions of the galaxies, the laws of thermodynamics, and the life story of the stars. All point to one conclusion: that the universe had a beginning. [381] In particular, the second law of

---

[377] Peter Atkins, *The Creation* (San Francisco: W.H. Freeman & Co., 1981), 115.
[378] William Lane Craig, *The Kalam Cosmological Argument* (London: Macmillan, 1979), 149.
[379] Stephen Hawking, "The Shape of Time," *The Universe in a Nutshell,* 30-65.
[380] Ibid., 3-27.
[381] Norman Geisler and Ron Brooks, "The Origin of The Universe," *When Skeptics Ask: A Handbook on Christian Evidences*

thermodynamics indicates that as time, space, and matter expand, the universe is running down like a giant wound-up alarm clock. This supports Einstein's theory that the universe will have an end.

Both the beginning and the end of time are places where the equations of general relativity cannot be defined. If time, space, and matter are like an expanding balloon, in what are they expanding? The problem of what was before the singularity lies somewhere along the boundary between physics and metaphysics. Wittgenstein has aptly said "we are unable to imagine spatial objects outside of space or temporal objects outside of time."[382] This introduces the idea of transcendence into our vocabulary. Time, space, and matter are expanding into something, a larger realm beyond our physics and a reality beyond the universe. Theists see this feature as the place to introduce God and His relationship to time into the equation.

C. Time as Partly Subjective, Partly Objective

Many philosophers have wanted to recognize time as being partly subjective and partly objective. Augustine identified time with the eternity of God in the sense that the continuation of divine existence would necessarily involve as its consequence duration, or time. [383] Although some philosophers, such as Russell, accused Augustine of replacing the common and public time of history and physics with a "private psychological time" (subjective time), clearly Augustine's *The City of God* presented an objective

---

(Wheaton, IL: Victor Books, 1989), 219-222.
[382] Ludwig Wittgenstein, *Tractatus Logico-Philosophicus*, trans. D.F. Pears and B.F. McGuinness (New York: Routledge, reprint 2002), #2.0121.
[383] Augustine, *The Confessions*, 262-7.

view of time.[384] Augustine had two concepts of time, one that was subjective and another that was objective. One can resolve these two perspectives by recognizing that Augustine was presenting an account of our experience of time but that embedded in his thought was the notion that history and prophecy presuppose the past and future as having some being.

Bergson recognized a multiplicity of durations, belonging to the acts of our consciousness as well as to external things.[385] Time has been viewed as becoming concrete in continuous movement. Movement only becomes time with the intervention of our intelligence. Therefore time is defined as the measure of movement. There is thus a notion that we never perceive time apart from movement and that all our measures of movement in temporal duration are borrowed from local movement and movement among the constellations.

Heidegger would say that public time is the time in which inner things and objectively present things are encountered. *Da-sein* understands itself in terms of its daily work and records the time that it must take for itself in terms of what is encountered. Motions such as that of the sun help us to date and measure time. Once measured, it becomes public time and is accessible in a way that has been unveiled phenomenally (that is, through sense perceptions). Because *Da-sein* has been thrown into the world, it "temporalizes" and gives itself time, taking account of its regular recurring passage.[386]

Augustine wanted to distinguish motion from time and disagreed with the Platonic description of time as the "measure of motion" and the idea that what

---

[384] Teske, 38-45.
[385] Stumpf, *Socrates to Sartre*, 436-437.
[386] Heidegger, "Temporality and within-timeness as the origin of the vulgar concept of time," 378-379.

constituted time was the motion of the constellations. He argued that if such things ceased to move, there would still be time. He indicated that although we measure time by the length of a motion in time, time is not the motion of a body.[387] The biblical Canon seems to add support to this in a passage that describes the sun standing still for about a whole day so Joshua could finish a battle (Joshua 10). We are also told that God caused the sundial in Hezekiah's palace to move backwards ten steps (2 Kings 20). In these instances, time became disassociated from certain coexisting motions.

D. Time as an Illusion

Shepherd called the cleavage between the eternal and the temporal to be one of the greatest delusions of consciousness.[388] The idea that true reality should not be associated with time or temporal flux is as old as the ancient Chinese, Hindu, and Buddhist versions of the cyclical view of history. Even the Greeks seemed to lack any hope of history going anywhere (Ephesians 2:11-12) and were at a loss over what to do with time. One manifestation of this was the attention they gave to searching for forms and ideals that were eternal, beyond time, and not subject to change.[389] Nietzsche tried to empty time of any meaning by stating that "the eternal hourglass of existence is turned over and over and you with it, a grain of dust."[390]

Spengler and Camus questioned whether time was

---

[387] Augustine, *The Confessions*, 275-277. For Plato, the meaning of time is change, and therefore in the absence of change there can be no time: Stumpf, "Plato," *Socrates to Sartre*, 78-79).

[388] A. P. Shepherd, "The Problem of Time," *The Eternity of Time* (London: Camelot Press, 1941), 11-18.

[389] John P. Newport, *Life's Ultimate Questions: A Contemporary Philosophy of Religion* (Dallas: Word Publishing, 1989), 42-50.

[390] D.W. Bebbington, *Patterns in History: A Christian View* (Downers Grove, IL: InterVarsity Press, 1979), 83.

a cyclical and absurd illusion.[391] Many existentialists also classify history as uncertain, a myth, or incapable of providing accurate facts supporting any meaning.[392] Heidegger advocated that time is not a thing and yet it remains constant in its passing away without being something temporal like beings in time are.[393]

Adherents of Eastern pantheistic monism embrace the idea that to realize one's oneness with the One is to pass beyond time. Time for them is unreal, and history is cyclical.[394] Einstein also felt that "For us believing physicists the distinction between the past, present, and future is only an illusion, even if a stubborn one." [395] Tipler's Omega point theory advanced a similar thought, suggesting that,

> In effect all the different instants of universal history are collapsed into the Omega point; "duration" for the Omega point can be regarded as equivalent to the collection of all experience of all life that did, does, and will exist in the whole of universal history, together with all non-living instants. This duration is very close to the idea of *aeternitas* of Thomist philosophy.[396]

The idea that time or the passage of time might be an illusion brings us to the margins of the idea of God's

---

[391] Oswald Spengler, *The Decline of the West*, 2 vols. (New York: Knopf, 1926, 1928), 107-110, 230-244; Robert C. Solomon and Kathleen M. Higgins, "No Exit: The Existentialism of Camus," *A Short History of Philosophy* (Oxford: Oxford University Press, 1996), 279-282.
[392] Sire, *The Universe Next Door,* 130-134.
[393] Heidegger, 371-398.
[394] Sire, *The Universe Next Door*, 151.
[395] Banesh Hoffmann and Helen Dukas, *Albert Einstein: Creator and Rebel* (New York: The Viking Press, 1973), 258.
[396] Frank J. Tipler, "The Omega Point as Eschaton: Answers to Pannenberg's Questions for Scientists," *Zygon: Journal of Religion and Science* 24 (1989): 229.

timeless existence. Theologians have speculated as to whether time is merely part of the present order, for God identifies Himself as the "I Am" and indicates that, from the human perspective, one day "Time shall be no more" (Revelation 10:6 NMB).[397]

E. Transitions

Towards the end of Wittgenstein's *Tractatus*, he conceded that "the solution of the riddle of space and time lies outside of space and time."[398] That brings us back to the idea of transcendence. Behe went a step further by concluding that what we experience is part of a design established by an Intelligent Agent.[399]

To speculate about whether time began with creation, as Augustine did, or creation began with time already present, is an unfathomable question. It is perhaps better perhaps to acknowledge that both are from God: "For in him all things were created: things in heaven and on earth, visible and invisible...all things have been created through him and for him" (Colossians 1:16). The universe in its totality was formed at God's command, so that "what is seen was not made out of what was visible" (Hebrews 11:3), and "God is the builder of everything" (Hebrews 3:4).

Problem #2: What Was God Doing before He Made Heaven and Earth? What Is His Current Relationship to Time?

Augustine's discussion of time in *The Confessions* came within a context of prayers for understanding. Augustine documented these prayers in the hope that they would arouse his readers' meditations towards

---

[397] Some embrace the myth of the passage of time to avoid unanswerable questions such as, "How fast does time flow?"
[398] Wittgenstein, 87, #6.4312.
[399] Michael J. Behe, "Science, Philosophy, Religion," *Darwin's Black Box* (New York: The Free Press, 1996), 252.

Transcendence.[400] There was also a sense in which he was trying to convey that God is omnipresent. Augustine presented the traditional Christian view of God being "eternally timeless"—a view diametrically opposed by various contemporary perspectives on the nature of divine eternity. Specifically, the disagreement is over whether God's relationship to time is temporal or timeless.

A. Divine Timeless Eternity

Augustine held to the classical Christian view of God's relationship to time, the view that God exists timelessly and eternally. Augustine concluded that nothing would exist if the will of the Creator did not first exist. He embraced the idea that God's creative Word was spoken eternally and that eternal Reason has no beginning and no ending. [401] Timeless eternalists such as Augustine argue that the statement that God is "eternal" means that He exists without beginning or end and cannot be contained in time (Psalm 90:2,4, 102:25-27). The statement that God is "timeless" means that He exists but He exists under no constraints of time. Augustine wanted his readers to firmly fix their minds on the "splendor of eternity [that] stands forever and compare it with the times that never last and see that no comparison is possible."[402] He understood that the "immeasurable abiding present"' of God is an almost incomprehensible concept.

B. Timeless: Hebrew or Greek?

Swinburne has suggested that Augustine's "timeless" concept of God was not rooted in Hebrew tradition but in Greek tradition and is therefore

---

[400] See Augustine, *The Confessions,* 257.
[401] Augustine, "Book XI," *The Confessions*, 260-263, 265
[402] Augustine, *The Confessions,* 265.

foreign to Scripture.[403] Looking at the way Scripture conveys time will help to clarify if this is true.

Time in the Old Testament was used to describe sacred occurrences and events in God's interaction with people. For the Hebrew, life was time (Psalm 90:3-12). History was perceived as a meaningful sequence of unfolding events proceeding towards the outworking of God's purposes; history had an eschatological goal which would be fulfilled in time. The biblical Canon depicts three stages to time: a beginning to history, an in-between time that God keeps track of in detail, and an approaching day of reckoning. Following this understanding, Christian theists have recognized that "history is a transcendentally significant story with a well-defined plot."[404] History is not reversible, repeatable, cyclic, meaningless, or an indefinite spiral of progress (Hebrews 9:27), but is directed, purposeful, and a form of revelation. History is portrayed as having a unity because God is purposefully working in the progression of events (2 Corinthians 5:18-20). Eschatological linear action distinguishes the biblical approach to time and history.

Scholars have debated whether Genesis 1 is prose history or poetry, similar to the Sumerian creation myths of that era.[405] Either way, the net import of Genesis 1:1 is that there is an absolute beginning—a beginning that includes the physical universe and time itself. Consequently God may be thought of as

---

[403] Richard Swinburne, "Time," *The Christian God* (Oxford: Clarendon Press, 1994), 72-95. Swinburne argued that the first thirteen centuries of the Church were influenced by Plato's view that the "fundamental things" were timeless.
[404] C.S. Lewis, "The Human Past," *The Discarded Image* (Cambridge: Cambridge University Press, reprint 1998), 174-184.
[405] Rikk E. Watts, *Making Sense of Genesis 1,* lecture given at Regent College 2002, http://www.asa3.org/ASA/topics/Bible-Science/6-02Watts.html, accessed December 4, 2017.

timeless.[406] Helm said, "In creation God [timelessly] brings into being the whole temporal matrix and knows at a glance the whole of His temporally ordered creation."[407]

One theological idea that characterizes this biblical approach to time is contained in the Greek word *kairos* (καιρός), which refers to an occasion, place, or situation that is set in its proper time.[408] Its Hebrew equivalent (מוֹעֵד — *aram* or *moed*) also refers to situations in God's time.[409] References to a decisive point in time generally stress the fact that it is divinely foreordained (Luke19:44, Romans 8:28-29). The idea of *kairos* is associated with God's sovereign control over encounters in a believer's life (2 Timothy 4:6, Luke 1:20) and the fulfillment of prophecy (Mark 1:15, 1 Peter 5:6, Revelation 1:3).[410] *Kairos* seems to be bound up with the biblical phrase, "the fullness of time" which refers to "filled time," time abundant with happening and meaning. History can be divided into periods that center in on a special *kairos*, where each *kairos* gains its true significance by its relation to the central *kairos*, the life, death, and resurrection of Christ.

The "timeless eternalist" view supports the understanding that because Jesus is God and because

---

[406] Passages used to support the timeless argument include: Genesis 1:5, John 1:1, 17:24, Proverbs 8:22-23, Isaiah 57:15, Jude 25, 2 Timothy 1:9; 1 Corinthians 2:7, Ephesians 1:4, 1 Peter 1:20, Revelation 13:8.

[407] Paul Helm, *Eternal God* (Oxford: Clarendon Press, 1988), 26-27.

[408] *Kairos* is "an occasion, i.e. set, or proper time, opportunity (convenient, due) season (due, short, while) time, a while." James Strong, *The Strongest Strong's Exhaustive Concordance* (Grand Rapids, MI: Zondervan, 2001).

[409] Gerhard Kittel et al., eds., "Kairos," *Theological Dictionary of the New Testament,* abridged in one volume (Grand Rapids, MI: Wm. B. Eerdmans, 1985), 389-390.

[410] Ibid., 389-390.

He is the "I am" (not "was" or "will be"), all things happen in the now for Him. Jesus said, "Before Abraham was born, I am" (John 8:58). The present "I am" of divine existence at once fills heaven and earth in one eternal "now." A further implication is that when Jesus was on the cross, He was able to see all humanity simultaneously in God's time and to reach across time and space to absorb all the sins of humanity into His own body.

The biblical Canon does not seem to extensively or grandly refer to "time" as an abstract something over and above events. We generally attribute this sort of abstract speculation and theorizing to the Greeks. As a result, the Hebrews and the Early Church do not seem to have discussed the same sort of abstract questions and speculations the heirs to the Greeks advanced. There are no Old Testament examples of the Hebrews engaging in discussions about whether time really existed or if they could "feel" time. It is philosophers from Augustine to the present who have demonstrated a preoccupation with the subjective and objective problems of time.

It seems that in order for Augustine to maintain that there was no time before God created the world, and to avoid the idea of God being idle for endless ages, he presented the concept of timeless eternity. The concept of divine eternity as timeless, as being always present without past or future, is said to have been derived from Plotinus. This construct does not appear to be found prior to Plotinus, nor does it seem to be clearly expressed after him until Augustine.[411]

Teske believed that without the concept of "eternity free from all succession," Augustine could not have successfully dealt with the Manichean question,

---

[411] Teske, 2-58, 46. Teske suggested that in the Enneads 3:7, Plotinus was not presenting an account of one sort of time among several, but of time.

"What was God doing before He made heaven and earth?" If Neoplatonism provided the conceptual apparatus of "eternalism" and influenced the way it was formulated and expressed, it would still be presumptuous to assume that biblical ideas were being replaced by Greek philosophical ideas. It would be folly to assume that the Church Fathers did not sift through secular cultural ideas, and not everything the Greek philosophers said was false. Some of their language and philosophical constructs have helped many Christians come to terms with certain biblical texts.

Augustine asked the question, "What was God doing before He made heaven and earth?" and concluded that:

> All things are spoken eternally (yet) all the things God makes are not eternal. Eternity, which is neither past nor future, dictates the times. You are before all the past in Your ever-present eternity and You are above all future things...but You are the Same and Your years fail not (they) stand still together as one day, today. Your today is eternity. What times (ages) could there have been which were not created by You? You made all times and before all times You are; nor was there ever a time in which there was no time. Since You made time itself, one cannot say that there was any time in which You had not made anything. No times are coeternal with You because you are permanent.[412]

Augustine did not solve the question "What was God doing before He made heaven and earth?" but he did conclude that time is a creation of God and that before God created anything, there was no time. Augustine's

---
[412] Ibid., 266-267.

concept of God was that He is the "I Am," a non-temporal Being who exists eternally timeless, complete all at once in the present without any past or future, with eternity being His very substance.

C. Divine Fullness and Perfection

The attractive element in the timeless eternity position is the idea of the divine fullness or self-sufficiency of God. The idea that God could be subject to temporal passage, with portions of His life being irretrievably finished, seems to be incompatible with God's sovereignty, perfection, and fullness. Temporalists focus on the dates of temporal events that involve God because an event is considered to be something that happens at some present temporal moment. However, eternalists advocate that nothing is earlier than God's life if God is timeless. What is timeless cannot be old because there is no past in eternity. A timeless God lives His whole life in a single present of unimaginable intensity. Because God, by definition, is a Perfect Being, He must have a perfect mode of existence. The fleeting nature of temporal existence seems to be incompatible and less perfect than a timeless existence.

Eternalism has its source in the idea of divine fullness, God being immutable, Scripture, and the Creator-creature distinction. Boethius articulated the traditional view of divine timelessness by stating,

> It is the common judgment, then of all creatures that live by reason that God is eternal. So let us consider the nature of eternity, for this will make clear to us both the nature of God and his manner of knowing. Eternity is the complete, simultaneous and perfect possession of everlasting life; this will be clear from a comparison with creatures

that exist in time.[413]

Aquinas also came to the conclusion that God sees everything as present and stated:

> all things that are in time are present to God from eternity, not only because He has the essence of things present within Him, but because His glance is carried from eternity over all things as they are in their presentiality.[414]

God's life lasts forever in the sense that at every time He exists. To use Heidegger's language, God's succession of "now" is uninterrupted and has no gaps; it is always "now."

D. Can Divine Timeless Eternity be Determined by a Precise Analysis of Language?

Several Bible verses are often cited as being consistent with a "timeless" interpretation of God and His relation to time. Hebrews 1:10-12 states:

> In the beginning, Lord, you laid the foundations of the earth, and the heavens are the work of your hands. They will perish, but you remain; they will all wear out like a garment. You will roll them up like a robe; like a garment they will be changed. But you remain the same, and your years will never end.

Psalm 90:2 declares: "Before the mountains were born or you brought forth the whole world, from everlasting to everlasting you are God." 1 Corinthians 2:7 and 2 Timothy 1:9 also refer to God existing before the world. Eternalists recognize that Scripture uses imprecise

---

[413] Boethius, *The Consolation of Philosophy*, trans. V.E. Watts (Harmondsworth, UK: Penguin, 1969), 5-6.

[414] Thomas Aquinas, "God's Eternal Knowledge," in Baruch A. Brody, ed., *Readings in the Philosophy of Religion: An Analytic Approach* (Englewood Cliffs, NJ: Prentice-Hall, 1974), 391.

language and that the case for God's timeless eternity must therefore be based on a construction of Christian doctrine. However, they argue that to only look at the language of time and change, which temporalists apply to God, is to ignore other language that asserts God's all-encompassing knowledge. See, for example, Isaiah 45:13, 46:9-10, 48:3-5, 1 Samuel 23:10-11, 1 Chronicles 28:9, Genesis 40:8, Psalm 139:16, John 6:64, Acts 2:23.

So how do eternalists make sense of biblical language that implies change in God and suggests God is in time—language that suggests God relents, learns, hopes, predicts, remembers, changes His attitudes and plans, or is surprised at an action?

Aquinas emphasized that God's will is unchangeable and therefore words that refer to God that imply change

> have a metaphorical turn according to a human figure of speech...to speak of God as repenting is to use the language of metaphor...the conclusion of this argument is not that God's will changes, but that he wills change.[415]

Calvin also posited an eternalist view, suggesting that biblical language attempts to describe God to us in anthropomorphic terms:

> Because our weakness does not attain to his exalted state, the description of Him that is given to us must be accommodated to our capacity so that we may understand it. Now the mode of accommodation is for him to represent himself to us not as he is in himself, but as he seems to us. God's plan [and] will are not reversed...but what he had from

---

[415] Thomas Aquinas, *Summa Theologiae*, trans. Thomas Gilby (London: Spottiswoode, 1966), 1a.19.7.

eternity foreseen, approved, and decreed, he pursues in uninterrupted tenor, however sudden the variation may appear in men's eyes.[416]

In other words, such language is a form of divine accommodation in order for dialogue with humans to transpire. If a timelessly eternal God is to communicate to physical, temporal creatures that exist in space and time, then He must do so in ways that perhaps are not literally true. Put another way, God never fully discloses Himself, and in so doing He never changes.

Wittgenstein's later anti-foundationalism, which rejected the idea that language always reflects the way the world really is, affords a "window" here for the timeless view, in that it opens up alternative possibilities for language other than the "correspondence theory of truth." [417] Koestler also acknowledged that language can become a screen that stands between the thinker and reality, where words and concepts such as "space" and "time" can become grammatical decoys or straitjackets that ensnare us in their paradoxes.[418]

E. Timeless and Omniscient?

Temporalists claim that eternalism and divine omniscience are incompatible. If God is outside of time, then there are propositions that such a God cannot know. Eternalists respond that to an eternal God everything is present all at once. God has eternally decreed the existence of creation and has a "timeless eternal" relation that is contingent with the

---

[416] Calvin, vol. 1, 227.
[417] Ludwig Wittgenstein, "Philosophical Investigations," in Baird and Kaufman, 151, 162-165.
[418] Arthur Koestler, *The Act of Creation* (London: Penguin Books, reprint 1989), 174-177.

temporal world. Because God is omniscient, His decisions are everlasting or timeless rather than preceded by an interval of indecision or ignorance. His intentions can be timelessly desired and willed.

The idea of a timeless eternal God acting in the world may seem to be contradictory. Deism presents an image of a detached God who may have timelessly created the temporal order but is not able to act within it.[419] This fits with Wittgenstein's cold comment that "God does not reveal Himself in the world." [420] However, this caricature of an unchanging God who is in an eternally frozen pose or off on some kind of a vacation is a not a biblical idea. The picture of a God who remains unconcerned and unaffected by human misery overlooks the theological point that God is eternally united with human nature in the Incarnation. It is here that the heart of God is revealed.

In contrast, the eternalist portrays a God who acts within time and may even act in response to what happens in time. To act is to bring about something as the result of intending, desiring, or willing that thing, to take purposeful action. God eternally wills that some event occur at some particular determined time. God, eternally willing something in time, does so in one eternal act of the will that has numerous temporally scattered effects. One timeless decision brings about different effects at different times. Not only can a timelessly eternal God will things in time without changing His will, but He may also eternally will His own reactions to some human action.

---

[419] James Sire, "The Clockwork Universe," *The Universe Next Door,* 46-58.
[420] Ludwig Wittgenstein, "Tractatus Logico-Philosophicus," in Baird and Kaufman, 148, 6.432.

F. The Problem of the Incarnation

The incarnation raises all kinds of complex questions, for God is united in man, and this provides us with a unique case of God acting in time. In God incarnate, He became localized, but does this mean finite? The incarnation does not help us understand what an unlimited God can do. for the incarnate God still upheld the world and never failed to be God (John 1:1-11).

It would seem that if God the Son is timelessly eternal (Colossians 1:17: "He is before all things") and yet incarnate in Jesus, then perhaps there was no time in His existence when the incarnation was not always willed. We must concede that since He became incarnate at a particular time in our history, there were times in that history before the incarnation and times after the incarnation. Yet the incarnation is a projection of the eternal triune God, for Jesus said, "Anyone who has seen me has seen the Father" (John 14:9).

John 8:58 indicates that Jesus was profoundly aware of the eternal dimension and dwelt in eternity in some sense the whole time He was present on earth. In time He sent ripples into eternity that changed the past and future. His reference to the appointment of the incarnation was a revelation of the divine plan for the ages in effect at all times.

An eternalist would say that there was no time when the Son of God was not willing Himself to be incarnate.[421] God did not exist and then at some later point decide to become incarnate because there is no change or succession possible in the timeless eternity of God's life.

It is probably impossible to present a completely

---

[421] Newport, "The Biblical Worldview and the Meaning of History," *Life's Ultimate Questions*, 87.

satisfactory analogy of a doctrine such as timeless eternity because it would require an accurate description of what it is like to be timeless. A temporalist's objection to God being timelessly eternal is that every event would take place at the same time. For example, my typing of this chapter would be considered to be at the same time as all eternity. A response to this is: how do we know that eternity really is a kind of time, as we know it? We don't, and we can only speculate. Part of what we mean when we say that God is inscrutable is that though we may believe that God is timeless, we cannot have a straightforward understanding of what His timeless life is. We cannot know as God knows.

In Book Eleven of *The Confessions*, Augustine cannot get past Genesis 1:1. Neither can the inspired authors: "He has made everything beautiful in its time. He has also set eternity in the human heart; yet no one can fathom what God has done from beginning to end" (Ecclesiastes 3:10-11) and "The secret things belong to the LORD our God, but the things revealed belong to us and to our children forever" (Deuteronomy 29:29).

3. The Opposing View: Divine Temporality

Merleau-Ponty proposed a heightened awareness of "the wonder of it all" that seemed to combine temporality and a launch into metaphysics. His approach presupposed a rich curiosity about the world that gives us permission to ask the why questions. He indicated that history and time should not be something that we try to detach ourselves from, as if they were just a collection of facts, because everything has meaning.[422]

---

[422] Maurice Merleau-Ponty, "What is Phenomenology?" in Baird and Kaufman, 280, 282, 284-5.

One dominant proposition of the contemporary theologians and philosophers of religion who embrace a temporal view is that time has meaning and God is meaningfully involved in time. In contrast to the classical position, they contend that a timeless life may not be the most perfect mode of existence of a perfect person.

Temporalists emphasize an anthropomorphic conception of God's temporal activity in time, arguing that it moves in a linear fashion from event to event towards a goal. Genesis 1:14-19 describes the temporal time-keeping mechanism God put into place on the fourth day, a sort of natural clock for measuring time: the rotation of the earth on its axis defines the day, the moon revolving around the earth establishes the lunar month, and the earth orbiting around the sun defines the year. Other constellations mark out other events.

Temporalists refer to God's actions in the world especially in terms of the word *chronos* (χρόνος), which is often used to refer to time in the sense of passing minutes and days.[423] *Chronos* refers to a section, measure, span, point, or limited portion of time (see Acts 1:7,21, 19:22, 1 Corinthians 16:7, Matthew 2:7,16, Luke 1:57, Revelation 2:21). *Chronos* times are God's times—He has established them (Acts 1:7) and is the Lord of history and time.[424]

Temporalists argue that before there was *chronos* time, God was timeless and not temporal, and once there was *chronos* time, God was temporal and not timeless. They say that God cannot be timeless during

---

[423] Kittel et al., 1337-1339. Temporal time terms in Hebrew are *yom* (which can refer to a 24-hour day or a segment of time but cannot be interpreted as referring to an infinite period of time) and *ereb,* and *boquer* (which refer to segments of a day): Hugh Ross, "Biblical Basis for Long Creation Days," *Creation and Time* (Colorado Springs, CO: NavPress, 1994), 45-46; Strong, 1542, 1525.
[424] Kittel et al., 1337-1339.

the time He is temporal. Temporalists want to adhere to a literal interpretation of biblical language rather than use Platonic terminology that contrasts the world of time "here" with a world of eternity "there."

A. Language, Religious Experience, and Temporal Being

Temporalists point out that we experience God in time and history, and biblical language is taken to be a reflection of this. Apart from language, we experience the reality of passing time in so many ways that belief in the objective reality of past, present, and future is a universal feature of human experience. Phenomenological analyses of temporal consciousness have emphasized the centrality of past, present, and future to our experience of time.

Husserl described our experience of time in terms of remembering the past and anticipating the future with both anchored in consciousness of the "now." The transformation of a "now" consciousness to a past consciousness and being replaced by a new "now" consciousness is "part of the essence of time consciousness."[425]

Friedman said, "The division between past, present, and future so deeply permeates our experience that it is hard to imagine its absence."[426] When God and biblical language are introduced to human temporal experience, the tendency is to project the human temporal consciousness of time into our conception of God. This leads us to see God as thinking successive thoughts, performing successive actions, and being related to changing things.

---

[425] Edmund Husserl, *The Phenomenology of Internal Time-Consciousness*, ed. Martin Heidegger, trans. James S. Churchill (Bloomington, IN: Indiana University Press, 1964), 86.
[426] William Friedman, *About Time* (Cambridge, MA: MIT Press, 1990), 92.

Heidegger said that humans engage in a lifelong endeavor to explore the meaning of being. When it comes to the issue of space and time, people may find it difficult to rise above the question of their own "being." In this sense, time and God's relation to time are "extraordinary" topics. Heidegger felt that philosophizing was about the extraordinary, asking questions such as, "Why are there beings instead of nothing?"[427] But the common concept of time, which conceives of time as infinite, is derived from our experience of temporality. Therefore, asking the ultimate why questions of "being" and "time" seem insurmountably inconclusive. [428] "*Da-sein*" (being there) in the world is a continuous experience of thinking about the meaning of everything there is, including how one exists in space and time. Therefore, *Da-sein* is grounded in temporality, in the phenomenon of human existence. Our experience of life involves us in a relationship with our past, present, and future that is encompassed in something larger than ourselves and will continue to exist when we die.[429] Because people are aware of the precarious nature of their temporal being, anxiety may lead them to evade, ignore, or deny their temporality. This in turn may lead them to choose to lead an "inauthentic" existence. [430] Biblical texts on the temporal

---

[427] Martin Heidegger, "Introduction to Metaphysics," in Baird and Kaufman, 102-127. See also Martin Heidegger, "Being in the world as the fundamental constitution of Da-sein," *Being and Time*, 49-58.
[428] Heidegger, *Being and Time*, 384-385. Heidegger felt that questioning what time is, whether it has any being or is a phantom, and whether it is inside or outside (that is, objectively present in the subject or in the object), causes one to bump into the limits of knowing.
[429] Ibid., 378, 383, 389.
[430] Baird and Kaufman, "Martin Heidegger," *Twentieth-Century Philosophy*, 97-101.

interventions of God in time address issues around inauthentic existence and human depravity.

B. God's Attributes and Temporal Relations with Humanity

Those who write on this subject often use the words "time" and "history" interchangeably. The outworking of many of God's attributes has personal reference points in time and in historical contexts. In order for one to be personal, one must possess certain properties that inherently involve time. [431] For example, verbal communication, rational activity, and states of consciousness, which grow out of qualities such as faithfulness and patience, operate within time. As a result, God interacts with us in time. This is an obvious conclusion from the definition of time as a dimension in which cause and effect take place.[432] It would seem that God's personal interactions with us in time and history are an example of His condescending to our humanity.

Temporalists argue that certain aspects of the concept of God require that He exist in time. Because God is alive, and living involves changing, God must change—and since only beings in time can change, therefore God is in time. Because God is alive and lives occur in time, therefore God is in time. Because God's actions are events, and events are assumed to only occur in time, God must be in time. Since causal relations link events or link people to events, and since God is a cause or an agent of cause of temporal effects,

---

[431] Daniel Dennett, "Conditions of Personhood," in Amelie Oksenberg Rorty, ed., *The Identities of Persons* (Berkeley, CA: University of California Press, 1976), 175-179.
[432] Richard Rice, "Biblical Support for a New Perspective," *The Openness of God* (Downers Grove, IL: InterVarsity Press, 1994), 16.

then He is in time.[433]

Since God coexists with temporal things, temporalists assume that means that He is in time and that He changes. For example God coexisted with the patriarchs in the Old Testament and then later with the apostles in the New Testament. It is also pointed out that God interacts with temporal things. For example, when we pray, He hears and responds. If God first hears and then responds, this must mean that He hears before He responds. Therefore, temporalists conclude that He hears and responds in time.

C. The Temporal Nature of God's Narrative History

Scripture portrays God as having a narrative history in the sense that there are purposeful changes in His actions, responses, and knowledge that have teleological implications. Comparisons are made with the temporal nature of human narrative history. MacIntyre argued that narrative history is the basic genre of human actions. His concept of "*teleos*" (having a goal or end in mind) is framed in the context of human temporality and human awareness that "time is passing." Because people think of themselves as being in a narrative, asking key questions such as, "What story am I a part of?" they look at texts that portray God anthropomorphically as suggesting that He also is in a narrative; therefore, they conclude that God is also temporal, in time.

The fundamental issue at stake is whether God has a history. Scripture offers us a narrative story of God's actions in creation whereby His story breaks into human stories. In *The Confessions*, Augustine

---

[433] William Lane Craig, "Divine Temporality," *Time and Eternity: Exploring God's Relationship to Time* (Wheaton, IL: Crossway Books, 2001), 77-114.

argued that the fall represents the "loss of the possibility of relationship to the whole story, or time's full narrative"; this challenges human beings with the ultimate question of whether they will give "the Author" authority "as the story unfolds."[434] Although humans' search for the "good" and humans' attempt to practice virtues hint at absolutes and transcendence, the fact that we "are never more than coauthors of our own narratives" and that "we enter a stage (temporal life) we did not design" could be construed as pointing to immanence.[435]

Wolterstorff analyzed some of the weightiest texts used to support divine timelessness (Psalm 90:1-4, 2 Peter 3:8, John.8:58) and concluded that these only allude to God existing before creation, not to Him being outside of time. Similarly, he argued that passages cited in support of God's immutability (Malachi 3:6, Psalm 102:27, James1:17) do not demonstrate that God is not in time; rather, they affirm that His years are without end, that He remains faithful to His covenant, and that He is never the source of evil. Wolterstorff conceded that some conceptual things—such as properties, numbers, and non-events—could be outside of time, but argued that God is not outside of time because He has a narrative history. (In contrast, timeless eternalists deny that God has a history; they say that the biblical narrative should not be interpreted as presenting events in God's history but rather events in human history.)[436]

Temporalists feel that the traditional position

---

[434] David Lyle Jeffrey, "The Book Without and the Book Within," *People of the Book: Christian Identity and Literary Culture* (Grand Rapids, MI: Wm. B. Eerdmans, 1996), 142-147.

[435] Alister MacIntyre, "After Virtue (In Part)" in Baird and Kaufman, 391-408.

[436] Nicholas Wolterstorff, "Unqualified Divine Temporality," in Gregory E. Ganssle, ed., *God and Time: Four Views* (Downers Grove, IL: InterVarsity Press, 2001), 187-213.

comes very close to Deism, implying that God does not intervene in human history and does not act in response to His creatures; otherwise, traditionalists could not argue that God is eternal, is out of time, and has no history. Craig argued that the only way a traditionalist could logically maintain belief in divine timelessness would be to adopt a static theory of time and deny the reality of "tensed facts" (events occurring in the past, present, or future) as well as temporal becoming.[437]

Temporalists consider God to be fully integrated in time and, to some extent, limited by it. They say that, instead of perceiving the entire course of human existence in one timeless moment, God comes to know events as they take place. He is dependent upon the world in some respects and learns something from what transpires:

> An action makes a difference. It brings about something that would not otherwise exist. In the case of specific acts, it brings about something that did not previously exist. To say that God acts, therefore, means that it makes sense to use the words *before* and *after* when we talk about Him. God makes decisions, and then acts. He decides before He acts, He acts after He decides. This is so simple that it sounds trivial, but it points to a fundamental truth about God. Not only does He bring about change, but also in a significant sense God Himself experiences change. After God acts, the universe is different. The concept of divine action thus involves divine temporality. Time is real for God.[438]

---

[437] Ganslle, *God and Time*, 115-160.
[438] Rice, 36.

Those who embrace this view suggest that only this perspective allows God to react to human choices as the Bible suggests He does. This view makes it very difficult to maintain a robust view of God's foreknowledge and also raises other philosophical difficulties.

D. God's Personal Love Is Enacted in the Temporal Realm.

By creating a temporal world God, has come into relationship with that temporal world. Temporalists believe that because God is rational and loves His creatures, He reacts appropriately to their suffering. God does not remain untouched by His creatures' temporality. It pains God to see His creatures suffer. In the final state of things, "the Kingdom of Heaven," there will be no more suffering (Revelation 7:17, 21:4), and therefore God will feel less pain. God is said to change between now and then. If God timelessly saw both present suffering and future happiness, His single, changeless, overall state of feeling would be inappropriate to at least one of them.[439]

Pike dismissed the "timeless" idea by discussing the idea of God as a person. He observed that temporal processes can describe the mental capacities of a person. He did not feel that a timeless being could intentionally engage in such mental activities, nor could another prompt a timeless being to provide responses located in time. He concluded that the concept of a timeless being contradicts the definition of a person and that such a being could not create or preserve a temporally extended universe.[440]

---

[439] Brian Leftow, *Time and Eternity* (Ithaca, NY: Cornell University Press, 1991), 48-67.
[440] Nelson Pike, *God and Timelessness* (New York: Schocken Books, 1970), 140-168.

E. The Incarnation and Physicality

The incarnation becomes a key argument for temporalists because it is an event in God's life that has a temporal date. They argue that whatever lives through temporally dated events exists in time. Time is associated so closely to notions of the physical that it becomes obvious that we run into difficulties with it in speaking of God, who is Spirit. If God sees everything as present, future, and past, this would make God's knowledge related to time, and this would mean that God is not timeless. On the other hand, if God sees everything as present, then God could not know anything as future.

F. Omniscience and Human Free Will

Temporalists address the issue of God's omniscience. They acknowledge that God knows what time it is now, but then argue that only someone who exists now can know what time it is now. Whoever knows that I am typing this chapter at 2:41 p.m. can say with truth, "It is now 2:41 p.m." But only at 2:41 p.m. can someone say this with truth. Temporalists say that because God knows things like this, He must be in time.[441]

If God is omniscient and a temporal world exists, then He must know tensed facts (to locate something in relation to the present). If God is timeless, it could be assumed that He does not know tensed facts. Because the world is in constant change, God's knowledge of what is happening is assumed to also be in constant flux.[442]

Furthermore, because God is omniscient, He knows all future human actions and holds no false beliefs. If He were timeless, His knowledge would not

---

[441] William Lane Craig, "Divine Temporality," *Time and Eternity*, 77-112.
[442] Ibid., 97-106.

change or depend on temporal events because eternal things are as fixed as the past. However, if people were to behave other than God expected, God could be accused of holding a false belief or people would be able to change God's timeless knowledge—God's timeless knowledge would depend on our temporal actions. If God is omniscient and timeless, we would not be able to do other than God believes we will, and this would lead to the conclusion that we are not free. But God is omniscient, and we are free; therefore, temporalists conclude that He is in time.[443]

4. A Way Forward: Mystery and Complementary Time

I began this discussion by looking at Augustine's question regarding time and briefly surveyed some subjective and objective interpretations of the issue. There are some (empiricists, logical positivists, Naturalists, and physicists) who dismiss the metaphysical propositions involved in the question. Many recognize the existence of time but deny that it has any overarching meaning or significance.

Given the law of cause and effect and a cosmology that points to the universe beginning in a singularity, it can be affirmed that time may have a beginning, as theistic arguments have suggested. But what was before the singularity, or what is outside of space and time, brings us to the boundary between physics and metaphysics. If time is an illusion, that, too, could bring us to the edge of God's presumed timeless existence. The theist concludes that all things visible and invisible are from God and that the phenomenon of time provides a framework for understanding dependence on a Creator.

Augustine's second question as to God's current

---

[443] Craig, "Divine Eternity and God's Knowledge of the Future," *Time and Eternity,* 243-265.

relationship with time brought us to the "timeless eternity" view. It is recognized that the timeless eternity concept is an insight borrowed from Greek philosophy to illuminate God's relationship with the temporal. The argument for God's timelessness is thus grounded in a construction of Christian doctrine, not on any precise language in the biblical Canon. To a timeless God, everything is present all at once, and His singular will brings about numerous scattered effects. To say that any part of God's character, attitude, or actions could change would be incompatible with divine fullness and perfection. The incarnation does not help us understand what an omnipotent God can do.

Temporalists use a literal interpretation of Scripture, seeing there a narrative history of specific events and dates in which God personally interacted with humans (preserving them, healing them, and performing miracles) in the temporal realm. Heidegger's phenomenological perspective that discusses the existential aspects of human "being" fits in with the temporalist view. Temporalists emphasize a dynamic conception of time. They argue that language is "tensed" because our experience of the world is "tensed"—past, present, and future are central to our conscious experience of time. For temporalists, the incarnation is the pinnacle event in time, demonstrating that God was limited, in part, by temporality. In their view, for God to know what is happening in time means that He must be in time.

Advocates of both the temporal and the timeless view have sought a proper philosophical-theological understanding of the divine, human beings, and time. This chapter has presented an overview of the numerous ancient and contemporary philosophical contributions and polarized perspectives swirling around Augustine's questions. Essentially, Augustine proposed a theory of "Divine eternity." The biblical Canon reveals that God is eternal and personal. Contemporary philosopher-theologians argue that this carries a conflict: If God is eternal, then He cannot have a personal relationship with humans in time, and if He personally interacts with humans in time, then He cannot be outside of time.

Is there any way forward out of this impasse? Theories of complementary time and the existence of mystery offer one possible way of making progress.

Hawking has attempted to combine Einstein's theory of relativity and Feynman's idea of multiple histories into one complete, unified theory that includes everything that happens in the universe and possibly other time dimensions outside of it. [444] Merleau-Ponty pointed out that ideas are only partial views and perception is never complete.[445] Given our incomplete perception of time, perhaps it would be more meaningful to speak of multidimensional time in which God exists rather than the singular dimension of time to which we are limited. Ross suggested:

> If time were two dimensional, for example, both a time length and a time width would be possible. Time would expand from a line into a plane. In a plane of time, an infinite number of lines running in an infinite number of directions would be possible.[446]

Ross's suggestion provides another option for understanding how God may transcend our concepts of time, but even this expanded version may be overly restrictive.

---

[444] Stephen Hawking, "A Brief History of Relativity,"*The Universe in a Nutshell*, 3-27.
[445] Maurice Merleau-Ponty, "What is Phenomenology?" in Baird and Kaufman, 276-285.
[446] Hugh Ross, *Creator and Cosmos* (Colorado Springs, CO: NavPress, 1993), 67.

Whitehead postulated that time and location are a necessary part of every metaphysical situation; therefore, any reality, including divine reality, must be related to at least one point somewhere in space and time. Whitehead's theory offers one more way of understanding God's action in the world and he has affirmed that God engages in space and time, but his ideas should be approached with caution.[447]

Temporal and eternal theories can become problematic when made into exclusive positions. Exclusive positions can lead to the jettisoning of a number of aspects of the biblically orthodox view of God's attributes and essence. Making God bound by time brings Him down to our level rather than being Sovereign over it. We should distinguish between God being Creator of a temporal world and God being temporal. God is unfettered by time and temporality. Whether God changes is a key issue. To say God is mutable is incompatible with God's supreme excellence and blurs the distinction between Creator and creature. While God's timelessness does follow from divine immutability, to equate God's immutability with radical immobility is a troubling doctrine. This would restrict God from taking any action at all. We need to maintain that God is omnipresent, omnipotent, omniscient, immutable, and perfect and yet embrace the mystery that He does have a relationship in time. Brunner rejected the Platonic formulation of Divinity and proposed that God's eternity be a "Sovereign rule over time and the temporal sphere," which would include God's "freedom to create and give us time."[448]

Given that the biblical Canon introduces ideas of

---

[447] Allison Heartz Johnson, *Whitehead's Theory of Reality* (New York: Dover Publications, 1962), 5.
[448] Emil Brunner, *The Christian Doctrine of God* (Philadelphia: The Westminster Press, 1950), 268-270.

both God's foreknowledge and human free will, we are prompted to embrace paradox. Because God foreknows future events does not mean that they are predetermined. Biblical history is salvation history, and that includes an understanding that humanity will be held accountable for its free choices.

Many view time as an absolute and as a single dimension measured by a fixed master clock. But maybe time is an independent thing, or a container of events, created by God to hold temporal things that God is totally active in and outside of. The biblical Canon could be interpreted as pointing to time being multidimensional, whereas humanity, perhaps partly because of depravity, is predominantly confined in one dimension of time. Although God may have sealed humanity in time for now, He has set eternity in our hearts (Ecclesiastes 3:11). Physical death, we are told, is the point when we step out of the time frame of human history and enter eternity.

Given the similarities between space and time, some feel that God's actions have temporal locations and therefore He must also have spatial location. It would seem that if God has a history, then, to be consistent, He might also have a location. The objection to this is that God is not limited to a body; He is Spirit and therefore could have a history without occupying a place.

Job 1:6 and 2:1 (NASB) seem to indicate time of another dimension, events in angelic realms: "Now there was a day when the sons of God came to present themselves before the LORD, and Satan also came among them." The book of Revelation depicts scenes taking place on earth in human history and scenes taking place in heavenly places at the same time. For example, Revelation 1:8 describes a period of silence in heaven lasting "about half an hour. The quality and pace of time in heaven seem to be different from those aspects of time on earth. The transfiguration of Jesus in the Gospels also seems unfettered by the usual rules and constraints of time as we commonly think of them. Men from ancient times appeared alive, and Jesus appeared to assume his future glorified body. When we consider the Gospel records of the capacities of Jesus' resurrection body to appear or disappear, we could conclude that resurrection bodies are equipped for multidimensional space and time travel.

Park has suggested the idea of at least two times as follows:

> Things have a twofold nature: the one invisible, unique, simple, and unworldly, and the other visible, multiple, varied, and distributed throughout the world. If this is so, then time is also two fold. There is a time for heaven and one for earth. The one remains and at the same time proceeds; the other is borne along in motion.[449]

Perhaps a way forward would be to see features of God's timeless eternity and His temporal relationship to the world as complementary. God's eternity could include engaging with temporality in real time, embracing all periods of time, without ceasing to be either transcendent or immanently relational. For some philosophers, this just doesn't make sense—but the biblical texts leave us with just such a paradox.

All reality has its being and vitality rooted in God (Acts 17:28: "in him we live and move and have our being"). Scripture indicates that humanity was created to live in a physical world and a spiritual reality at the same time.

If we bring together the New Testament Greek terms—*chronos* (time as measured), *kairos* (times and

---

[449] David Park, *The Image of Eternity: Roots of Time in the Physical World* (Amherst, MA: University of Massachusetts Press), 1980), 103.

seasons), and *aionios* (the eternal or everlasting life)[450]—they add dimension to our understanding of the complementary and complex nature of time. The Greek words *aion* (αἰών, age) and *aionios* (αἰώνιος, eternal or eternity) are terms where time and eternity merge, suggesting indefinite time. They are used for the temporal world's duration (Matthew 13:39, Hebrews 9:26, 1 Corinthians 10:11, Romans 16:25, Philemon 15) and for the idea that eternity embraces a succession of *aeons* (Ecclesiastes 1:9-10). The idea also crops up in Acts 3:21 and Jude 13. We find the double formula of "for ever and ever" in Hebrews 1:8, and Ephesians 3:21. Those who are redeemed from this *aeon* (Galatians 1:4) will enter into the future *aeon* (Hebrews 6:5).

There are attributes of God which are related to both invisible and visible time. That God acts in visible time does not mean that He gets caught up in the operation of the universe and loses His omnipotence or omniscience. The dichotomy sometimes created by eternalists and temporalists dissolves when we consider that the appearing of Jesus for His Church is an event in eternity that merges into our time frame at some particular date (1 Thessalonians 4:13-5:11, 1 Corinthians 15:51-58). The limits of human reason prevent us from fully comprehending God's manner of existence. To press beyond these limits leads to abstract speculation or confusion.

In dealing with language, Prigogine and Stengers contended that for many systems or objects there are languages and points of view that may be complementary:

---

[450] Kittel et al., 31-32. The New Testament also uses the Greek word *aion* for "age," usually referring to an indefinite period of time marked by certain moral and spiritual characteristics. John 17:3 refers to "eternal life," 2 Peter 1:11 to the "eternal kingdom," and Hebrews 6:2 to "eternal judgment."

> They all deal with the same reality, but it is impossible to reduce them to one single description. The irreducible plurality of perspectives on the same reality expresses the impossibility [for people to grasp] a divine point of view from which the whole of reality is visible. The real lesson to be learned from this consists in emphasizing the wealth of reality, which overflows any single language, any single logical structure.[451]

Such wealth suggests an ultimate reality that is personal and yet remains eternal. Perhaps it would be helpful to remember that Wittgenstein believed that most philosophical problems could be traced to a misuse of language. The subject of God's relation to time presses language to the limits and could be recognized as the kind of topic he would have consigned to silence.[452] Wittgenstein's discussion of "language games" does offer a way to bring clarity to the metaphysical questions of philosophy argued here. When Eternalists and temporalists debate at length over the meaning of language, they seem to be emphasizing different aspects of the same reality.[453] Neither biblical language nor the doctrine of the Trinity are explicit enough to wholly dismiss all aspects of the temporalist or the eternalist view. Biblical words for time may not be a sound basis for reflection on biblical concepts of time. So we are left with interpretive perspectives gathered from the contexts in which the words are used. The language used in the Bible is not precise enough to resolve the

---

[451] Ilya Prigogine and Isabelle Stengers, *Order Out of Chaos* (New York: Bantam Books, 1984), 225.
[452] Wittgenstein, "Tractatus Logico-Philosophicus" in Baird and Kaufman, 141-149.
[453] Wittgenstein, "Philosophical Investigations," in Baird and Kaufman, 149-165.

philosophical questions concerning time and eternity.

It would be appropriate to reflect on Gadamer's insights on hermeneutics here. Gadamer suggested that a reader is not always open to the meaning of a text and that all understanding inevitably involves some prejudice that makes the reader "deaf" to what is there. Our understanding of texts is historically affected because of our place in history. Furthermore,

> All correct interpretation must be on guard against the limitations imposed by imperceptible habits of thought and must direct its gaze on the texts themselves. A person who is trying to understand a text is always projecting. The initial meaning emerges only because one is reading the text with particular expectations in regard to a certain meaning.[454]

Certain dogmatic positions in the timeless and temporal arguments suggest that Gadamer's critique might be applicable here.

Influential changes in cosmology and a theological shift from the "historical timeless view" to the "contemporary temporal view" might give the impression that biblical texts are shaped by context and historical change and that they do not have a fixed meaning. But both positions assume, to some degree, a pure version of truth that is supposed to be in every text (that refers to God and time) and that is to be discovered through a careful reading. Some philosopher-theologians seem to be reading in a "logocentric" way, taking texts at literal face value to prove that the Bible is full of evidence for a doctrine of time; they assume that we can rationally discover the essential "fixed central truth" within such texts. However, Derrida warned that because we have a

---

[454] "Hans-Georg Gadamer" in Baird and Kaufman, 178-205.

tendency to read into a text from our own context, we should be careful in claiming that we understand the original intention or fixed essential truth.[455] Both theological positions on God and time want to exclude other interpretations. But Derrida was rightly suspicious of all such claims to fixed truth in the Platonic sense. There is no guarantee that a perspective has accessed truth simply by saying, "This is the timeless truth." Derrida might also point out that our notions of time are connected with our notions of cosmology and that that would raise the question, "How do we know that our present understanding of cosmology is the final truth?"[456]

It is easy to succumb to the idea that the inspired author's words are "the words" or "the last words" on the subject. But some texts do not easily or wholly disclose their original intent. (If the biblical Canon was clear on time, we would not have had to turn to philosophy to aid our understanding.) Derrida has aptly indicated that even if we have some grasp of the author's intention, that might still not be the word, and there might be more meaning to the text that the author was not aware of.[457] Because this subject falls under the banner of biblical revelation, we would have to say with Derrida that neither the human author nor the interpreter gets the last word.

Many temporalists view God as being timeless before creation and then engaging in a relationship to time in a temporal fashion. Yet God, who is eternal, can also be personal, transcending time and combining it into His ultimate reality.

To say that God is bound by time and therefore limited is theologically unsound and problematic. The

---

[455] "Jacques Derrida" in Baird and Kaufman, 349, 351, 364, 347-366.
[456] Ibid., 358.
[457] Ibid., 347-366.

opposite extreme is also problematic. To postulate that God is timeless and therefore unable to be temporally personal reduces Him to the God of a single description of physics. As well, to speak of God as being exclusively "timeless" runs the risk of abstracting Him from the world so that He cannot be thought of as influencing the world's life directly. Polarized positions on God's relation to time face the problem of a personal God entering into a relationship with finite beings that do not match His actual being. The biblical Canon asserts that God is not limited by time as we are; He is "the King eternal," or "the King of the ages" as some Bible versions translate it (1Timothy 1:17; 2 Peter 3:8). God's unbounded essence transcends all polarized categories that try to classify Him as either temporally personal or transcendently impersonal, for He is both simultaneously.

The incarnation is a staggering doctrine, for it is difficult to speak about it without projecting our temporal creaturely time onto God. How can we talk about the hypostatic union when we find our language is up against an ultimate boundary? Our difficulty is that we are unable, in one and the same language, to speak consistently and unambiguously of the intersection of divine and human reality. And yet maybe creation and the incarnation are the only helpful pointers to understanding God's relationship to space and time.

Because God is self-existent, creation *ex nihilo* (creation from nothing) implies that He has absolute priority over all space and time. The place of God in Jesus should be an open concept rooted in the space and time of this world yet open to the transcendent presence of God. Though He was incarnate within the physical space of the body He assumed, He was not confined by it.

We can remind ourselves that another

demonstration of the mystery of God's relationship to time is the fact that the incarnation culminated in the resurrection. The doctrine of the resurrection cannot do without its other empirical correlates such as the empty tomb. The incarnation should not be seen as placing space and time limitations on God, but it points to the fact that humanity is bound to space and time in relating to Him. We interact through Jesus in two dimensions, as it were, in space and time and through His Spirit. Torrance stated:

> In the incarnation the eternal reality of God has actually intersected with our creaturely reality. The difficulty that faces us is that this span of space-time is a coordinate system of divine and human, eternal and temporal, invisible and visible, spiritual and material relations, and we want to coordinate them in one and the same language. But that is exactly what we cannot do. It is because people keep on trying to do this that they continually introduce confusion into theology often lapsing into false dualisms.[458]

Tillich has aptly said, "Looking at God, we see that we do not have Him as an object of our knowledge, but He has us as the subject of our existence."[459]

To ask what God's experience of divine eternity is like is a different kind of question. In fact, we should be careful in trying to imagine what the life of God is like. This does not mean that we are reduced to Wittgenstein's silence, but part of what it means to say that God is unfathomable is to also admit that we do not know what it is like for God to be timeless. At best, perhaps the most that we can say is that, from God's

---

[458] Thomas F. Torrance, *Space, Time and Incarnation* (London: Oxford University Press, 1969), 76.
[459] Paul Tillich, *The New Being* (New York: Charles Scribner's Sons, 1955), 77.

own perspective, He knows and does what He does in the flash of a single now. He exists at every time that ever exists. In concluding his discussion on the mysterious relationship God has with time, Augustine prayed:

> Lord, how deep are the inner recesses of your secrets. Certainly if there were a mind gifted with such vast knowledge and foreknowledge as to know all the past, present, and future, that mind [would be] wonderful beyond belief, stupendous, and awe-inspiring....How high You are! And the humble in heart are the house in which You dwell.[460]

One idea of Du Bois resonates here. The struggle to see ourselves in relationship to God in time makes us conscious of "two warring ideals in one body" and produces the desire to "merge [our] double self into a better and truer self." [461] Augustine saw that the purpose of Christ's coming was to set us free from sin and time. He stated, "Then when the fullness of time came, he came to set us free from time. Once we have been set free from time, we will come to that eternity."[462] There we will dwell with "the only God, our Savior, through Jesus Christ our Lord, [to whom] be glory, majesty, dominion, and authority, before all time and now and forever. Amen" (Jude 1:25 NASB). One can reasonably understand what is being implied here but only enter it by faith.

---

[460] Augustine, *The Confessions*, 284, #31.
[461] "W.E.B. Du Bois, "The Souls of Black Folks," in Braid and Kaufman, 42-49.
[462] Teske, 31.

CHAPTER 7
Lessons from the Fall of Constantinople

How do we come to terms with the historic fall of Constantinople, a Christian city that valiantly attempted to embrace the interrelationship between faith and reason?

Three places that Western travelers and pious tourists often visit in the interest of expanding their understanding of history are Jerusalem, Rome, and Constantinople (now named Istanbul, in the country of Turkey). I have great memories of traveling to Turkey in the autumn of 2013. Among the highlights of the trip was a visit to the historical sites of the ancient church in Ephesus. Ephesus was where the elderly apostle John came to finish his life's ministry, bringing along Mary, the mother of Jesus, after Christ's crucifixion. It was also one of the places visited by Paul on his missionary journeys.

I was particularly fascinated to see what was left of the old Byzantine capital city of Constantinople and the ancient church basilica called the Sophia Hagia. This was one of the largest churches in Christendom for a thousand years, until the Renaissance, and was once called "the eye of all the world." It is intriguing to realize that the Byzantine Empire once stretched from the United Kingdom to North Africa, Arabia, and Asia. Constantinople was a very prosperous city, designed to be the center of the Christian world. It sits on a horn of land, with one side in Europe and the other side in

Asia. The city lay astride the land route from Europe to Asia and the seaway from the Black Sea to the Mediterranean and had an excellent and spacious harbor. Construction of Constantinople began in 324 AD, and the city was dedicated on May 11, 330 AD. It was created to be the new capital of the Roman Empire by Emperor Constantine the Great, after whom it was named. Constantinople was considered the cradle of Eastern Orthodox Christianity and one of Europe's most glorious cities, boasting a population of approximately half a million people. The multinational Byzantine Empire was one of the most enduring empires, lasting 1,123 years. The belief system behind its creation and continued existence was centered in Orthodox Christianity. The city was a cultural center whose achievements included the establishment of a unified code of law, the first public education system, and the first university. It was a city of scholars and artists who preserved ancient literature and knowledge from antiquity. The city had a reputation for having the largest collection of Christian relics, including the true cross and John the Baptist's head.

Constantinople was famed for its massive defenses, its impenetrable walls, and its magnificent palaces, domes, and towers. From the 5th century on, the city provided a solid defense for the eastern provinces of the old Roman Empire against barbarian invasions. Besides its immediate 18-meter-tall walls, the city was also protected by a 60-kilometer chain of walls across the peninsula. Many scholars argue that these sophisticated fortifications allowed the eastern half of the empire to develop unmolested while Rome and the western half of the empire collapsed. With the rise of Islam, Constantinople became the last bastion of Christian Europe, repelling Islamic expansion and influence. As Europe's first line of defense, the

Byzantine Empire served as a firewall against Arab advances in the 7th and 8th centuries, allowing Europe to slowly recover during the centuries following the collapse of Rome.

Constantinople was also famed for architectural masterpieces such as the Church of Hagia Sophia (the Church of Holy Wisdom), the palace of the emperors, the hippodrome, the Golden Gate, and arcaded avenues and squares. Constantinople contained numerous artistic and literary treasures. For centuries, it was the largest and richest urban center in the Eastern Mediterranean, mostly as a result of its strategic position commanding the trade route between the Aegean Sea and the Black Sea. It would remain the capital of the eastern, Greek-speaking Empire for over a thousand years. At its peak, roughly corresponding to the Middle Ages, it exerted a powerful cultural pull and dominated economic life in the Mediterranean. Visitors and merchants were especially struck by the beautiful monasteries and churches of the city, in particular the Hagia Sophia. I have stood in the former palace grounds and seen trees over a thousand years old still flourishing. Constantinople was especially important for preserving in its libraries manuscripts of Greek and Latin authors throughout a period when instability and disorder caused the mass destruction of similar libraries in Western Europe and North Africa. On the city's fall, many of these were brought by refugees to Italy and played a key part in stimulating the Renaissance and preparing Western Europe for the transition to the modern world. The cumulative influence of Constantinople on the West, over the many centuries of its existence, is incalculable. In terms of technology, art, and culture, as well as sheer size, Constantinople was without parallel anywhere in Europe for a thousand years.

1. Decline and Fall

In the 12th century, Constantinople was the largest and wealthiest city in Europe. But eventually the Byzantine Empire began to decline and shrink in size, until the once mighty empire was reduced to just its capital city and the immediate environs. Finally, the capital itself fell to the Ottoman Empire (as part of the Muslim conquest) in 1453. Though there are complex reasons for the fall of Constantinople, in many ways, the decline and fall of the Byzantine Empire parallels the decline and fall of the ancient Kingdom of Israel as documented in the Old Testament—and for many of the same reasons.

Constantinople fell to an invading army of the Ottoman Empire on Tuesday, May 29, 1453. The 200,000-man Ottoman army, assisted by a 1,000-ship fleet, was commanded by 21-year-old Ottoman Sultan Mehmed II, who wanted to take Constantinople "because he could." Facing this army, perceived to be "as numerous as the stars," was a city whose population was now only about 50,000 people (including about 7,000 in the army). The city fell following a seven-week siege that began on Friday, April 6, 1453, the day after Orthodox Easter. The Sultan Mehmed offered the Emperor and his people safety if they willingly surrendered; otherwise, he warned, Constantinople would be subject to the fate of all infidel cities that resisted Muslim conquest. The Christian emperor refused.

On the evening before the fall of Constantinople, as the Ottoman army prepared for the final assault, large-scale religious processions and church prayer services were held in the city. A last solemn ceremony was held in the Hagia Sophia Church, in which the emperor and representatives of both the Latin and Greek branches of the Christian Church, as well as nobles from Eastern and Western Europe, participated. They spent time in repentance, asking for forgiveness and seeking God's help.

The next morning, the city was overrun. One who escaped said the invading soldiers came like an army of ants pouring into the city. A few lucky civilians managed to escape, and a small number of Italians escaped by quickly retreating to their boats. Mehmed II had sent an advance guard to protect key buildings such as the Hagia Sophia Church, but no such restraint was evident in the rest of the city.

In his book *Lost to the West: The Forgotten Byzantine Empire That Rescued Western Civilization*, historian Lars Brownworth described the horror that followed:

> The carnage was terrible. Turkish soldiers fanned out along streets that were soon slick with blood, covering the ground so thickly with corpses that in some places it could hardly be seen. The Venetians and Genovese managed to get to their ships and escape... but the rest of the population was doomed. Women and children were raped, men were impaled, houses were sacked, and churches were looted and burned. After three days of chaos, Mehmed restored order and ended the bloodshed and looting.[463]

The horror is further revealed in an eyewitness account by George Sphrantzes, a close friend of the emperor and a government minister:

> As soon as the Turks were inside the City, they began to seize and enslave every person who came their way, all those who tried to offer resistance were put to the sword. In

---

[463] Lars Brownworth, *Lost to the West: The Forgotten Byzantine Empire That Rescued Western Civilization* (New York: Crown Publishing Group, 2009), 298.

many places the ground could not be seen, as it was covered by heaps of corpses. There were unprecedented events: all sorts of lamentations, countless rows of slaves consisting of noble ladies, virgins, and nuns, who were being dragged by the Turks by their headgear, hair, and braids out of the shelter of Churches, to the accompaniment of mourning. There was the crying of children, the looting of our sacred and holy buildings. What horror can such sounds cause! The Turks did not hesitate to trample over the body and blood of Christ poured all over the ground and were passing his precious vessels from hand to hand.

Christ our Lord, how inscrutable and incomprehensible your wise judgments! Our greatest and holiest Church of Saint Sophia, the earthly heaven, the throne of God's glory, the vehicle of the cherubim and second firmament, God's creation, such edifice and monument, the joy of all earth, the beautiful and more beautiful than the beautiful, became a place of feasting; its inner sanctum was turned into a dining room; its holy altars supported food and wine, and were also employed in the enactment of their perversions with our women, virgins, and children. Who could have been so insensitive as not to wail Holy Church?[464]

Another eyewitness account appears in the book *They Saw It Happen in Europe 1450-1600:*

Nothing will ever equal the horror of this harrowing and terrible spectacle. People

---

[464] *The Fall of the Byzantine Empire: A Chronicle by George Sphrantzes 1401-1477*, trans. Marios Phillipides (Amherst: University of Massachusetts Press, 1980), 174.

frightened by the shouting ran out of their houses and were cut down by the sword before they knew what was happening. And some were massacred in their houses where they tried to hide, and some in churches where they sought refuge.

The enraged Turkish soldiers...gave no quarter. When they had massacred and there was no longer any resistance, they were intent on pillage and roamed through the town stealing, disrobing, pillaging, killing, raping, taking captive men, women, children, old men, young men, monks, priests, people of all sorts and conditions...There were virgins who awoke from troubled sleep to find those [soldiers] standing over them with bloody hands and faces full of abject fury. This medley of all nations, these frantic brutes stormed into their houses, dragged them, tore them, forced them, dishonored them, raped them at the cross-roads and made them submit to the most terrible outrages. It is even said that at the mere sight of them many girls were so stupefied that they almost gave up the ghost.

Old men of venerable appearance were dragged by their white hair and piteously beaten. Priests were led into captivity in batches, as well as reverend virgins, hermits and recluses who were dedicated to God alone and lived only for Him to whom they sacrificed themselves, who were dragged from their cells and others from the churches in which they had sought refuge, in spite of their weeping and sobs and their emaciated cheeks, to be made objects of scorn before being struck down. Tender children were brutally snatched from their mothers' breasts and girls were pitilessly given up to strange and horrible unions, and a thousand other terrible things happened.[465]

Mehmed II allowed his troops to plunder the city for three days as was customary. According to the Venetian surgeon Nicolò Barbaro, "All through the day the Turks made a great slaughter of Christians through the city." We would call this a genocide. According to Philip Mansel, thousands of Christian civilians were killed, enslaved, or deported. The following is an historical document describing what happened to those in the Hagia Sophia:

> The Army converged upon the vast square that fronted the great church of Hagia Sophia whose bronze gates were barred by a huge throng of Christian civilians (priests, nuns, etc.) inside the building, hoping for divine protection. (This would become a slaughter house.)
>
> The church was full of Christians. The [church service was ending with a song]. At the sound of the uproar outside, the huge bronze gates of the building were closed. Inside the congregation prayed for the miracle that alone could save them. They prayed in vain. It was not long before the doors were battered down. The worshippers were trapped. After the doors were breached, the troops separated the congregation according to what price they might bring in the *slave markets*.
>
> A few of the elderly and infirmed were killed on the spot; but most of them were tied

---

[465] C.R.N. Routh, ed,. *They Saw It Happen in Europe 1450-1600* (Oxford: Blackwell Publishers, 1965).

or chained together. Veils and scarves were torn off the women to serve as ropes. Many of the lovelier young women and youths and many of the richer-clad nobles were almost torn to death as their captors quarreled over them. Soon a long procession of ill-assorted little groups of men and women bound tightly together was being dragged to the soldiers' military camp, there to be fought over once again. Some of the prettiest young women were saved alive for a fate worse than death...to become concubines in the harem of the Sultan Mehmet II. The priests had continued to pray at the altar, until they were taken too. When Sultan Mehmed (II) saw the ravages, the destruction and the deserted houses and all that had perished and become ruins...Tears came to his eyes and sobbing he expressed his sadness. "What a town this was! And we have allowed it to be destroyed!"...the horror of the situation exceeded all limits.[466]

The capture of Constantinople marked the end of the Roman Empire, an imperial state which had lasted for nearly 1,500 years. The Ottoman conquest of Constantinople also dealt a massive blow to Christendom, as the Ottoman Muslim armies were now free to advance into Europe without an adversary to their rear. The name of the city was later changed to Istanbul, and the Hagia Sophia Church was turned into a mosque. Constantinople was defeated by an Islamic regime that was determined to conquer the known world—and in fact would overrun Eastern and Central Europe, reaching the gates of Vienna, Austria, as other Muslim forces had advanced through Spain

---

[466] Steven Runciman, *The Fall of Constantinople 1453* (Cambridge University Press, 1965), p. 147.

and into southern France. The Muslim advance was a very serious threat to Western Europe and had a significant impact during the early 16th century, including impacts on the Protestant Reformation.[467] Christians suffered terribly as a result of this conquest. Muslims, on the other hand, considered this to be a jihad victory over Christianity.

Historian Mark Noll has cited the fall of Constantinople as one of the "decisive moments in the history of Christianity":

> It goes without saying that looking back on the past helps us gain new understanding on the present. History shows us how we got where we are today, and reminds us that we are part of a much larger story. We look back to the past to help us gain new meaning on the present. It is a mistake to forget the past. The past was the path to the present. Though there is complexity to the story of the fall of Constantinople...I have pondered whether there are some insights and enduring lessons that can be gleaned from the fall of Constantinople.[468]

I am sure that many academic disciplines have provided useful commentary on what lessons we can learn from the historic fall of Constantinople. I will use a theological grid in attempting to understand what made this once great city vulnerable. I am not dismissing military, political, and sociological explanations. Rather, I hope to add supplementary explanations to those kinds of commentary. A theological understanding of the fall of Constantinople

---

[467] Eric Metaxas, *Martin Luther: The Man Who Rediscovered God and Changed the World* (New York: Penguin Random House, 2017), 391.
[468] Mark Noll, *Turning Points: Decisive Moments in the History of Christianity* (Baker Academic, 1997).

suggests that the city fell because of two general enemies, the same forces that even today are enemies of the Christian worldview. Ultimately, they city of Constantinople could not overcome these two enemies.

2. The Enemy Within

A. Betrayal of Theological Beliefs

According to historical reports, many in Constantinople had betrayed their own theological principles, straying from the statement of faith on which their empire and community were established. Many were nominal Christians. The cumulative effect of a diluted lukewarm version of Christianity was such that many nominal Christians (such as the Janissaries and Arianists) eventually found it easy to join Islam. It appears that modern Greece has learned this lesson, as about 95 per cent of its population profess adherence to the Orthodox faith, right up to the border of Muslim Turkey.

B. Failure to Maintain a High View of Christ

One of the most profound questions Jesus asked His followers was: "Who do you say that I am?"

One lesson that can learned from the lives of several biblical figures is that spiritual weakness and atrophy usually never happen all of a sudden. We are told in Song of Solomon 2:15: "Catch for us the foxes, the little foxes that ruin the vineyards, our vineyards that are in bloom." The little things that we let slide eventually can ruin everything else. Christendom in the eastern half of the old Roman Empire didn't all of a sudden become weak; its weakness was the cumulative impact of centuries of decisions that had resulted in a Christianity that was not Christocentric but liberalized, nominalized, and characterized by diminished spiritual life and vitality.

As happened in ancient Israel, the shrinking of the Byzantine Empire came as a result of flawed biblical theology. Believers were so confused in their theology that they found it easy to join another faith. This can only happen if people do not have a solid grounding in the Bible. The rise of Islam was facilitated by disunity among Christians and by the Arian heresy that had been so strong in North Africa and other parts of the eastern Mediterranean. The Arian view of Christ is quite compatible with the Islamic view of Christ in that it allows Him to be a great prophet, but not fully divine. Such a low view of Christ allowed people with an Arian Christology to fall prey to Islam, and this greatly facilitated its rise. The key point is that theology matters and that bad theology in the long run has huge consequences—often generations down the road.

In our modern context, many nominal and liberal Christians have drifted to the position that Jesus was simply a great prophet. There is similar confusion over the authority of Scripture. This, in turn, can affect conclusions on many other theological and ethical matters. In contrast, the writers of the New Testament had a very clear understanding of who Jesus is. Paul argued in Colossians 2:9 "In Christ all the fullness of the Deity lives in bodily form." John reported Christ's words in Revelation 1:17-18: "Do not be afraid; I am the First and the Last. I am the living One; I was dead, and now look, I am alive for ever and ever! And I hold the keys of death and Hades."

C. Ethnocentrism

History documents that the dominant attitude in the Byzantine Empire shifted from a focus on multinational unity based on the Orthodox Christian faith to a focus on the ethnic superiority of the Greeks. This inevitably created first and second class

Christians and contributed to many ethnic regions departing from the Byzantine transregional unity. Thus, the geographic expanse of the Byzantine Empire and of Christendom began to shrink. There was a need for a reminder of the truth of Galatians 3:28: "There is neither Jew nor Gentile, neither slave nor free, nor is there male and female, for you are all one in Christ Jesus."

D. Intrusion of the State and Cultural Convention into the Church

In the later years of the Byzantine Empire, there was a great amount of instability. Leadership changed about every four years, often due to power struggles and internal disputes. Each new leader had a different vision and direction, which destabilized the present and undermined any attempt to build a solid future.

This instability and confusion also affected the Eastern Church. This was because it was in a compromised state because of its subjection to the civil ruler. The term "Caesaropapism" is often used to describe this approach—the idea that the civil ruler (in this case, the Byzantine emperor) should be in a position comparable to that of the Pope in the Western Church. The Byzantine emperor dominated and ruled the Eastern Church, making it simply one more department of the State. This intrusion of the political sphere into the life of the Church was a serious threat. It is necessary for Christians to be able to separate their devotion to Christ and the biblical Canon from their responsibilities as citizens of the State. When the rulers of the State try to control the Church and make it serve the State, the faith community has a serious problem that may cause it to lose sight of its purpose and destiny.

3. The Enemy Without

The Byzantium Empire was also unable to withstand assaults from its enemies without.

A. The Reality of Evil

Constantinople had been betrayed and attacked during the Fourth Crusade by Crusaders from Western Europe (in 1204), greatly weakening the Byzantine Empire and its ability to defend even its capital city. But the Empire and city were also vulnerable because they were faced by the massive Ottoman army, equipped with the new invention of giant cannons. These weapons speedily shattered the walls of Constantinople, which had previously been thought to be impregnable.

The simple observation here is that suffering because of the choices and actions of other people is one of the dark aspects of human life. The prospect of Christians suffering in this life because of their faith is also very real. A primary text that describes this is found in Hebrews 11:35-40:

> There were others who were tortured, refusing to be released so that they might gain an even better resurrection. Some faced jeers and flogging, and even chains and imprisonment. They were put to death by stoning; they were sawed in two; they were killed by the sword. They went about in sheepskins and goatskins, destitute, persecuted and mistreated—the world was not worthy of them. They wandered in deserts and mountains, living in caves and in holes in the ground. These were all commended for their faith, yet none of them received what had been promised, since God had planned something better for us so that only together with us would they be made perfect.

Bad things happen to people who don't deserve it, and that is something that we have to understand and accept.

B. The Reality of Spiritual Conflict

There is no neutral zone. From a theological perspective, we are either advancing the Kingdom of God through practicing discipleship and living out missional theology, or we are hindering the dominion of Christ by our diminishing spirituality. The threat to a vibrant faith and the flourishing of faith communities is ever present. It is not flesh and blood that presents the threat but powers and principalities, manifested through political and institutional systems, false beliefs, false religions, and ungodly philosophies that set themselves up against a Christian worldview (Ephesians 6:12).

When we look at the history of the Church, we see that the Church has faced a variety of experiences (both positive and negative) that may or may not be a part of our own current experience. In many places in the world (such as North Korea, Iran, Iraq, Syria, Afghanistan, and Sudan), Christians are severely persecuted or enslaved because of who they are and what they believe. When it was besieged, Constantinople was largely abandoned by the Western Church. Why? Because the Western Church perceived Constantinople as peripheral to its interests. And also because the relationship between the Western Church and the Eastern Church was not healthy. Because of this disunity, the majority of those in the Western Church refused to help Constantinople.

Ignoring the critical reality of other believers facing genocide is troubling, and yet it has a contemporary ring to it. Do we as Christians pray for the persecuted Church around the globe? It is not because of a lack of knowledge. We can easily go onto the Internet and see information on the countries where Christians are most persecuted and pray for them. They are part of the body of Christ, the same body of Christ that we belong to. Hearing that Christians are being persecuted and even wiped out in countries such as Iraq shouldn't just tickle our ears. It should fuel our prayers. It should move us. If we refuse to help, pray, and care, then we are part of the problem.

We may think that what happens on the other side of the world does not affect us, but it does. Because the majority of the Western Church refused to help Constantinople, it fell, and that created an even greater problem. Now that Constantinople was no longer serving as a firewall or buffer zone, the Ottoman armies were able to march right into Europe. The lesson from this for me is that the loss or fall of other Christians we could have helped may come back to haunt us. If we refuse to help others when they are facing a threat, we may be alone when we face similar challenges. We must not leave our Christian brothers and sisters and their leaders alone on the front lines.

Another lesson here is that there is great danger for the local church when its leadership and its congregation lose their focus on the outward mission of Christ and sink back into an inward focus on church politics, disunity, and infighting.

4. Conclusion

For the secular liberal, this whole discussion about the fall of a remnant of the Byzantine Empire and the loss of a part of Christendom may seem irrelevant. Why even bother to integrate faith into the discussion? After all, from a socio-evolutionary point of view, Christianity is viewed as unnecessary scaffolding to be kicked away once we have evolved, climbed higher, and embraced "free thinking"—thus setting up an empire of another kind. But perhaps having a fixation with empire building is part of the human condition.

In my opinion, the development of Christendom, in its various forms, has been an anomaly. Trying to build a Christian city, nation, or empire inevitably has its problems because of the theological tenet of the total depravity of humanity. We are not a nice species, and anything we build will inevitably be tainted and even undermined by sin. Furthermore, nothing here lasts—not Calvin's Geneva, not the Byzantine Empire, not Charlemagne's Holy Roman Empire. Nothing we build—outside of anything that may be classified as belonging to the eternal—lasts. Empires have come and gone. History and reason tell me that faith frequently gets corrupted by empire building. Although Christians may pray with the Lord's Prayer, "Your will be done on earth as it is in heaven," ultimately the faith community needs to be reminded that what we are really looking forward to is "the city with foundations, whose architect and builder is God" (Hebrews 11:10) and "the Holy City, the new Jerusalem, coming down out of heaven from God" (Revelation 21:2). Keeping an eye on the future horizon, we are looking forward to the time when "The kingdom of the world has become the kingdom of our Lord and of his Messiah, and he will reign for ever and ever" (Revelation 11:15)!

CHAPTER 8
Signs of Hope as Christendom Declines
(A Chapter for Those Weary of the Church's Cultural Captivity)

It doesn't take a rocket scientist to recognize the increasing domination of secularism in Canada, North America, and the West and that Christendom is in the historical rearview mirror. There are many characteristics of the Christendom that used to exist that are hardly worth lamenting. In this chapter, I want to suggest some reasonable signs of hope. My vision is that as the caricature of Christendom declines, it will allow a more orthodox form of faith-praxis (faith and practice) to emerge. It will be good for the Church to blow in some fresh air. In some sense, the topics that I address in this chapter are an outworking of a process of wrestling with certain issues in Christendom over the last four decades.

I recollect as an adolescent growing up in a church that had 1,200 members and sent out lay missionaries from the congregation to every continent in the world. I recollect a sense of optimism in the 1970s in that church, an "expectation that soon this [missionary] enterprise [would be a part of] realizing God's kingdom on earth." [469] I remember completing my

---

[469] Darrell L. Guder, *The Continuing Conversion of the Church* (Grand Rapids MI: Wm. B. Eerdmans, 2000), 15.

Bachelor of Theology degree and driving home on graduation day, singing and feeling elated over that chapter of my faith journey. But four-and-a-half years later, I would stand on another graduation platform, receiving a Bachelor of Arts in social sciences degree from Simon Fraser University, a left-wing secular university. I remember that day feeling somewhat disillusioned with Churchianity after all the critiques of the Church I had heard in lectures during those years of study—of the Church's failures in culture, of the Church's misconduct and abuses when running Residential schools for Native children, [470] of the abuses and cultural genocide inflicted on First Nations people, [471] of the cultural imperialism and colonial destructiveness of the Christian missionary enterprise,[472] of the patriarchy of the Church, and so forth. In the words of Bosch, more than ever before in its history, I could see that Christian mission was in the firing line.[473] It was the first time I had begun to think that something was very wrong and that modern culture was increasingly out of step and diverging from the old certainties of Christendom. I became aware that there was "a profound inconsistency in our institutions." [474] In a liberal university, I was encountering Christendom being rationally brought into question. The liberal university was raising deeper questions in regards to the tension building

---

[470] Guder discussed the optimism of modernity and called the "pulling and pushing of primitive cultures [a] colonial enterprise." Guder, *The Continuing Conversion of the Church*, 4.

[471] Guder also discussed the "unquestioned assumption of western Christians" in imposing their "normative cultural forms of faith" in the colonial enterprise. Guder, *The Continuing Conversion of the Church*, 13-14.

[472] David J. Bosch, *Transforming Mission: Paradigm Shifts in Theology of Mission* (Maryknoll, NY: Orbis Books, 1991), 4.

[473] Ibid., 2.

[474] Guder, *The Continuing Conversion of the Church*, 192.

between culture and the institution of the Church. (At the time, this was being referred to as the "culture wars.")

In hindsight, I can see that from my mid-teens on, my life had become slowly enmeshed with the institution of the Church. As a young person, I had never given much thought to or dared to question the fundamentalist, conservative version of Christianity that I was being bequeathed and was being shaped in. Sixteen years of university and graduate school pressed me to think deeper and remove my rose-colored glasses. Today, I would consider myself a progressive Protestant. I might perhaps be perceived by some to be theologically liberal, but my core convictions remain firmly anchored in orthodoxy. However, over the last thirty-five or more years, I have gradually come to realize that some things are not working and that some notions and practices of the Church are considered inexcusable by non-Christian people. I slowly discovered that people in my secular networks were seeing the institution of the Church not as a conduit to faith but as an obstacle for them to come to faith and an impediment to hearing the Good News that God loved them.

I had not been told Christendom was over[475] until I encountered Reginald Bibby's book of Canadian sociological research titled *Fragmented Gods*. Bibby graciously confronted the Church's optimism with the statistical fact that the Church's high-water mark for attendance in Canada was around 1967 and attendance has been declining ever since.[476] Despite this new understanding of the changing role of the institution of the Church, I still took consolation in the

---

[475] Ibid., xii.
[476] Reginald W. Bibby, "The Great Canadian Attendance Drop-off," *Fragmented Gods: The Poverty and Potential of Religion in Canada* (Toronto: Irwin Publishing, 1987), 11-23.

thought that, whatever happened to a flawed institution, that could not highjack God's loving agenda for humanity.[477] I reasoned: *Why should God be blamed for what an institution does or fails to do? It is unnecessary to confuse faith in God with faith in an institution that has systemic issues.*

One other noteworthy set of experiences also helped to open my eyes to a "growing sense of the 'cultural captivity' of the gospel and of churches' compromise with their surrounding contexts."[478] This was my cross-cultural experiences pastoring in an Italian-Canadian church and a Chinese-Canadian church. It is very true that mission is something that God gives us and that we tend to resist it. Working with Italian Protestants, who at the time were barely a generation away from an Italian Roman Catholic framework, caused me to think about why my mainstream Canadian Protestant theological framework felt different from theirs. They seemed to have a greater focus on salvation including works. Their celebration of the *santa cena* (Holy Supper/communion) was always highly attended and was treated in a sacramental way, as if grace was being transferred simply because they were partaking of the Eucharist. They may have had a Protestant sign on their church, but these believers still approached the faith life in a culturally Italian-Catholic manner. Pastoring cross-culturally "challenged assumptions" and highlighted my own "cultural captivities, blind spots and reductions of the gospel."[479] I gained a new

---

[477] Patrick W.T. Johnson, *The Mission of Preaching: Equipping the Community for Faithful Witness* (Downers Grove, IL: InterVarsity Press, 2015), 89-90. Johnson said: "Christ is not bound to the agency of the church and is free to offer himself to the world directly."
[478] Guder, *The Continuing Conversion of the Church*, 17.
[479] Johnson, 193.

critical awareness of my own Christian subculture, and that helped me reconsider some crucial texts in the biblical Canon.

As a vocational clergyman in a Chinese-Canadian church, I encountered parts of that congregation's culture that were harmonious with the gospel and other parts that were hostile to or threatened by the gospel. I witnessed some "cultural components [that] led to organizational forms that [I considered] not faithful to the gospel mission." I recognized that "The culture can take the organized Church captive."[480] For example, filial piety, patriarchy, and the hierarchical nature of Chinese culture occasionally got in the way of the Good News of the gospel. [481] Filial piety (deference to elders) [482] kept the next generation dependent on the older generation, which controlled decision making in the church; this did not allow the next generation to grow up, take on key leadership roles, or easily bring their friends from other nationalities into the church. Asian cultural values such as hierarchy, conformity, deference, respect for tradition and elders (filial piety), Confucian-based perspectives, and an inability to resolve conflict—all hindered the ability of local-born Chinese in Chinese Canadian churches to engage in cross-cultural mission among the larger Canadian society where they lived and worked every day. I discovered that it was not only

---

[480] Guder, *The Continuing Conversion of the Church*, 147.

[481] Most Chinese churches begin with a structure and leadership style influenced by traditional Chinese culture. Often the overseas-born Chinese leaders run the church in the same way as they run their families, with a top-down approach and a paternalistic leadership style.

[482] The atrocious reality for some next generation Canadian-born Chinese in Chinese churches is that they are slamming into powerful hierarchical, patriarchal, and paternalistic personalities and cultural barriers, often filtered through filial piety and Confucian values.

Caucasian churches that practiced forms of segregation but also Chinese churches. Their cultural church practice, their knee-jerk reaction against the intrusion of historic Western colonial church practices, and their xenophobia kept other people away.

Pastoring in a Chinese congregation opened my eyes to the fact that "Christians from non-Western cultures read their Bibles without a Western lens."[483] In fact, it was a discovery for me to learn that these churches had evolved patterns of church life that were very different from the ones I was used to. This led me to consider the lens which I bring to canonical texts and to my understanding of Christian faith and mission. The ethnic churches I served in had been established as Canadian home mission churches among ethnic groups, which had abandoned some of the cultural "limitations imposed on them in the translation process"[484] and had reshaped how they communicated God's love. Initially, I felt that my conception of the faith was normative orthodoxy; I was slowly learning that it was just *one way* of living and presenting the true faith. I began to deeply question whether my interpretation of canonical texts would connect in a relevant way in cross-cultural contexts I had visited, such as China. I had to face the fact that my understanding of these texts should not be viewed as normative—they were Western and did not translate very well. I was coming to terms with the fact that

> Mission as *Missio Dei* necessarily relativizes Western understandings and practices of mission. God cannot be restricted to what has been and is happening in Western cultural

---

[483] Guder, *The Continuing Conversion of the Church*, 17.
[484] Ibid., 91.

Christianity. God's work is universal in its intention.[485]

Because I do a lot of cross-cultural work doing *kerygma* (proclamation and itinerant speaking), I really do want to offer Good News to other cultures in ways that it can be received and understood. I think there are many people like me who have grown up with the Church and have realized that new wine cannot be kept in old wineskins. The gospel needs to be contextualized to every culture, and there is an ongoing need to change the way we do things. We are in desperate need of seeing signs of hope. As Christendom declines in the Western cultural context, there are signs of hope that I think can be realized. I will discuss some of these in the rest of this chapter.

1. Getting Back to a Pre-Christian Kind of Culture Where the Gospel Can Be Heard Again

One sign of hope as Christendom declines must be getting away from the public caricatures of the Church—institutional hegemony, parochialism, pontification, condescension, and sectarianism—all of which have done enormous damage in the name of "historic Christianity." We must get back to a pre-Christian kind of culture where people can hear the gospel again. Every time we talk about the Church, I have a relative who works from a frame of reference of growing up in the Canadian Anglican Church. Everything has changed since then, and I am constantly having to unpack assumptions rooted in a Christendom that no longer exists. Unfortunately, the secular community seems to be more able to express what the Church is *against* than what the Church is *for*. The Church is called to be a witness to the Good News of what God has done for lost people that we

---

[485] Ibid., 20.

can't do for ourselves, the Good News that God is good, loving, and knowable.

2. Getting Back to Being Inclusive so the Gospel Can Be Heard Again by Everyone

We discover in the biblical Canon and through religious experience that God seeks, finds, and restores people. And when God redeems a life and commissions that life, "there is no form of human creativity or virtue that is a necessary perquisite for this calling. It comes from outside ourselves...[and] is the result of God's initiative and mission."[486] Another sign of hope as Christendom declines in the West would be a move away from the Church functioning as a non-inclusive institution that marginalizes people in the community. Those currently marginalized include the poor, the LGBTQ2 community, those who don't wholly embrace institutional church beliefs, those who don't hold church membership, the divorced, those with mental health issues, those with addictions, those of a different race, people with a different socio-economic status, and Muslims. It would be helpful for us to review the inclusiveness of Jesus' mission.

The institution of the Church functions to guard the institution, and legal membership has been one of its safeguards. The Church's relationship with the State has contributed to the development of legal membership that affords certain rights and privileges to certain people who sign up to be members. I believe church institution policies associated with legal membership have created a wedge between members, attendees (those who attend but choose not to take membership due to various convictions), and outsiders in the broader community. In this sense, the institution of the Church has been "control-driven for

---

[486] Ibid., 60.

public order, institutional security, [and] protection of power"—something we may "need to repent of [and] be converted [away from]."[487] If we follow Jesus' example, we should start with accepting people as we find them, not pontificating over them. It has been noted:

> The compassion with which the community cares for its own as well as its neighbors [those next to it] incarnates the gospel. The dependence upon God's forgiveness is incarnated in the way that the community forgives, practices tolerance, [and] bears one another's burdens.[488]

I think it is a flawed argument to equate Christian identity with institutional church membership, with all of its attendant organizational rights and privileges. People who are part of the faith community are those the Holy Spirit draws to Himself, not those who have met the organizational criteria of signing a document of membership, joining the club, sitting up straight in a pew, paying a tithe, and volunteering to perform various duties in the parish.

I served as a pastor in the Mennonite Brethren denomination, where believer's baptism and membership were granted together. The denominational theological conviction was that people were welcomed into the faith community at baptism; that is when these people became "one of us." Furthermore, membership was granted only if a person had been baptized by *believer's baptism*. By policy, membership could not be granted to people who wanted to transfer in from another denomination and maintained that their baptism as babies and their later confirmation constituted *bona fide* baptism; the Mennonite Brethren Church insisted that these

---

[487] Ibid., 141.
[488] Ibid., 159.

people had to be baptized again when they were able to consent to and understand their baptism. Furthermore, the particular church in which I pastored practiced a "closed table" for communion; that is, it was open only to those who had undergone believer's baptism. This created all kinds of practical problems for me when I was trying to work with people who had come out of other church traditions. They felt that they did not need to be baptized again, they were upset that membership in the faith community was tied to believer's baptism, and they resented that they were barred from partaking in communion or serving in the church. I had had no hand in writing these church board-enforced polices; in fact, I loathed them. I could see that in practice they were creating different classes of believers, which I am convinced is unbiblical. I just don't see God creating this many manmade barriers to people drawing near to His presence. Augustine drew attention to the fact that not all of God's people are found in the institution of the Church and not all in the institution of the Church are God's people, members of the family of God.[489]

Getting back to being inclusive is really about getting back to the heart of God's mission. God wants "to heal his rebellious creation" and intends to bless all peoples, and part of that can be through His elect and called out ones.[490] We are called to serve the Lord's purposes, and we don't get the right to say who is or is not welcome in the family of God. Unfortunately, there are many church institutional policies designed to protect in-group, class, and personal values rather than kingdom values. We are called to be missionaries but often lack a heart for whole categories of people. We excuse ourselves by saying that reaching out to

---

[489] Augustine, *The City of God,* trans. Marcus Dods (Peabody, MA: Hendrickson Publishers, 2008).
[490] Guder, *The Continuing Conversion of the Church,* 32-33.

these groups is for Christians who have special gifts to minister to the homeless, the divorced, gay people, people with mental health issues, people from other ethnic and religious backgrounds, those in halfway houses, those recently released from prison, and so forth. We are called to focus on God's redemption and on loving our neighbor. In this sense, our identity as the people of God is "an identity-in-mission."[491]

Another of my observations is that the focus of too many churches is not multicultural or ecumenical. It might be useful for Christians to intentionally attend and serve in a church with a dominant ethnicity and culture different from their own. This would force them to intentionally think through some of their assumptions about the witness of the Church and about how the gospel is intended to unify believers in a way that transcends cultural divisions. I have served in several non-Anglo congregations and share Guder's conclusion that "no particular culture...may be regarded as normative for the gospel community."[492] I observed that many with Chinese backgrounds were drawn to the Chinese church in which I served as a clergyman because I was Caucasian (鬼佬, *Gweilo* or *gwáilóu*).[493] They perceived that my employment there meant the church was more open in its theology and practices.

I am not sure that the Church recognizes its non-inclusive practices as part of its "constant rebellion against God"; we forget that it has always been possible for [people] to encounter God's Word and work in history and to ignore it, reject it, distort it, or manipulate it for selfish ends."[494] In other words, God takes a loving risk with the people who are entrusted

---

[491] Bosch, 81.
[492] Ibid., 69.
[493] The term *gwáilóu* literally means "ghostly man."
[494] Bosch, 74.

with the message—a risk because His witnesses are sinful, rebellious, and unworthy too. God continues to communicate to the sinful believing community so that they may enter into the experience of salvation and be able to respond to His loving promptings. But instead of opening ourselves to the unfettered flow of God's Spirit, we create forms of religion (idolatrous tradition, stale religiosity, and in-group privilege) to control Christian teaching, tame God, and make the gospel manageable. In this sense, "sin as control continues to challenge the integrity of Christian witness,"[495] and our supposed religious impulses are really "expressions of the heart to use God to serve human purposes."[496]

Currently, it appears that the desire to risk crossing boundaries with the message of God's love has been shrinking. This is at least partly because of our awareness of the Western colonialism and cultural imperialism in which we have often wrapped our missionary endeavors. However, the message of God's love still needs to be "conveyed into every language and culture,"[497] modifying it into forms that those receiving it can understand.

I began writing this chapter at a time when millions of refugees were fleeing violence in Syria and Iraq. In the process, I listened to some confusing messages within church networks about what should be done by the Church in regards to this humanitarian crisis. A number of negative voices were being raised against this demographic because they were predominantly Muslim—in spite of the atrocious devastation they had experienced! It could be said that the Church's indifference to the suffering of these

---

[495] Ibid., 76.
[496] Ibid., 77.
[497] Ibid., 79.

refugees conveys a gospel that is too small.[498] My heart was deeply moved by images coming out of Greece and Italy and Germany of people opening their hands and hearts to the needy. For me, a social gospel also has to be part of the Church's response to human suffering. The Good News of God's love has to have hands and feet as well as a voice to name the Name. Bosch has made the point that the Church exists for others and for God's mission, not for itself. If the Church is to be the Church as it was intended to be, it must come to terms with its own unfaithfulness.[499]

3. Moving the Focus from Professional Programs to People So the Gospel Can Be Heard Again

There needs to be a recognition of the tendency of the Church and of Christians to try to control and manage the gospel, making it conform to culture and thus diluting the message. It has been noted that people gather in churches with culture-tainted expectations and church life becomes distorted by ambitious goals, consumer habits, and competitive instincts.[500] In this milieu, the gospel gets reduced to programs. It has been properly noted that "the fulfillment of missional vocation is not a program [or a] method."[501] I served with one church where at least two executive pastors thought they were bringing renewal to the church by restructuring the organization and its programs. Johnson was quick to dismiss this "understanding of the church...as a collection of programs and services administered by religious professionals offered to a consumer

---

[498] Guder, *The Continuing Conversion of the Church*, 102.
[499] Bosch, 377-397.
[500] Eugene H. Peterson, *The Pastor: A Memoir* (New York: HarperCollins, 2011), 105.
[501] Johnson, 207.

congregation."[502] Restructuring doesn't bring about the conversion of the church. For years, I got very tired of "hammering out" with church boards the various church ministry programs that we would run throughout the coming year for the congregation. With the exception of a few evangelistic plans, much of the programming functioned as an in-group social club for the congregation. Guder commented that "There is probably no better example of the reductionist view of the gospel and the church's mission than the organizational chart of many...congregations, where evangelism is a program assigned to one of several committees."[503]

With the demise of Christendom, I suspect the program orientation of the institutional Church will diminish and things that belong to being a fellowshipping faith community will remain. In that process, I believe there is an opportunity for the Church to review its embedded theology and deliberately re-examine what the gospel is all about. This, too, is a sign of hope. I believe there is increasing evidence of a desire to "deal responsibly and critically with the heritage of [historical Church] decisions as they shape us and often restrict our faithful witness."[504] I believe that there is increasing awareness that "we are not called to preserve reductionisms that weaken the church's faithful witness."[505] In this regard, Guder pointed out that "Cultures do not stand still. They evolve and change, and so must the work of translating. As our Western cultures move beyond the forms of Christendom, new translation hurdles arise."[506] Herein lies hope—that

---

[502] Ibid., 122.
[503] Guder, *The Continuing Conversion of the Church*, 136.
[504] Ibid., 193.
[505] Ibid., 133.
[506] Ibid., 93.

we review our reductions of the gospel in order to pursue a more faithful response to God's love. My observation is that the best the Church has been able to do is stumble clumsily toward being a community of witness to the truth of the in-breaking of God. It seems to me that there is a need to come back to basics, to be able to pray, "Lord, I depend on You to walk the maze of being a witness." It is refreshing to acknowledge that "mission is…derived from the nature of God [and is a] movement from God to the world" and therefore "moves the subject beyond the level of program or method."[507] The mission of God—initiated by God, not human beings—is Good News, and God's mission "makes clear that [people] in their lostness, find hope in what God has done for them, not in what they might imagine they can do for themselves."[508]

I have learned from my former blindsightedness that too often the Church relies on programs to change people—discipleship programs, Bible college programs, Christian education programs, and so forth. The subtle problem is that we are depending on reason, information, knowledge, and education to change people's hearts. Some of our most respected denominations, theologians, and clergy have too often depended on programs for transformation. The Western Enlightenment has given priority to solving problems through reason, information, and knowledge, neatly packaged as learning programs. However these learning programs are often detached from human life and may circumvent the relational and Spirit-empowered elements that we need to encourage one another in our faith journey—elements acquired through community prayer, fellowship, and shared devotional practices. It is a theological flaw to

---

[507] Ibid., 20.
[508] Ibid., 47.

believe that all problems can be solved by reason or a church program. Peterson commented:

> Programs [have] developed into the dominant methodology of "doing church." Far more attention [is] given to organizing and giving leadership to programs than anything else. [The] problem here: a program is an abstraction and inherently nonpersonal. A program defines people in terms of what they do, not who they are. The more program, the less person...Treating souls for whom Christ died as numbers or projects seem[s] to me something like a sin against the Holy Spirit.[509]

When we make the Church about programs, we disregard the resources we have in relational ministry, hospitality, and prayer that sustain us in the muddle of spiritual life and spiritual challenges. Programs may not be that helpful for Christians who are going through suffering. If there is one message we can garner from the book of Job, it is how important it can be for hurting people to have real, accessible friends.

Many of our churches are contexts for public monologues—speeches—when the real need is for believers to be able to unpack preached texts, to make real life connections, and to discern God's mission and providential leading in their journey. A related problem here is that the Church has too often made public preaching "the primary form of witness [which has] tended to narrow the understanding of witness to that which is oral and that which is said [in] churches by preachers on Sundays."[510] This is reductionist. God calls, equips, and empowers His witnesses so that

---

[509] Peterson, 254-255.
[510] Guder, *The Continuing Conversion of the Church*, 62.

their life and service communicate their testimonies of God's saving activity and initiative.

One sign of hope I foresee is that, with the demise of Christendom, the Church will move away from an institutional focus to a dynamic relational focus that will truly nourish and encourage participants. As is happening in China (a country that puts minimal emphasis on the institution of the Church), we may see believers gathering more often in small groups and home gatherings where the Good News can be heard, shared, discussed, and understood without institutional filters. Canada could be only one legislative change away from a time when churches could lose their freedom to speak on subjects such as the right to life, marriage and sexual expression, and so forth. It would be prudent at this juncture for us to learn from Christians in countries such as China, Cuba, Turkey, Iran, and North Korea that suppress the public expression of Christianity. They may teach us to put less importance on the institution of the Church and put the focus back on being sustainable and multiplying communities of faith.

4. Getting Past the Institutional Church's Conceptions of Discipleship So the Gospel Can Be Heard Again

Another sign of hope as Christendom declines could be the Church reevaluating its understanding of discipleship. Formerly, the Christian education (Sunday school) department of the Church institution used to tackle this issue with Bible-education programs offered from the cradle to the grave. Churches would run an hour-long class either before or after the main worship service, with the intention of deepening people's faith lives. Over the last number of decades, a lot of churches have dissolved the Christian education hour and opted for longer worship services, giving more focus to music liturgies. Some theological colleges are reporting that the net result of less focus on Christian education and greater focus on worship is that students are coming to their institutions with far less knowledge of the Bible; the teachers have had to lower the bar on what they are teaching because of a higher measure of biblical illiteracy.

A missional church should be learning what it means to be a disciple of Christ, but, as Johnson pointed out, people can study the Bible for personal benefits and negate calling and vocation. That is, formation for mission gets missed.[511] The benefits of salvation are given to us in order that we will bear witness to the world. A key "purpose of scripture is the formation of the community for witness."[512] With the demise of Christendom, is it time for the Church to evaluate what discipleship should look like? What are the different components of discipleship? Is intentional mentoring a key component? What could be the effect on future leadership if the Church doesn't address this issue? Why is discipleship so critically significant to being a witness to the Good News? Why did Jesus elevate the importance of discipleship (apprenticing after the life model of Jesus), and how does that tie in with mission?

I am convinced that questions such as this can be looked at in a new way, without confusing them with maintenance ministry. The Church can begin again to talk about how discipleship, in part, is walking with God and trusting him as we navigate the web of life and encounter God's providential assignments and incidents. The Church can begin again to have a conversation about how living soaked in Scripture, and an active prayer life can help sustain people and

---

[511] Johnson, 115-116.
[512] Ibid., 195.

keep them focused on living as a witness to the Good News. The Church can begin again to talk about discipleship as a "decisive turn to both God and neighbor...discovering new dimensions of loving God and neighbor" based on a revelation of the "reign of God."[513]

One further warning. As Darrel Guder has warned, "too much talk about discipleship is a reduction of what it is...the discipling is not an end in itself, it is the means of the goal...leading to sending."[514] Ultimately, "the call to discipleship is a call into God's reign and is an act of grace" where we will "be with Him."[515] A biblically-based discipleship looks at how the text calls, forms, shapes, and sends us into our missional vocation. Being a disciple of Christ means following Christ, which has many expressions as Christians all share in missionary authority. Recently I sat with a board on which I serve. We asked the question: why is there so much biblical illiteracy among the younger generations in the Church (millennials and generation Z). We realized that it is tied to the demise of Christendom. I also realized that conversations such as this are the first step toward addressing that concern. They are a sign of hope that there is a willingness to tackle this issue in a way that is contextual, integral, and missional.

5. Getting Past the Institutional Church's Relationship with the State So the Gospel Can Be Heard Again

Another sign of hope as Christendom declines might be purer intentions in the practice of the faith and the communication of the Good News. The Church

---

[513] Bosch, 83.
[514] Darrell L. Guder, "Missional Theology Lecture #1," Carey Theological College, January 23, 2017.
[515] Bosch, 38-39.

benefits from its preferential relationship with the State in various ways—tax exemptions on church property, tax deductions for charitable giving, tax exemptions for clergy housing, the legal right to officiate marriages, and government subsidies for social services the Church provides to society. These are some of the lingering linkages between the State and the Church bequeathed from Christendom.

In contrast, if we look at the Church in other countries where Christendom never existed, we see a much different picture. There Christians have never been given tax breaks on church properties or charitable giving, clergy don't receive tax breaks on housing costs, the Church has no relationship with the State allowing it to perform legal marriages, and the Church is not recognized by the State for its provision of social services. As we look at the condition of the churches in those international contexts, we see Christians who give and serve because the Scriptures teach giving and serving, not because it is beneficial at tax time. Churches there are not enclaves of societal privilege but communities for gathering and worshiping, often while being oppressed by the broader society. In those international contexts, the Church is not entwined with the State.

With the demise of Christendom in the West, I can foresee here as well the breaking of some of these final ties to the State. This will challenge the Church to dig deeper into what it means to give to the work of the Lord rather than to the institutional Church. The Church might be able to rediscover that we should not confuse who the Church is with our institutional structures and professional clergy. The Church might also dig deeper into its sacred texts and see that it is God, not the State, who ultimately and actually affirms and recognizes a marriage, since marriage finds its idea in God's created order.

In exercising the privilege that the State has given it to officiate at legal marriages, I have discovered that the Church has often practiced discrimination. Some of the choices to refrain from officiating at a wedding are understandable, and some are not. In some churches, if a couple do not fit into the church's theology on marriage, the church will refuse to marry the couple (and the State protects the Church's right to refuse). In essence, what many of these church leaders do is send a couple down the street to a more liberal church (or to City Hall) to get married and then ask the couple to come back and tithe and serve in their church. For instance, some churches have refused to marry a couple if one of the partners has been divorced. This is ridiculous. In many cases, you cannot unscramble the egg once damage has been done with a previous marriage. If the church won't marry some couples, those couples can go to City Hall (the State) and get married anyway. So what has the church accomplished with its discriminatory policies on marriage? Why not use the opportunity to counsel the couple, offering Good News and grace?

For the past seven years, my wife and I have been doing premarital counseling in our home for various couples who were not able to get married (or did not feel comfortable with getting married) in the churches that they had previously attended (or that they currently attended). I have encountered many couples who have been hurt by the Church. In many cases, the churches they had previously attended (or currently attended) had discriminatory policies that would prevent them from getting married there. For example, they might not be church members, or they might be nominal in their Christian practices, or one of the partners did not attend church (even if that partner was open to faith-based premarital counseling). I have never advertised that I do premarital counseling, but somehow many couples have contacted me. My wife and I do premarital with them in our home over a six-week period, and then I officiate at their wedding, often in a secular context. All of the premarital counseling we do is faith-based. I get to talk about the Good News (that God loves them) and the biblical foundation of marriage (that marriage is God's idea). We explore their own faith journeys and how faith is important to building a stronger marriage, family, and future. What I treasure most is when one of the partners has not been a part of the Church or has left the Church as a youth. I have the privilege of helping these individuals to unpack some of their confused understanding about what it means to be a Christian and of introducing them to Christ. All of the weddings that I officiate are faith-based. I use Scripture, I pray with the couples, and I encourage them (but don't force them) to further explore the resources of Christian faith in building their lives. This has been a great honor for me to be a part of, but it has been an opportunity forfeited by the institutional church.

This past fall, I received an invitation to attend a gay marriage banquet of an in-law family member. I had to think that through, and I concluded that I would be a more authentic witness if I attended. About half the family did not attend over religious convictions taught in their churches, and the other half did attend after reflecting on their religious convictions. One author has commented that "The mission field in which we find ourselves requires that the church diversify its ways of communicating [as] we need to become more creative in finding ways to translate the message."[516] By my attendance at the marriage banquet, I communicated to this family

---

[516] Guder, *The Continuing Conversion of the Church*, 157.

member that my familial relationship to him was important and that I cared about him. I have known him since he was six years old. He told me that he was surprised that I came, and he was very grateful.

I am an itinerant minister and therefore more independent than some ministers, who have to report monthly to church boards regarding their public attendance at external functions. In this regard, I believe that the institutional Church, in many denominations, binds the hands of clergy so that they are not able to freely exercise some of this kind of freedom. These churches view their clergy as representing their institution, and this is another case where "rules trump relationships."[517] I believe this hinders God's servants from being a witness to the Good News that God loves people and that Christians can be conduits of that love.

Society has been transforming the Church. Maybe it's time for the Church to review its position, reconsider its strategy, and reexamine the Church's historical relationship with the State.

6. Getting Past How Christendom Has Distorted the Pastoral Identity So the Gospel Can Be Released

One of the factors supporting the continuation of Christendom is the vested interest of the clergy. I suspect many clergy promote the current privileged position of the institutional church, in particular because it aids their job security. Perhaps another sign of hope as Christendom declines might be the diminishment of the deep separation between clergy and laity. The exalted and privileged position of clergy in the institutional church is called clericalism. My conviction is that this situation troubles many Christians, and many outside the Church are

---

[517] Peterson, 163.

alienated when they detect a sense of clerical entitlement, pride, class, and privilege. A skeptical world and grieving congregations can both cringe when they witness clergy exercising a leadership style based on power and authority that does not reflect accountability, humility, and servanthood. It's a frightful thing that a church can become so clergy-centered that even the minister believes that much of his/her thoughts are also God's thoughts.

I remember being at a rally where David Suzuki, a former professor in the genetics department at the University of British Columbia, was present. He commented on US President George Bush Jr., who had remarked that "God told me to go to war" against Iraq. Suzuki said, "That scares the hell out of me." I couldn't help thinking that Suzuki's concern in the civic arena has a parallel in the Church. Some clergy, because of their power-based position and the clergy-centered nature of the institutional church, frequently use the "God card," declaring, "God told me..." in order to extend their influence. Sadly, too often laity cannot discern that some statements made by clergy are simply the clergy's opinion.

I remember being at a men's breakfast. One young clergyman stated from the platform that people with PhDs never did much in the Church. I noted that there were at least three men with doctoral degrees in the audience. The young man's statement was offensive and half-baked at best. Theologian John Stackhouse has commented:

> We might be tempted to defensively blame our brightest young people for avoiding pastoral occupations out of worldly motives. But let's consider a more provocative possibility. Perhaps our prudent God is just not calling our most intelligent young people to pastor us. Perhaps he is using them

elsewhere because the typical North American church would simply waste those gifts."[518]

It has been said that in spite of the lip service paid to the doctrine of the priesthood of all believers, Reformation churches have largely continued to be clerical because many did not refocus the Church and its offices upon mission. [519] Evelyn and James Whitehead have noted:

> In their status as children of God, however, adults do not fare as well as children of the clergy. This dependency, more acceptable in an era of educated clergy and generally uneducated laity, is experienced today as a hazard not only to psychological development but to religious growth...we would argue that after forty it may be healthiest to call no one father.[520]

Some feel that one of the biggest obstacles to people hearing the gospel today is the Church's failure

---

[518] John Stackhouse, "Our Pastoral Brain Drain," *Church: An Insider's Look at How We Do It* (Grand Rapids, MI: Baker Books, 2003), 56.

[519] Ibid., 134. This problem surfaced in a discussion I had with a Canadian denominational leader. He said, "We need more church-planter pastors." I made the observation that that requires bivocational pastors (pastors who financially support themselves through marketplace employment). I also noted that his denomination will only license and ordain full-time clergy. That is evidence of a clergy-centered, institution-focused practice, rather than recognizing the value of bivocational and lay clergy pastoral giftings. What is the point of encouraging church-planting or lay pastors if the denomination won't empower them to do the full job (including ordination and being licensed to officiate marriages)? Such an antiquated system perpetuates a hierarchical form of clericalism.

[520] Evelyn Eaton Whitehead and James D. Whitehead, *Christian Life Patterns: The Psychological Challenges and Religious Invitations of Adult Life* (New York: The Crossroad Publishing Company, 2003), 137.

to properly understand pastoral identity. I find it refreshing that God keeps working with people and Christians despite human failure. There are many examples of this in the biblical Canon, including Adam and Eve, Cain, Abraham, and Joseph and his brothers. God continues to always move toward His saving purposes for creation.[521] God is constantly making His Good News known and addressing what is systematically problematic in our lives. The issue of pastoral identity is no exception. Guder noted that the conversion of the Church will necessarily mean the conversion of many of our concepts and practices of church office, ordination, and leadership. [522] The purpose of God in giving pastoral gifts is to equip the faith community for works of service in doing mission and sharing the Good News of God's love. However, too frequently we see pastoral identity being squeezed into other molds and purposes. One of the molds that pastoral identity gets shaped into is the business management model of servicing faith communities. One author has commented on how "North American …denominations [have] expanded and restructured after the model of the American corporation …organiz[ing] the continuing Christianization of American culture." [523] This is happening in church institutions where "the values and assumptions of the competitive market can take over the church and make it into a business."[524] The pastor is being viewed as a manager, someone who "gets things done" and "makes things happen," rather than as a "person who is placed in the community to pay attention and call attention to 'what is going on right now' between men and women, with one another and with God—this

---

[521] Ibid., 38.
[522] Ibid., 164.
[523] Ibid., 5.
[524] Ibid., 147.

kingdom of God."[525] Unfortunately this idea of "running an ecclesiastical business"[526] and competing in a "religious market"[527] is pervasive. The business management model of running the Church is running it into the ground and "reshaping evangelism into a program of church business."[528]

I hope that the demise of Christendom might bring a corrective back to the Church in regards to the pastoral identity. I hope a pastor will increasingly be seen as one who calls people to worship God,[529] one who teaches people to pray,[530] and one who equips people for mission. I find a great deal of encouragement in Peterson's corrective on pastoral identity:

> I didn't want to be a religious professional whose identity was institutionalized. I didn't want to be a pastor whose sense of worth derived from whether people affirmed or ignored me. I didn't want to be a pastor in the ways that were most in evidence and most rewarded in the American consumerist and celebrity culture.[531]

I deeply resonate with Peterson's vision of what a pastor should be:

> I want to be a pastor who prays...I want to be a pastor who reads and studies. This culture...squeezes the God sense out of us. I want to be observant and informed enough to help [the] congregation understand what we are up against...I can't do this just by trying

---

[525] Peterson, 5.
[526] Ibid., 112.
[527] Ibid., 13.
[528] Guder, *The Continuing Conversion of the Church*, 196-197.
[529] Peterson, 136.
[530] Ibid., 142.
[531] Ibid., 242.

harder. I want to be a pastor who has the time to be with you in leisurely, unhurried conversations so that I can understand and be a companion with you as you grow in Christ...I want to be a pastor who leads you in worship, a pastor who brings you before God in receptive obedience, a pastor who preaches sermons that make scripture accessible, present and alive...to give you a language and imagination that restores in you a sense of dignity as a Christian in your homes and workplaces and gets rid of these debilitating images of being a "mere" layperson...I want to be an unbusy pastor.[532]

One further comment I would like to make here is that the importance of the pastoral role in mission is one that I think has been blown out of proportion. I notice that the Church puts a great deal of emphasis on commissioning its pastors and missionaries and occasionally those in some other helping professions, but it tends to ignore Christians in other professions, as if their calling to mission is farther down the pecking order. Other professions need to be recognized as sharing in the mission of the Church. In fact, I would take it one step further and ask why we don't have commissioning services for those who work in business, legal, teaching, and other professions.

7. Getting Back to Being a Community That Recognizes Addressing Social Justice Issues Can Help Open People's Ears to the Gospel

The secular community seems to know more about what the Church stands *against* than what the Church stands *for*. Many of these perceptions are related to social justice issues. For example, many segments of

---

[532] Ibid., 278.

the Church are known for being places that are not egalitarian with regard to women, ethnic groups, and people from the LGBTQ2 demographic. Unfortunately, the Church seems to be more known for standing against abortion, homosexual practice, pornography, alcohol and drugs, euthanasia, gambling, suicide, and other religions, rather than being known for witnessing to the love of a God who is invested in reaching people and being a blessing to their lives. The Church should be "a community in which human categories of social discrimination and privilege are set aside."[533] It is necessary to question what has happened to "the missionary lifestyle of the congregation."[534] If God is a missionary God, then His people should be a missionary people. The institution of the Church is known for pressuring people (especially staff and congregations) to hold certain perspectives.

I remember having a human resources (HR) problem while on a pastoral staff. I called the denominational headquarters for some assistance on this matter. I was told: "You can have us come in to straighten this out, but then you must resign." In other words, my choice was either to put up with a dysfunctional staff member or to choose unemployment. If I was working in a secular context, this matter would have been mediated by a labor relations agency, a union, or a lawyer. But in the church context, there was little concern to follow the basic laws of the land and in particular the Employment Standards Act. I have learned that churches in a single denomination in our province can have up to half a dozen cases in the law courts in a year in regards to church staff issues. For example,

---

[533] Ibid., 138.
[534] Ibid., 186.

one church secretary was going to go on maternity leave, and just weeks before her maternity leave was to begin, she was laid off so that the church could hire another full-time church secretary with no domestic interruptions. The pregnant secretary took her case to court, and the church lost. Only then did the denominational officials come in and scold that church's board for not practicing justice. Cases such as this are examples of churches not practicing justice, but they are also examples of people exerting their right to self-defense. When some of these cases become public, they soil the testimony and witness of the Christian community. The MeToo movement certainly adds additional focus to this discussion.[535]

One sign of hope I see with the demise of Christendom is that the Church can no longer hide behind its closed doors on issues of social justice. The secular community will no longer give the institution of the Church amnesty just because it is supposed to be an organization that is above reproach. I believe that as the Church, its officers, and its executives are held more accountable to the laws of the land, the Church must clean up its act and practice justice—not just according to the law but according to the higher law of love (Matthew 22:37). If that happens, the church will recapture its lost witness to society as people see how much we love one another (John 13:35).

Deeply related to this is the problem of reducing the gospel to individual salvation and the benefits it brings rather than it including the call to be witnesses.

---

[535] For an example of how the MeToo movement has crossed into religious circles, see Bob Smietana, "Willow Creek Promises Investigation Amid New Allegations Against Bill Hybels," *Christianity Today*, April 21, 2018,
https://www.christianitytoday.com/news/2018/april/bill-hybels-willow-creek-promises-investigation-allegations.html, accessed April 2018.

Some have discussed how the pendulum can swing too far in either direction—from the Church renouncing involvement in the world to the Church focusing on social justice to the point that it is reduced to promoting a program of social change.[536] Our call is to serve God's mission, which will spill over into social justice areas but which will focus on witnessing about the God who seeks a relationship with people. Bosch noted that a key concept in the apostle Matthew's missionary consciousness was that Christians "bear fruit."[537] This involves a commitment to God's reign, to justice and love, and to obedience to the entire will of God. Mission involves helping believers to become sensitive to the needs of others, opening their eyes and hearts to recognize injustice, suffering, oppression, and the plight of those who have fallen by the wayside.[538] Mission involves helping those suffering from "poverty, discrimination and violence."[539] The gospel also includes peace-making,[540] reconciliation, refusing vengeance,[541] and love of the enemy.[542]

8. Getting Back to Being a Community Where Theological Training for Mission Is for the Whole People of God So More People Can Be Equipped to Channel the Good News

If indeed there is no area of life outside God's reign,[543] then it makes sense that the breadth of theological training should be made available to as many believers as possible to help equip more people

---

[536] Guder, *The Continuing Conversion of the Church*, 122-124.
[537] Bosch, 66.
[538] Ibid., 83.
[539] Ibid., 11.
[540] Ibid., 120.
[541] Ibid., 109-114.
[542] Ibid., 71.
[543] Guder, *The Continuing Conversion of the Church*, 38; Johnson, 75; Bosch, 32-33, 150.

for service in the *missio Dei*. Evelyn and James Whitehead, have commented:

> When no access to religious leadership is provided for maturing adults, their religious maturation can be stunted—and this by the Church! [544] ...If religious leadership is restricted to a small group of persons, whether priests or other professionals, the community will be deprived of a healthy variety of ministers. By blocking the development and expansion of ministry, the Church imperils the handing on of the faith.[545]

If the New Testament is a missionary document,[546] why are we only making theological training available to some of the "missionaries"? Why are our theological institutions only allowing some privileged Christians to be equipped to lead a life worthy of the calling?[547] Currently, most of the theological institutions in my country and in the West generally predominately focus on training for the clergy. There is a need to make theological training up to the doctoral level available to *all* believers, rather than further entrenching clericalism. This could also be done in a more relational and less clinical manner in the context of homes and cluster groups, with praxis in God's mission as the focus of training. My best understanding is that all Christians are sent out with a testimony and are enabled by the Holy Spirit, and that God is at work through each witness. Thank God that the Holy Spirit is continuing to convert us by helping us to translate, proclaim, and hear the Word and by empowering our faith response. It is important

---

[544] Whitehead and Whitehead, 137.
[545] Ibid., 140.
[546] Bosch, 55.
[547] Guder, *The Continuing Conversion of the Church*, 58.

to remember that the mission of God announces that the kingdom of God is near, breaking in, present in Jesus Christ and still coming.[548]

9. Getting Back to What Preaching Is Supposed to Be So People Can Be Equipped and More People Can Hear the Gospel

Another sign of hope as Christendom declines might be that there are fewer "vocational preachers" who have no calling from God but who have chosen the role and pursued ordination as just another career choice. We have inherited from Christendom the idea that a person can obtain a Master of Divinity degree (an academic achievement), be ordained and called "Reverend" (a professional credential), and therefore be considered qualified to preach. Johnson noted that a legacy of Christendom's clerical paradigm is that ordination and education get confused with having sufficient authority to preach.[549] Ordination in this sense can undermine the priesthood of all believers and create a hierarchical rather than a communal understanding of preaching. This puts too much focus on the preacher, especially since preachers are supposed to point away from themselves to Christ. (Remember John the Baptist's comment in John 3:30: "He must become greater; I must become less.") Who can really claim he has "mastered divinity"? Who really deserves to be called "Reverend"? These titles are awkward at best and should be replaced with a more biblical term, recognizing one who has been called and gifted to preach and prepare God's people for service and witness. There is a need to recognize that the content and authority of preaching should come from the preacher's encounter with God.[550]

---

[548] Ibid., 67.
[549] Ibid., 44, 45, 50.
[550] Ibid., 45, 47, 49.

With the current escalating closure of churches in Canada, I can only hope that people seeking to be "career" clergy would be detoured from making such an occupational choice. I also hope that those who do follow the arduous road of preaching would be the ones truly called by God, so that the preacher's testimony and engagement with the biblical Canon would carry humble authority. Missional preaching must be based on a missional interpretation of Scripture so that the preaching participates in God's mission of redemption.[551] Such preaching will bear witness to the goodness of God, who intervened in history through Jesus, in the crucifixion and resurrection, bringing liberation and freedom to those who place their faith in Christ. The entire Bible should be "read through the interpretive matrix of Jesus [as] a missionary document,"[552] with an understanding that its purpose is to equip believers for witness, through centering, contextualizing, or kindling. I envision preaching will have to change, as ministers need to be retooled to think missionally. In many churches, preaching is focused on maintenance (therapeutic, storytelling, entertaining) rather than based on the understanding that preaching is the exposition of God's Word to equip the saints for the work of ministry.[553]

Johnson has made the case that "performative" preaching simply has not helped to equip Christians to understand their faith and share it. "Formative" preaching, on the other hand, increases the congregation's competence and confidence in carrying out the primary elements of Christian faith;[554] that is, it equips the congregation for its own witness.[555] We

---

[551] Ibid., 177.
[552] Ibid., 187.
[553] Guder, *The Continuing Conversion of the Church*, 135.
[554] Johnson, 10-11.
[555] Ibid., 29.

should recognize that the maintenance of the mission community is not the main priority, since the central focus of our vocation is to be Christ's witnesses. The Church itself is not the goal of the gospel, but rather the Church is called to be the witness to and the servant of the gospel.[556] Preaching can often be reduced to providing an emotional service station to help people cope with life. However, "the eschatological nature of the gospel" means that not all problems have an immediate solution; the victory of God may not be realized speedily or in this lifetime.[557] Preaching in some cases misrepresents the gospel, reducing it to a way to obtain "happiness, self-fulfillment, self-realization, prosperity...[and] meet individual needs for the assurance of salvation."[558]

I envision that some preaching may adopt a conversational form and be done in home contexts, perhaps similar to the contexts in which preaching was done in the first two centuries of the Church—in smaller groups, with more dialogue and discussion, and with more of a formative purpose. Another sign of hope I see with the demise of Christendom might be that communities include those who are not ordained but who are gifted with the Word to help equip the congregation in the weekly preaching.

10. Conclusion

Change is part of life. Reason tells me that it is necessary to envision changes that enhance integral expressions of faith. I am intrigued by the comment that the only way that "the evangel voice" can truly be at the heart of ministry will be through the continuing conversion of the Church.[559] The current reduction of

---

[556] Guder, *The Continuing Conversion of the Church*, 199.
[557] Johnson, 34.
[558] Guder, *The Continuing Conversion of the Church*, 135.
[559] Ibid., 27.

the gospel seems to be intended to try to control God and to reinterpret the gospel as a means to private salvation.[560] I have been trying to persuade readers of this book to recognize that the Church has been susceptible to cultural captivity and a lamentable reduction of the gospel.[561] There is a need to recognize that we are constantly challenged with cultural compromise and that this needs to be dealt with through repentance and healing. We all have a need to yield to the Good News and to hear the call of Christ to be faithful and dependent on His forgiveness and grace.

It needs to be recognized that though Christendom is history, the Christian's faith calling has never changed. Secular Christendom has long historical roots in the West, where a fragmented Christian worldview was integrated into an informal cultural hegemony. Christendom and true Christianity are very different. Christendom has always been a form of syncretism—a diluted mix of secular culture and Christian ideals, a blending of incoherent beliefs. True Christianity carries the Good News of God's remedy for the sin problem and humanity's separation from God. The Good News is that God, through the sacrificial death of Christ on the cross and His subsequent resurrection from the dead, has provided a way for us sinful human beings to experience peace with God. The Good News proclaims that God loves the world and that whoever calls on Him in faith will know God and the grace, forgiveness, and new quality of life He can bring. Whoever calls on the name of Christ will discover that God hears and welcomes everyone, with no discrimination. The Good News of Christianity is one of the greatest signs of hope this

---

[560] Ibid., 131.
[561] Ibid., 201.

side of heaven. It is grounded in faith and rationally provocative.

EPILOG
Athens to Jerusalem

Recently I undertook a study trip, traveling throughout Germany in the regions of Brandenburg, Saxony, Thuringia, Rhineland, and Northern and Central Bavaria. I visited the cities of Berlin, Wittenberg, Leipzig, Eisleben, Erfurt, Coburg, Wiesbaden, Nuremberg, Augsburg, Eisenach, Worms, and Munich. It was the tail end of Oktoberfest, with a full schedule. The highlights included visits to art galleries, well-preserved medieval villages (Rothenberg, Nuremberg, Oberammergau), castles (Wartburg, Coburg, Linderhof), and medieval churches. As I traveled, my attention was drawn to some of the scars from the former Russian occupation of the eastern part of the country—gray vacant decrepit buildings and ruins, remnants of the Berlin wall, and the Checkpoint Charlie crossing that divided Berlin between 1961 and 1989 during the Cold War. In Berlin, I saw some of the former Nazi torture chambers, the Holocaust memorial, and various bombed-out buildings. One of the buildings was the Kaiser Wilhelm Memorial Church, called the "broken tooth," its damaged spire a reminder of Second World War air raids. I also visited the Nazi rally grounds in Nuremberg. As I stood there, just feet away from the place where Hitler had made his speeches in the late 1930s, I pondered two recent conversations I had had with German seniors who had survived the Allied forces' bombing as children in Berlin by hiding out in bunkers. I was deeply reminded that ideas have consequences.

Two themes run through this book. The first is an affirmation of the complementary factors of reason and faith to potentially draw lives into accepting the evidence for the existence of God and ultimately into knowing God. The second, a minor theme, is that ideas have consequences and that there is a need for a paradigm shift to one that requires a culture of change and reform. The second theme is particularly reflected in Chapter 8.

A key focus for me in Germany was on the European Reformation and Martin Luther's legacy as a change agent. A secondary research focus was the German theologian Dietrich Bonhoeffer, better known for being a Second World War conspirator against Adolf Hitler's Nazi agenda and a martyr for the cause of the liberation of Germany. Both men, in different periods of history, struggled over the question of what reason has to do with faith.

1. Martin Luther

Luther wanted to bring about reform, founded on a love of freedom, reason, and trust in God. In 1517, Luther sparked a transition from medieval thinking to the Reformation. Some believe Luther's legacy contributed to the development of free inquiry, democracy, and limited government. My earliest memory of being exposed to the history of the European Reformation was in grade eight in public school. Later, in my undergraduate studies on the history of the Church, I learned more about this monk/scholar who was well versed in Hebrew and Greek and translated the Bible into the German language.

2017 marked the 500-year anniversary of the European Reformation, and frankly I was surprised at how little public media attention was given to it, considering that its legacy parallels the impact of the Renaissance. Author Eric Metaxas commented that:

> Much of what we now take for granted may be traced directly to [Luther]...for example, the...modern idea of the individual—and one's personal responsibility before one's self and God rather than before any institution, whether church or state—was unthinkable before Luther...and the similarly modern idea of "the people," along with the democratic impulse that proceeds from it, was created—or at least given voice—by Luther too. And the more recent ideas of pluralism, religious liberty, and self-government all entered history through the door that Luther opened to the future in which we now live.[562]

Luther's attempt at reform began with himself and then with the Catholic Church. Many conclude that he initiated the Reformation with the writing of his Ninety-five Theses, which were supposedly nailed to a cathedral door in Wittenberg. Luther called for a Reformation in doctrine in which people would put their whole confidence in Scripture as the source of belief and in faith in Christ, not good works, as the way to receive God's pardon for sin. He was calling for theological change, which coincided with the rise of German nationalism, discontent with the papacy, the growth of humanism, and the Renaissance.

In his recent book on Luther, Eric Metaxas explored Luther's journey with the question: "At what point [does] loving the church mean questioning the church?"[563] Luther believed that "the problem with the

---

[562] Eric Metaxas, *Martin Luther: The Man Who Rediscovered God and Changed the World* (New York: Penguin Random House, 2017), 1.
[563] Ibid,, 50.

church's understanding of grace would be at the heart of larger misunderstandings [and] theological errors."[564] For Luther,

> the very essence of Christian theology [was that] God reached down...all the way...to our broken humanity...and in doing so underscored this truth about us...we are dead and in need of resurrecting...If we do not recognize that we need eternal life from the hand of God, we remain in our sins and are eternally dead...he can only reach us if we are honest about our condition.[565]

Luther's theology of the cross was that:

> we cannot reason our way to God...we can only reason so far. At some point, we come to an end and are stuck. It is at this point that we must stand and wait for God's revelation to come to us.[566]

Luther came to a realization that in his time:

> the greatest minds of the church were genuinely unaware of having become unmoored from the rock of Scriptures ...Luther sincerely hoped that somehow he might awaken them.[567]

Luther believed that "it was faith that created the Christian and body of Christians, called the church."[568] In other words, the Church is a people, not an institution. His theology led him to rediscover the idea of the "priesthood of all believers" and question the "structure of the church [and the creation of] a

---

[564] Ibid., 86.
[565] Ibid., 97.
[566] Ibid., 131-132.
[567] Ibid., 150.
[568] Ibid., 168.

special caste of people who alone had privilege to preach and pastor."[569]

Luther would be persecuted for his convictions and stand trial for them, most notably at the Diet of Worms in Germany. It is there that he made his now famous speech:

> Unless I am convinced by the testimony of the scriptures or clear reason, for I do not trust in the Pope or in the councils alone...I am bound to the Scriptures...and my conscience is captive to the Word of God. I cannot and will not retract anything, since it is neither safe nor right to go against conscience. I cannot do otherwise. Here I stand. God help me.[570]

Metaxas commented that:

> There isn't a historian of the last five centuries who could argue against the idea that Luther's stand that day at Worms—before the assembled powers of the empire, and against the theological and political and ecclesiastical order that had reigned for centuries, and therefore against the whole of the medieval world—was one of the most significant moments in history. It ranks with the 1066 Norman Conquest and the 1215 signing of the Magna Carta and the 1492 landing of Columbus in the New World...If ever there was a moment where it can be said the modern world was born...surely it was in that room on April 18, 1521 at Worms.[571]

Luther prepared the ground for future reformers to emerge, people such as Zwingli and Calvin. Luther's reform coincided with the development of Gutenberg's printing press, which helped spread his ideas in the

---

[569] Ibid., 187-186.
[570] Ibid., 216.
[571] Ibid., 218.

public domain. Eventually, Lutheran churches were established throughout Western Europe. The Reformation also influenced other Protestant movements, such as that of the Anabaptists, which produced further theological changes and reforms.

I see Luther as a prototype for one willing to engage in reform and make change happen. In his generation, he challenged a Catholic worldview infected with Aristotelian philosophy and tradition. The point is that ideas have consequences and they take us places spiritually, socially, and collectively we may not have anticipated, either for good or for ill. Luther's call for change wasn't popular in his time, and perhaps some of my call for change in Chapter 8 may also be considered to sit on the "wrong side" of history. However, if history is any indicator, change starts with individuals, who are often not in the majority but who contribute to creating a different future based on personal and social reform. Such change often starts with reason and moves in faith.

2. Dietrich Bonhoeffer

Dietrich Bonhoeffer, an academic in Hitler's Nazi Germany, also wrestled with how one interfaces faith and reason. Bonhoeffer advocated a "religionless Christianity," one that moved beyond the "abbreviated Christianity" seen in Christendom. He longed to see a "time for the lordship of Christ to move past Sunday mornings and into the whole world."[572] Bonhoeffer's conviction was that God was not just God over what we don't know but also over what we do know. In other words, he was bridging faith into reason. The inference is that we "stop pretending that God wants to live in the religious corners we reserve for him." In

---

[572] Eric Metaxas, Bonhoeffer, *Pastor, Martyr, Prophet, Spy* (Nashville, TN: Thomas Nelson, 2010), 466-467.

dissolving the dualism separating the sacred and the secular, we are saying a "yes to God," which is also a "yes to the world he created."[573] Bonhoeffer lived in confusing times, when the logic of German National Socialism, (the Nazi philosophy rooted in Nietzschean social Darwinism) became very blinding. It has been noted that:

> for many Germans, their national identity had become so melted together with whatever Lutheran Christian faith they had it was impossible to see either clearly. After four hundred years of taking for granted all Germans were Lutheran Christians, [few] really knew what Christianity was anymore.[574]

In contrast, Bonhoeffer's reasoning brought him to a place of faith. Bonhoeffer spoke about the Christian life as basically not being about what we can logically figure out by reason, but as having "everything to do with living one's whole life in obedience to God's call through action."[575] In the midst of a world and culture of turmoil, Bonhoeffer asked:

> Who stands fast?...Only the [person] whose final standard is not reason, principles, conscience, freedom or virtue, but who is ready to sacrifice all this when...called to obedient and responsible action in faith and in exclusive allegiance to God—the responsible [person] who tries to make [their] whole life an answer to the question and call of God.[576]

Grüße an Gott
Musings after Germany, November 15, 2018

---

[573] Ibid., 467-468.
[574] Ibid., 174.
[575] Ibid., 446.
[576] Ibid.

Bibliography

Alston, William. "Divine Action: Shadow or Substance?" In Thomas F. Tracy, ed., *The God Who Acts: Philosophical and Theological Explorations.* University Park, PA: Pennsylvania State University Press, 1994.

Alston, William. "Perceiving God." *The Journal of Philosophy,* LXXXIII (1986).

Aquinas, Thomas. *Summa Theologiae.* Translated by Thomas Gilby. London: Spottiswoode, 1966.

Archibald, Adam, *A Discussion of Quantum Physics & its implications for a serious theory of reality.* http://www.tardis.ed.uk/~adama/quantum.html, accessed June 28, 2002.

Atkins, Peter. *The Creation.* San Francisco: W.H. Freeman & Co., 1981.

———. *Creation Revisited.* Harmondsworth, UK: Penguin, 1994.

Augustine. *The City of God.* Translated by Marcus Dods. Peabody, MA: Hendrickson Publishers, 2008.

———. *The Confessions.* Translated by Rex Warner. New York: Mentor Books, 1963.

Baird, Forrest E., and Walter Kaufman, eds. *Twentieth-Century Philosophy.* Upper Saddle River, NJ: Prentice-Hall, vol. 5, reprint 2000.

Banks, R., and Paul Stevens. *The Complete Book of Everyday Christianity.* Downers Grove, IL: InterVarsity Press, 1997.

Bauer, Walter. *A Greek-English Lexicon of the New Testament and Other Early Christian Literature.* Chicago: The University of Chicago Press, 1979.

Bebbington, D.W. *Patterns in History: A Christian View.* Downers Grove, IL: InterVarsity Press, 1979.

Begbie, Jeremy S. *Voicing Creation's Praise: Towards a Theology of the Arts.* Edinburgh: T. & T. Clark, 1991.

Behe, Michael J. *Darwin's Black Box: The Biochemical Challenge to Evolution.* New York: The Free Press, 1996.

Best, W.E. *Eternity and Time.* Houston, TX: W.E. Best Book Missionary Trust, no date provided.

Bettelheim, Bruno. *The Uses of Enchantment.* New York: Vintage Books, 1989.

Bettenson, Henry, ed. *Documents of the Christian Church.* 2nd ed. London: Oxford University Press, 1963.

Bibby, Reginald W. *Fragmented Gods: The Poverty and Potential of Religion in Canada.* Toronto: Irwin Publishing, 1987.

Blanchard, John. *Does God Believe in Atheists?* Darlington, England: Evangelical Press, 2000.

Boethius. *The Consolation of Philosophy.* Translated by V.E. Watts. Harmondsworth, UK: Penguin, 1969.

Bosch, David J. *Transforming Mission: Paradigm Shifts in Theology of Mission.* Maryknoll, NY: Orbis Books, 1991.

Bradly, F.H. *Appearance and Reality.* 2nd ed. Oxford: Clarendon Press, 1930.

Braude, Stephen. *The Limits of Influence: Psychokinesis and the Philosophy of Science.* London: Routledge and Kegan Paul, 1986.

Brody, Baruch A., ed. *Readings in the Philosophy of Religion: An Analytic Approach.* Englewood Cliffs, NJ: Prentice-Hall, 1974.

Brown, Colin. *Christianity and Western Thought: From the Ancient World to the Age of Enlightenment.* Downers Grove, IL: InterVarsity Press, 1990.

———. *Philosophy and the Christian Faith.* London: InterVarsity Press, 1973.

Brownworth, Lars. *Lost to the West: The Forgotten Byzantine Empire That Rescued Western Civilization.* New York: Crown Publishing Group, 2009.

Brunner, Emil. *The Christian Doctrine of God.* Philadelphia: The Westminster Press, 1950.

Cairns, Earle E. *Christianity through the Centuries.* Grand Rapids, MI: Zondervan, 1981.

"Category: Arguments for the existence of God." Wikipedia. https://en.wikipedia.org/wiki/Category:Arguments_for_the _existence_of_God), accessed December 9, 2017.

Calvin, John. *Institutes of the Christian Religion.* Edited by John T. McNeill. Philadelphia: The Westminster Press, 1960.

The Collected Works of St. John of the Cross. Translated by Kieran Kavanaugh and Otilio Rodriguez. Washington, DC: ICS Publications, 1979.

Colson, Chuck, and Nancy Pearcey. *How Now Shall We Live?* Grand Rapids, MI: Wm. B. Eerdmans, 2000.

Complete Works of St. Teresa. Translated by E. Allison Peers. London: Sheed and Ward, 1978.

Cooper, David E., and Robert Hopkins, eds. *A Companion to Aesthetics.* Malden, MA: Blackwell Publishers, reprint 1997.

Copan, Paul, and Ronald K. Tacelli, eds. *Jesus' Resurrection Fact or Figment? A Debate between William Craig and Gerd Ludemann.* Downers Grove, IL: InterVarsity Press, 2000.

Craig, William Lane. "Did Jesus Rise from the Dead?" In Michael J. Wilkins and J.P. Moreland, eds., *Jesus Under Fire: Modern Scholarship Reinvents the Historical Jesus.* Grand Rapids, MI: Zondervan, 1995.

———. *The Kalam Cosmological Argument.* London: Macmillan, 1979.

———. *Knowing the Truth about the Resurrection.* Ann Arbor, MI: Servant Books, 1988.

———. *Time and Eternity: Exploring God's Relationship to Time.* Wheaton, IL: Crossway Books, 2001.

Crossan, John Dominic. *Jesus: A Revolutionary Biography.* San Francisco: HarperCollins, 1994.

Cupitt, Don. *Mysticism after Modernity.* Oxford: Blackwell Publishers, 1998.

Davis, Caroline. *The Evidential Force of Religious Experience.* Oxford: Clarendon Press, 1989.

Davis, Stephen, T. *God, Reason and Theistic Proofs.* Grand Rapids, MI: Wm. B. Eerdmans, 1997.

———. "Survival of Death." In Philip Quinn and Charles Taliaferro, eds., *A Companion to Philosophy of Religion.* Malden, MA: Blackwell Publishers, 1997, reprint 2000.

Dennett, Daniel. "Conditions of Personhood." In Amelie Oksenberg Rorty, ed., *The Identities of Persons.* Berkeley, CA: University of California Press, 1976.

Dillard, Annie. *Holy the Firm.* New York: Harper and Row, 1977.

———. *Pilgrim at Tinker Creek.* New York: Harper and Row,

1988.

Dubay, Thomas. *The Evidential Power of Beauty.* San Francisco: Ignatius Press, 1999.

Eakin, Emily. "So God's Really in the Details?" *New York Times,* Saturday, May 11, 2002, http://www.selfknowledge.org/resources/pressnyt_eakin.htm

Eberle, Gary. *Sacred Time and the Search for Meaning.* Boston: Shambhala Publications, 2003.

Edwards, William D., et al. "On the Physical Death of Jesus Christ." *The Journal of the American Medical Association* 255, no. 11 (March 21, 1986).

Elwell, Walter, ed. *Baker Theological Dictionary.* Grand Rapids, MI: Baker Book House, 1996.

Eusebius. *Ecclesiastical History, Nicene and Post-Nicene Fathers.* vol. 1, 2nd series, http://apostlesrec.com/wilderness/saints/jmsjrslm.htm, accessed July 8, 2002.

Fingelkurts, Alexander A., and Andrew A. Fingelkurts. "Is our brain hardwired to produce God or is our brain hardwired to perceive God? A systematic review on the role of the brain in mediating religious experience." *Cognitive Processing* 10 (November 2009): 293-326.

Freshwater, Mark. E. *C.S. Lewis and the Truth of Myth.* Boston: University Press of America, 1988.

Friedman, William. *About Time.* Cambridge, MA: MIT Press, 1990.

Ganssle, Gregory E., ed. *God and Time: Four Views.* Downers Grove, IL: InterVarsity Press, 2001.

Gay, Peter. *Freud: A Life for Our Time.* New York: Doubleday Books, 1988.

Geisler, Norman. *Baker Encyclopedia of Christian Apologetics.* Grand Rapids, MI: Baker Books, 1999.

———. *The Battle for the Resurrection.* Nashville, TN: Thomas Nelson, 1989.

Geisler, Norman, and Ron Brooks. *When Skeptics Ask: A Handbook on Christian Evidences.* Wheaton, IL: Victor Books, 1989.

Gill, Jerry. "Wittgenstein and Religious Language." *Theology Today* 21 (April 1964): 59-72.

Glaspey, Terry W. *Great Books of the Christian Tradition.*

Eugene, OR: Harvest House Publishers, 1996.
Gormley, Beatrice. *C.S. Lewis: Christian and Storyteller.* Grand Rapids, MI: Wm. B. Eerdmans, 1998.
Gotshalk, D.W. *Art and the Social Order.* New York: Dover Publishing, 1962.
"Gottfried Wilhelm Leibniz: Space and Time." http://www.philosophypages.com/ph/leib.htm, accessed November 20, 2002.
Goulder, Michael. "The Empty Tomb." *Theology* 79 (1976).
Great Dialogues of Plato. Translated by W.H.D. Rouse. New York: Mentor Books, 1984.
Green, Jay, ed. *Interlinear Greek-English New Testament.* Grand Rapids, MI: Baker Books, reprint 1996.
Greenleaf, Simon. *The Testimony of the Evangelists.* Grand Rapids, MI: Baker Books, reprint 1984.
Grenz, Stanley J. *A Primer on Postmodernism.* Grand Rapids, MI: Wm. B. Eerdmans, 1996.
Grime, Paul. "The Changing Tempo." *Christian History* XIL, no. 3 (1993).
Grudem, Wayne. *Systematic Theology.* Grand Rapids, MI: Zondervan, 1994.
Guder, Darrell L. *The Continuing Conversion of the Church.* Grand Rapids, MI: Wm. B. Eerdmans, 2000.
———. "Missional Theology Lecture #1." Carey Theological College, January 23, 2017.
Habermas, Gary. "Resurrection Claims in Non-Christian Religions." *Religious Studies* 25 (1989).
———. *The Resurrection of Jesus: An Apologetic.* Grand Rapids, MI: Baker Books, 1980.
Hamer, Dean. *The God Gene: How Faith Is Hardwired into Our Genes.* Toronto: Random House of Canada, 2004.
Harpur, Tom. *For Christ's Sake.* Toronto: McClelland and Stewart, 1993.
Harris, Murray. *From the Grave to Glory.* Grand Rapids, MI: Zondervan, 1990.
Hawking, Stephen. *The Universe in a Nutshell.* New York: Bantam Books, 2001.
Hawking, Stephen, and Roger Penrose. *The Nature of Space and Time.* Princeton, NJ: Princeton University Press, 1996.

Heidegger, Martin. *Being and Time.* Translated by Joan Stambaugh. Albany: State University of New York Press, reprint 1996.

Helm, Paul. *The Doctrine of Creation.* Edited by Colin Gunton. Edinburgh: T. & T. Clark, 1997.

———. *Eternal God.* Oxford: Clarendon Press, 1988.

Herbert Spencer. www.utm.edu/research/iep/s/spencer.htm, accessed December 6, 2002.

Hick, John. *The Metaphor of God Incarnate.* London: SCM Press, 1993.

Hindmarsh, D. Bruce. *The Faith of George MacDonald: A Biographical and Critical Examination of the Theology Represented in His Sermons and Letters.* Vancouver: Regent College, 1989.

Hodge, A.A. *Outlines of Theology.* Grand Rapids, MI: Zondervan, 1980.

Hoffmann, Banesh, and Helen Dukas. *Albert Einstein: Creator and Rebel.* New York: The Viking Press, 1973.

Hooper, Walter. *C.S. Lewis: A Companion Guide.* UK: HarperCollins, 1996.

Hospers, John, ed. *Introductory Readings in Aesthetics.* New York: The Free Press, 1969.

Houston, James, ed. *Religious Affections.* Minneapolis, MN: Bethany House, 1996.

Humphreys, D. Russel. *Starlight and Time.* Colorado Springs, CO: Master Books, reprint 1995.

Hunnex, Milton, D. *Charts of Philosophies and Philosophers.* Grand Rapids, MI: Zondervan, 1986.

Husserl, Edmund. *The Phenomenology of Internal Time-Consciousness.* Edited by Martin Heidegger. Translated by James S. Churchill. Bloomington, IN: Indiana University Press, 1964.

James, William. *The Varieties of Religious Experience: A Study in Human Nature.* London: Collins, 1960.

Jeffrey, David Lyle. *People of the Book: Christian Identity and Literary Culture.* Grand Rapids, MI: Wm. B. Eerdmans, 1996.

Johnson, Allison Heartz. *Whitehead's Theory of Reality.* New York: Dover Publications, 1962.

Johnson, Patrick W.T. *The Mission of Preaching: Equipping the Community for Faithful Witness.* Downers Grove IL: InterVarsity Press, 2015.

Josephus' Antiquities, Ecclesiastical History, Nicene and Post-Nicene Fathers, vol. 1, second series, http://apostlesrec.com/wilderness/saints/jmsjrslm.htm, accessed July 8, 2002.

Kant, Immanuel. *Critique of Pure Reason.* Translated by Norman K. Smith. New York: Saint Martin's Press, 1965.

———. *Religion within the Limits of Reason Alone.* Translated by Theodore Greene and Hoyt Hudson. 2nd ed. New York: Harper and Row, 1960.

Kilby, Clyde. *The Christian World of C.S. Lewis.* Grand Rapids, MI: Wm. B. Eerdmans, 1964.

Kittel, Gerhard, et al., eds. *Theological Dictionary of the New Testament.* Abridged in one volume. Grand Rapids, MI: Wm. B. Eerdmans, 1985.

Koestler, Arthur. *The Act of Creation.* London: Penguin Books, reprint 1989.

Kuhn, Thomas S. *The Structure of Scientific Revolutions.* Chicago: University of Chicago Press, 1962.

Ladd, George E. *I Believe in the Resurrection of Jesus.* Grand Rapids, MI: Wm. B. Eerdmans, 1975.

Leftow. Brian. *Time and Eternity.* Ithaca, NY: Cornell University Press, 1991.

L'Engle, Madeleine. *A Wrinkle in Time.* New York: Bantam Doubleday Dell Books, reprint 1989.

———. *Walking on Water: Reflections on Faith and Art.* Wheaton, IL: Harold Shaw Publishers, 1980.

Lewis, C.S. *Christian Reflections.* Edited by Walter Hooper. Grand Rapids, MI: Wm. B. Eerdmans, 1967.

———. *The Discarded Image.* Cambridge: Cambridge University Press, reprint 1998.

———. *God in the Dock.* UK: William Collins, Sons, reprint 1979.

———. *The Great Divorce.* New York: MacMillan, 1946.

———. *That Hideous Strength.* New York: MacMillan, 1965.

———. *The Lion, The Witch and The Wardrobe.* UK: William Collins, Sons, reprint 1990.

———. *Mere Christianity.* New York: Macmillan, 1960.

———. *Miracles.* New York: Macmillan, reprint 1978.

―――. *Prince Caspian*. UK: William Collins, Sons, reprint 1990.

―――. *Till We Have Faces*. UK: HarperCollins, reprint 1991.

Lewis, C.S., ed. *Essays Presented to Charles Williams*. Grand Rapids, MI: Wm. B. Eerdmans, 1981.

Little, Paul E. *Know Why You Believe*. Downers Grove, IL: InterVarsity Press, reprint 2000.

MacDonald, George. *Diary of an Old Soul*. Minneapolis: Augsburg, reprint 1994.

―――. *Phantastes*. Grand Rapids, MI: Wm. B. Eerdmans, reprint 1994.

―――. *The Princess and the Goblin*. UK: Wordsworth Editions, reprint 1995.

Markos, Louise. "Myth Matters." *Christianity Today* 45, no. 6 (April 23, 2001).

Martindale, Wayne, and Jerry Root, eds. *The Quotable Lewis*. Wheaton, IL: Tyndale, 1989.

Mascetti, Manuela Dunn. *Christian Mysticism*. New York: Hyperion, 1998.

McCullagh, C. Behan. *Justifying Historical Descriptions*. Cambridge: Cambridge University Press, 1984.

McDermott, Gerald R. *Seeing God*. Downers Grove, IL: InterVarsity Press, 1995.

McDowell, Josh. *The New Evidence That Demands a Verdict*. Nashville, TN: Thomas Nelson, 1999.

McDowell, Josh, and Don Stewart. *Understanding the Occult*. San Bernardino, CA: Here's Life Publishers, 1982.

McKenzie, L. *Pagan Resurrection Myths and the Resurrection of Jesus*. Charlottesville, VA: Bookwrights Press, 1997.

Merriam-Webster's Collegiate Dictionary, 11th ed. Springfield, MA: Merriam-Webster, 2004.

Metaxas, Eric. *Bonhoeffer, Pastor, Martyr, Prophet, Spy*. Nashville, TN: Thomas Nelson, 2010.

―――. *Martin Luther: The Man Who Rediscovered God and Changed the World*. New York: Penguin Random House, 2017.

Miethe, Terry L., ed. *Did Jesus Rise from the Dead? The Resurrection Debate between Gary R. Habermas and Antony G.N. Flew*. San Francisco: Harper and Row, 1987.

Monte, Christopher, F. *Beneath the Mask: An introduction to theories of personality*. Chicago: Holt, Rinehart and

Winston, 1991.

Moody, Raymond. *Life after Life.* New York: Bantam, 1975.

Moreland, J.P., and William Lane Craig. *Philosophical Foundations for a Christian Worldview.* Downers Grove, IL: InterVarsity Press, 2003.

Morison, Frank. *Who Moved The Stone?* Grand Rapids, MI: Zondervan, reprint 2002.

Naugle, David K. *Worldview: The History of a Concept.* Grand Rapids, MI: Wm. B. Eerdmans, 2002.

New Bible Dictionary. Wheaton, IL: Tyndale House Publishers, 1986.

Newport, John P. *Life's Ultimate Questions: A Contemporary Philosophy of Religion.* Dallas: Word Publishing, 1989.

Nielsen, Kai. *Philosophy and Atheism: In Defense of Atheism.* Buffalo, NY: Prometheus Books, 1985.

———. "Perceiving God." In J.J. MacIntosh and H.A. Meynell, eds., *Faith, Scepticism and Personal Identity.* Calgary: University of Calgary Press, 1994: 1-16.

Noll, Mark. *The Scandal of the Evangelical Mind.* Grand Rapids, MI: Wm. B. Eerdmans, 1994.

———. *Turning Points: Decisive Moments in the History of Christianity.* Baker Academic, 1997.

O'Brien, Elmer. *Varieties of Mystic Experience.* Canada: Mentor-Omega Books, 1965.

Opie, Peter and Iona. *The Classic Fairy Tales.* New York: Oxford University Press, 1974.

Otto, Rudolf. *The Idea of the Holy.* 2nd ed. London: Oxford University Press, 1958.

Pagels, Elaine. *The Gnostic Gospels.* New York: Vintage Books, 1989.

Park, David. *The Image of Eternity: Roots of Time in the Physical World.* Amherst, MA: University of Massachusetts Press, 1980.

Pascal, Blaise. *The Mind on Fire.* Portland, OR: Multnomah Press, 2006.

Pearce, Joseph. *Tolkien: Man and Myth.* San Francisco: Ignatius Press, 1998.

Pell, Barbara. *Faith and Fiction.* Waterloo, ON: Wilfred Laurier University Press, 1988.

Penelhum, Terence, ed. *Faith.* New York: Macmillan, 1989.

Perschbacher, Wesley, ed. *The New Analytical Greek Lexicon.* Peabody, MA: Hendrickson Publishers, 1990.

Peterson, Eugene H. *The Pastor: A Memoir.* New York: HarperCollins, 2011.

Phillips, D.Z. *Religion without Explanation.* Oxford: Basil Blackwell, 1976.

Pike, Nelson. *God and Timelessness.* New York: Schocken Books, 1970.

Plantinga, Alvin. "Is Belief in God Rational?" In C.F. Delaney, ed. *Rationality and Religious Belief.* Notre Dame, IN: University of Notre Dame Press, 1979.

———. "Is Belief in God Properly Basic?" *Noûs* 15:1 (March 1981).

Plantinga, Alvin, and N. Wolterstorff, eds. *Faith and Rationality: Reason and Belief in God.* South Bend, IN: University of Notre Dame Press, 1983.

Plotinus. *Enneads.* Translated by Stephen Mackenna and B.S. Page. http://www.vt98/academic/books/plotinus/enneads, accessed February 22, 2016.

Plutnick Rod, and Sandra Mollenauer. *Introduction to Psychology.* New York: Random House, 1986.

Pojman, Louis P., ed. *Philosophy of Religion.* 4th ed. Cengage Learning, 2002.

Prigogine, Ilya, and Isabelle Stengers. *Order Out of Chaos.* New York: Bantam Books, 1984.

"Probable First Cause." Editorial. *Christianity Today*, July 8, 2002: 25.

QuickVerse. version 5. Iowa: Parsons Technology, 1998.

Quinn, Philip L., and Charles Taliaferro, eds. *A Companion to Philosophy of Religion.* Malden, MA: Blackwell Publishers, 1997, reprint 2000.

Raised from the Dead: A 21st Century Resurrection Story. London, ON: Christ for all Nations video, 2001.

Rawlings, Maurice S. *To Hell and Back.* Nashville, TN: Thomas Nelson, 1993.

Rice, Richard. *The Openness of God.* Downers Grove, IL: InterVarsity Press, 1994.

Rienecker, Fritz. *Linguistic Key to the Greek New Testament.* Edited by Cleon L. Rogers. Grand Rapids, MI: Zondervan, 1980.

Rookmaaker, H.R. *Art Needs No Justification*. Downers Grove, IL: InterVarsity Press, 1978.

Ross, Hugh. *Creation and Time*. Colorado Springs, CO: NavPress, 1994.

———. *Creator and Cosmos*. Colorado Springs, CO: NavPress, 1993.

Routh, C.R.N., ed. *They Saw It Happen in Europe 1450-1600*. Oxford: Blackwell Publishers, 1965.

Runciman, Steven. *The Fall of Constantinople 1453*. Cambridge University Press, 1965.

Russell, Bertrand. BBC interview on *Face to Face*, 1959, https://www.youtube.com/watch?v=yw8n2asHj7Q

Ryken, Leland. *Triumphs of the Imagination: Literature in Christian Perspective*. Downers Grove, IL: InterVarsity Press, 1979.

Saint Teresa of Avila: Collected Works. Translated by Kieran Kavanaugh and Otilio Rodriguez. Washington, DC: ICS Publications, 1976.

Sayers, Dorothy. *The Mind of the Maker*. San Francisco: HarperCollins, reprint 1987.

Schaeffer, Francis A. "Art and the Bible." *The Complete Works of Francis Schaeffer: A Christian Worldview*, vol. 2, book 5. Westchester, IL: Crossway Books, 1982.

Schmidt, Roger. *Exploring Religion*. Belmont, CA: Wadsworth Publishing Co., 1988.

Schoen, Edward. *Religious Explanations: A Model from the Sciences*. Durham, NC: Duke University Press, 1985.

Shepherd, A.P. *The Eternity of Time*. London: Camelot Press, 1941.

Sire, James W. *Discipleship of The Mind: Learning to Love God in the Ways We Think*. Downers Grove, IL: InterVarsity Press, 1990.

———. *The Universe Next Door*. Downers Grove, IL: InterVarsity Press, 1988.

Smart, J.J., ed. *Problems of Space and Time*. New York: Macmillan, 2nd printing, 1968.

Smart, J.J.C., and J.J. Haldane. *Atheism and Theism*. Oxford: Blackwell Publishers, 1996.

Smietana, Bob. "Willow Creek Promises Investigation Amid New Allegations Against Bill Hybels." *Christianity Today*, April 21, 2018.

https://www.christianitytoday.com/news/2018/april/bill-hybels-willow-creek-promises-investigation-allegations.html, accessed April 2018.

Solomon, Robert C., and Kathleen M. Higgins. *A Short History of Philosophy.* Oxford: Oxford University Press, 1996.

Solomon, Jerry. *Arts, Entertainment, and Christian Values.* Grand Rapids MI: Kregel Publications, 2000.

Spengler, Oswald. *The Decline of the West.* 2 vols. New York: Knopf, 1926, 1928.

Sphrantzes, George. *The Fall of the Byzantine Empire: A Chronicle by George Sphrantzes 1401-1477.* Translated by Marios Phillipides. Amherst: University of Massachusetts Press, 1980.

Spong, John Shelby. *Resurrection: Myth or Reality?* San Francisco: HarperCollins, 1995.

Stackhouse, John. *Church: An Insider's Look at How We Do It.* Grand Rapids, MI: Baker Books, 2003.

———. *Humble Apologetics.* New York: Oxford University Press, 2002.

Stackhouse, Thomas. *A History of the Holy Bible: From the beginning of the world to the establishment of Christianity.* Edited by George Gleig. Longman, Hurst, Rees, Orme, and Brown, University of Iowa, 1817.

Stein, Alan. "Soviet cosmonaut Gherman Titov begins a two-day visit to Century 21 Exposition on May 5, 1962. History Link.org, http://www.historylink.org/File/10104, accessed November 15, 2017.

Strobel, Lee. *The Case for Christ: A Journalist's Personal Investigation of the Evidence for Jesus.* Grand Rapids, MI: Zondervan, 1998.

Strong, James. *The Strongest Strong's Exhaustive Concordance.* Grand Rapids, MI: Zondervan, 2001.

Stumpf, Samuel Enoch. *Socrates to Sartre: A History of Philosophy.* New York: McGraw-Hill, 1994.

Swinburne, Richard. *The Christian God.* Oxford: Clarendon Press, 1994.

———. *Epistemic Justification.* Oxford: Clarendon Press, 2001.

———. *The Existence of God.* Oxford: Clarendon Press, 1991.

———. "God and Time." In Eleonore Stump, ed., *Reasoned Faith.* Ithaca, NY: Cornell University Press, 1993.

Tarnas, Richard. *The Passion of the Western Mind.* New York: Ballantine Books, 1991.
Templeton, Charles. *Farewell to God: My reasons for rejecting the Christian faith.* Toronto: McClelland and Stewart, 1996.
Teske, Roland J. *Paradoxes of Time in Saint Augustine.* Milwaukee, WI: Marquette University Press, 1996.
Tillich, Paul. *The New Being.* New York: Charles Scribner's Sons, 1955.
Tipler, Frank J. "The Omega Point as Eschaton: Answers to Pannenberg's Questions for Scientists." *Zygon: Journal of Religion and Science* 24 (1989).
Todd, Anderson. "Transposition of Joy in C.S. Lewis." MA thesis, University of Waterloo, 2014.
Tolkien, J.R.R. *The Fellowship of the Ring.* New York: Ballantine Books, 1991.
———. *The Hobbit.* UK: HarperCollins, reprint 1991.
Torrance, Thomas F. *Space, Time and Incarnation.* London: Oxford University Press, 1969.
———. *Space, Time and Resurrection.* Grand Rapids, MI: Wm. B. Eerdmans, 1976.
Tresmontant, Claude. *The Origins of Christian Philosophy.* New York: Hawthorn, 1963.
Trevethan, Thomas L. *The Beauty of God's Holiness.* Downers Grove, IL: InterVarsity Press, 1995.
Underhill, Evelyn. *The Essentials of Mysticism.* New York: E.P. Dutton, 1961.
Van Bebber, Mark, and Paul S, Taylor. *Creation and Time.* Gilbert, AZ: Eden Communications, reprint 1996.
Von Balthasar, Hans Urs. *The Glory of the Lord.* 2 vols. San Francisco: Ignatius Press, 1989.
Walvoord, John F. *"Jesus Christ Our Lord.* Chicago: Moody Press, reprint 1985.
Watts, Rikk E. *Making Sense of Genesis 1.* Lecture given at Regent College 2002, http://www.asa3.org/ASA/topics/Bible-Science/6-02Watts.html, accessed December 4, 2017.
Weil, Simone. *Waiting on God.* London: Routledge and Kegan Paul, 1950.
Wenham, John William. *Easter Enigma._*Grand Rapids, MI: Academie Books, 1984.
West, Ryan, and Adam C. Pelser. "Perceiving God through

Natural Beauty." *Faith and Philosophy* 32 (July 2015): 293-312.
Whitehead, Evelyn Eaton, and James D. Whitehead. *Christian Life Patterns: The Psychological Challenges and Religious Invitations of Adult Life.* New York: The Crossroad Publishing Company, 2003.
Who Is This Jesus: Is He Risen? Fort Lauderdale, FL: A video presentation by D. James Kennedy and Coral Ridge Ministries, 2001.
Wiebe, Donald. *The Irony of Theology and the Nature of Religious Thought.* Montreal: McGill-Queens University Press, 1991.
Wiebe, Philip H. "Evidence for a Resurrection." Unpublished article, Trinity Western University, 2002.
———. "Kai Nielsen on Perceiving God." Unpublished paper presented at Trinity Western University, fall 2001.
———. *Theism in an Age of Science.* Lanham, MD: University Press of America, 1988.
———. *Visions of Jesus.* New York: Oxford University Press, 1997.
Williams, Charles. *Descent into Hell.* Grand Rapids, MI: Wm. B. Eerdmans, reprint 1996.
Wilson, Ian. *The Bleeding Mind: An Investigation into the Mysterious Phenomenon of Stigmata.* London: Paladin, Grafton Books, 1991.
———. *The Blood and the Shroud.* New York: Touchstone, 1998.
Wilson, John. "The Geography of the Imagination." *Christianity Today* 41, no. 10 (September 1, 1997).
Windt, Peter. *An Introduction to Philosophy: Ideas in Conflict.* New York: West Publishing Company, 1982.
Wittgenstein, Ludwig. *Tractatus Logico-Philosophicus.* Translated by D.F. Pears and B.F. McGuinness. New York: Routledge, reprint 2002.
Wolterstorff, Nicholas. *Art in Action.* Grand Rapids, MI: Wm. B. Eerdmans, 1980.
Wright, N.T. *Who Was Jesus?* Grand Rapids, MI: Wm. B. Eerdmans, 1993.
Yates, J. *The Timelessness of God.* Lanham, MD: University Press of America, 1990.
Zagzebski, Linda. "Vocatio Philosophiae." In Kelly James Clark, ed., *Philosophers Who Believe.* Downers Grove, IL:

InterVarsity Press, 1993.

Zimdars-Swartz, Sandra. *Encountering Mary: From La Salette to Medjugorje.* Princeton, NJ: Princeton University Press, 1991.

www.ingramcontent.com/pod-product-compliance
Lightning Source LLC
Chambersburg PA
CBHW070532010526
44118CB00012B/1109